Guide for
Outdoor Building & Maintenance

GUIDE FOR
Outdoor Building & Maintenance

Reston Publishing Company, Inc.
A Prentice-Hall Company
Reston, Virginia

Richard Demske & L. Donald Meyers

Library of Congress Cataloging in Publication Data

Meyers, L   Donald
    Guide for outdoor building and maintenance.

    1. Dwellings—Maintenance and repair.   2. Building.
I. Demske, Richard   joint author. II. Title.
TH4817.M5   690'.8   76–43098
ISBN 0–87909–316–1

© 1977 by Reston Publishing Company, Inc.
   A Prentice-Hall Company
Reston, Virginia 22090

  10 9 8 7 6 5 4 3 2

PRINTED IN THE UNITED STATES OF AMERICA

CONTENTS

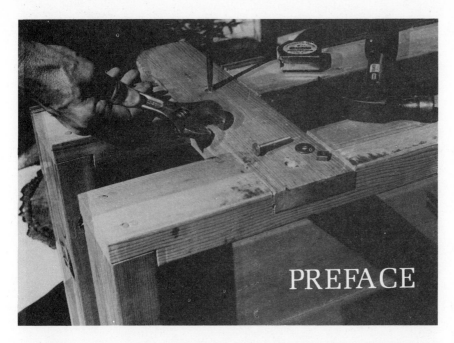

PREFACE

Enjoying outdoor life has become increasingly more appealing to many of us who are caught up in the nine-to-five pressures and counter pressures that accompany earning a twentieth-century living. Somehow, everyday industrial, commercial or professional work routines, however rewarding, can seem less confining when we can follow them with work in the sun, work we don't have to do, or work we want to do for our family.

There also is something immensely satisfying about doing work that enables us to actually make something physically complete and immediately usable. Working with one's hands is an age-old way of renewing contact with earth, wood, metal and tools. The satisfactions are real and the building projects outlined in this book are simple and useful. Try them. We think you'll like them.

None of the jobs in this book is particularly difficult. Some take a little more time, some a little more practice, and some a little more muscle. All can be accomplished, one way or another, though, by any handy, not-particularly-skilled, interested person.

*   *   *

Quite a few organizations have helped us with this book. We can not name them all here, but we would like especially to thank staff members at the American Plywood Association, Western *viii* *

Wood Products Association, the Portland Cement Association, Cornell University Cooperative Extension, the California Redwood Association, as well as many fellow citizens in various U.S. government agencies.

L.D.M.
R.D.

Guide for
Outdoor Building & Maintenance

Figure 1 1. Some of the nice things you can do with your backyard: All of them—decks, fences, outdoor furniture, patio covers, etc.—are discussed in detail in the appropriate chapters. Note the conspicuous knots in the less expensive but attractive garden grade redwood .

1:

Outdoor Living Today

At one time, outdoor living meant sitting on the front stoop nodding to passersby, with an occasional family picnic in the park (not much fun for Mom and Dad, who had to prepare the food and drink, load up the family Hupmobile and chug, chug out to the open spaces). But that was in the days of the city dweller, long before the mass exodus to the suburbs.

Today, it is not just the wealthy who have the luxury of the backyard swing and quiet contemplation in the gazebo. The omnipresent middle class has imbued its beloved suburbia with the emoluments of the rich—genial patios, quiet gardens, handsome decks, and elaborate barbecues. The most obvious example of how the mighty have fallen—or, perhaps, how the lowly have risen—is the swimming pool. Once it was the supreme status symbol of movie stars and Wall Street tycoons. Now, there's a pool for every budget, and woe to the poor suburbanite who doesn't have some type of dipping facility close at hand.

Even more ubiquitous than the swimming pool is the patio, terrace, deck, or whatever—now accepted as a must for almost every home—an "outdoor living room" in the real sense of the word. In warmer climates outdoor living is, of course, more popular than elsewhere, but even in the extreme northern areas of our continent, a home seems naked and incomplete without some sort of outdoor dining and lounging facility.

Since world food shortages and high prices have intruded on daily living, vegetable gardens have also made a remarkable comeback, reminiscent of the "victory gardens" of World War II. But, practical as they are, vegetable gardens still take second place to beauty. Landscaping and gardening are the primary concerns of the homeowner who strives to make his land an appropriate setting for his jewel—his home. Still

Figure 1-2:   The ultimate in backyard luxury is a built-in pool, like this heart-shaped Buster Crabbe design. Pools and all their accoutrements are no longer the province of the wealthy; the rest of us have taken poolside pleasures to "heart" too.

another popular outdoor interest is constructing play areas and amusements for the children, structures for outdoor tools, walks, driveways, and other elements of the landscape.

A thirst for the outdoors shows itself in other ways, too. The intense interest in preserving the environment, the great popularity of camping, and other forms of outdoor recreation (only slightly curtailed by energy problems) demonstrate the scope of the trend toward living with the freshness and sweetness of Nature.

And here we come to the *raison d'être* of this book. We hope in these pages to inspire some ideas that will add to your own outdoor living comfort, ease and pleasure—whether you are just now discovering the great outdoors at home, or whether you are already committed to it and are seeking new refinements and pleasures in such living.

Do It Yourself?

Outdoor projects are a natural for the do-it-yourselfer. While rather heavy work is involved in some of them, the careful craftsmanship that may be required for more intricate indoor projects such as furniture building or fine woodworking is less important for outdoor work. The backyard is kind to beginners, who can usually produce satisfactory results there, although more sophisticated projects might turn out rather badly and sour the novice on do-it-yourself forever.

This is not to say that a certain amount of skill and artistry is not required or that the jobs outlined in this book can be accomplished without care, planning and hard work. On the contrary, care and planning are essential for any job well done, and hard physical labor is involved in outdoor work more than in any other. But you can do a lot of the things in this book with no more basic training than knowing how to read a rule, drive a nail, or understand the difference between up and down on a level. Some of the projects in the following pages will be quite easy, some more difficult. But there are very few that cannot be successfully completed by the homeowner with only rudimentary grasp of do-it-yourselfing.

The Benefits of Outdoor Work

Most outdoor labor takes place in the spring and fall, those months when it is just plain nice to be outside. On the first warm spring day, even such routine tasks as raking fallen leaves and cleaning up the yard can be enjoyable. It's the city-dweller's way of communing with nature and one of the few times the harried suburbanite gets to enjoy the half-acre he worked so hard for.

Actually, the work is incidental on those fine green days in spring

Figure 1-3: Notice how exterior improvements benefit the inside, too. Before and after photographs of this living room show how the patio improves the view, particularly when seen through the new sliding doors (*courtesy of Andersen Company*).

and in the crisp fresh chill of autumn. The real reason for being outdoors is to smell the air, hear the birds, or bask in the breeze. In other parts of the world, the people often just sit and enjoy, but our New World Puritan ethic tends to make us uncomfortable if we are "lazing" around. So we pick up a shovel or a broom and make it feel legitimate. If we accomplish something along the way, all well and good, but it isn't essential. What is important is getting outside and breathing the air.

But working outside is beneficial to the body as well as the soul. If you want a semi-painless way of losing a few pounds, try planting a few shrubs; or, if you *really* want to lose weight and restore those sagging triceps, put in a concrete driveway—and/or patio, walkway, and steps. Nothing can top a loaded wheelbarrow for vigorous exercise.

GETTING IN SHAPE FOR OUTDOOR WORK

Outdoor work is good for body and soul. But there is a caveat or two. Your soul will be able to handle it all right, but your body might not withstand the sudden change from sedentary to gung-ho. If you haven't lifted anything heavier than a pencil or a nine-iron in recent years, you should seriously prepare your body for the jolt.

Although every type of exercise has its cultists, there is plenty of medical evidence that jogging is the best all-around body shaper-upper. But don't overdo it—or any other exercise. Even for a man in his late twenties, 50 jog steps a day is enough to start with. As you get used to it, gradually increase your exercise time over a month to six weeks until you are up to a half hour workout. But, for every five pounds of over-weight, slow down your schedule a day or two. And remember, when the weather doesn't permit outdoor exercise, you can run in place indoors. To do it effectively, bring the knees up high at a rapid pace for approximately thirty seconds at a time.

If you think that playing golf is keeping you in shape, you may be only half right, and even less than that if you use a golf cart. Make that a motorized jitney and your health handicap goes way up. Even walking, per se, does not do enough to condition your whole body since it uses only about 40 percent of the body capacity. You must utilize at least 60 percent of your bodily capacity before any effect can be felt on muscle tone.

Some other recommended methods for getting into condition are pushups and situps. Start off with five of either and work up, one more a day, to 20. Once you can do that many without any strain, you can be considered in pretty good shape for outdoor projects.

Some physical fitness professionals recommend barbells, as long as you don't try to lift more than 20 pounds at a time. And read a good book on weightlifting or take lessons—before you start. Severe back injuries and other mishaps can result from incorrect lifting and bending. Swimming is still another way to keep the entire body in shape.

6 *

In any case, you don't have to be a magnificent physical specimen to swing a hammer or putter a little in the garden. The less strenuous outdoor activities are, as a matter of fact, good physical conditioners by themselves. On the other hand, you should not attempt to lay concrete, set railroad ties, or carry building stone unless you are in pretty fair shape. Be guided by your own good judgment. Avoid heavy work if you have a heart condition or a bad back. Most of the projects in this book can be performed by most people, however. There are many that can be done by anyone, male or female, and the vast majority take only a minimum of physical exertion. If you know your body needs conditioning, by all means, start an exercise regimen, but don't put off outside work until you're Superman. Start with the easier jobs and work up to the more strenuous ones.

FINANCIAL BENEFITS OF DO-IT-YOURSELF

In addition to the betterment of body and soul, there is one other important benefit, and that is the good it does your pocket. Costs for most of the projects shown here would be prohibitive for the average family if workmen were hired or if the projects were bought complete (assuming they could be found). Although inflation and shortages have added greatly to the prices of building materials, they are still a relatively minor expense compared to the cost of having professionals put them together. With every one of the projects in this book, you are investing "sweat equity" in making your home more valuable.

How much, exactly, do you save by doing it yourself? That question is impossible to answer on a general basis, but you can find out the savings on any particular project by asking for estimates from professionals and then comparing the average price with what it costs you. If the project comes with complete plans, show them to the contractor, carpenter, or whomever and ask what he would charge to do it. If there are no specific plans, such as with a concrete walkway, draw a rough sketch with accurate dimensions and ask for estimates from that—or have the contractor come out and look at the layout, even though you have no firm intention of hiring. This may seem unfair at first glance, but there is often a good chance that his costs may be low enough so that you can hire him after all.

Basically, the difference in cost between do-it-yourself and professional depends on how labor-intensive the job is. On the one hand, digging a ditch is all labor and no materials. If you do it yourself, you save all the costs. You save very little, on the other hand, when you erect a prefabricated tool shed, because most of the work is already done for you—and charged to you. A project like a brick-in-sand patio will cost considerably less if you do it yourself because there is a lot of tedious handwork in laying the brick and leveling the sand underneath. Hiring a bricklayer for this type of work is an expensive luxury.

Figure 1-4: An inviting backyard like this probably won't repay its owners more than half of the "dollar" investment, but it makes the house easier to sell—not to mention the pleasant privacy such an investment guarantees to the homeowners (*courtesy of California Redwood Association*).

8 *

We are, of course, overlooking one very important aspect—that your time is worth money, too. Here, again, the value of your time is relative. A physician who takes time off from his practice to lay bricks is losing, not gaining—financially, at least. But if you work on salary and have time that ordinarily would be spent in front of the boob tube, your do-it-yourself work is money found.

INCREASING THE VALUE OF YOUR PROPERTY

There is no question but that outside improvements increase the value of your property to some extent. It is a mistake, however, to think that the resale value of your home is increased by what you pay. There are very few home improvements, inside or out, which repay 100 % on their investment. The primary consideration for any home improvement should be its importance to your family and not its resale value.

Still, some home improvements bring a higher percentage of return than others, and it is wise to consider this factor when you decide to make a permanent investment. You should also recognize that home prices in certain neighborhoods tend to level out so that improvements

Figure 1-5: Here again beauty and use may outweigh investment returns, but these outdoor improvements are not likely to be regretted.

reach a point of diminishing (or no) return. On a street of $30,000 houses, for example, you might improve yours up to a value of $35,000. But you can sink $20,000 more into improvements and not get much more than $35,000 for it.

Generally, outside improvements do not pay off as much as inside ones or home additions. Basic landscaping for a brand new home is a necessary evil which adds little to the worth of the home. (Shade trees are an exception.) Expensive plantings and elaborate gardens are not really worth much to anyone except you. A swimming pool may be worth most of its price in an area where swimming pools are "in" (especially in warm climates), but in the wrong neighborhood a pool may actually be more of a hindrance than a help on resale. Although a patio or deck is a must for most homes, you will probably get back only half what it costs you. Adding walks and driveways will make salable a home that may not be without them, but they will probably not bring the price up very much. And fancy concrete work such as circular driveways won't be worth much more than plain versions of the same.

In the long run, outdoor projects should be considered more in the light of family enjoyment than as an investment. After all, you are the ones living there, and you may well be there for a long time to come. Please yourself first of all, and if the investment pays off when you do resell, all the better. But remember the years of pleasure you had are worth a lot more than the few dollars you get when you sell.

What To Build and Why

Chances are that most people already have some project in mind when they consider outdoor remodeling. But if you just have the urge to build something out in the fresh air and don't know what, skim quickly through the following pages, and something is bound to appeal.

Don't forget the children, for example. Providing definite play areas with the necessary facilities to keep them occupied is as important to your summertime enjoyment as it is to theirs (see Chapter 12). Maybe you can simply make a large frame of 2x8s staked to the ground and dump in a load of clean sand, then let the kids' imagination take over. Or you might build them a jungle gym, a play house, or a fort. Give the older ones room to exercise. A tennis court is great where there is room (and money). Or hang a basket and backboard on a pole or from a garage roof (it's a lot cheaper). A level grassy area is all that's needed for badminton. (Even Mom and Dad can prove their agility with these facilities.)

In any event, keep the play area as remote as possible from the relaxing area, unless you have very small children, in which case you want to be able to see them. Make an overall plan before you start building so you can take all these factors into account. Then you can make the best and most pleasant use of your property. See Chapter 2.

Figure 1-6: Years of neglect made this old wood siding unpaintable, but this new western red cedar siding will weather naturally and not require further maintenance. These shingles come in eight-foot strips for quick application (*courtesy of Shakertown Corporation*).

Maintenance of Lawn & Garden   * 11

Sadly, outdoor living is not all play and no work. The lawn does continue to grow in summer (although it is accommodating enough to slow down considerably, even as you and I, during the hottest months), and some care is required to see that it remains healthy. And every now and then the house itself needs some freshening up, lest its shabby appearance give us pangs of guilt as we view it from our reclining chair on the patio. Painting should be done earlier in the season, though, before the heat becomes intense (better for you, better for the paint job).

If you want to keep these irksome chores down to a minimum, it may be well to put up some low-maintenance siding, such as cedar, aluminum, or plastic shingles. And, when you put in grass, be sure to use the slow-growing kinds. That way you can enjoy the fruits of your labor with a free mind. The warm months are for relaxing and savoring the beauties of nature in the comfortable confines of our own homes. We hope that this book will be of some help in realizing the benefits of outdoor living.

GENERAL INFORMATION ABOUT WOOD & ITS MAINTENANCE

This book will cover the gamut of outdoor activities—landscaping, gardening, concrete, brick and stone work, pool selection and building, etc. But a lot of pages are devoted to woodwork of various kinds. There is important general information about outdoor woodworking that will be discussed here to avoid repetition in every project.

* Always specify exterior plywood, hardboard, adhesives, hardware, etc., when ordering materials. Nails should be hot-dipped galvanized, or made of aluminum. Some things, such as dimension lumber (2×4s, etc.) are not categorized as indoor or outdoor, but be sure to let your dealer know that your project is an outdoor one regardless.
* Some woods, such as redwood and red cedar, are naturally more weather and insect resistant than other woods. If you can afford it, and the project calls for it, use these woods rather than the others. The better the grade of wood (for example, clear, all-heart redwood and incense cedar) the longer it should hold up, but the less-perfect grades (such as garden-grade redwood) are good, too, and are to be preferred over non-decay-resistant woods.
* If you can't afford the decay-resistant woods, or the project calls for other kinds, there are a lot of alternatives, but always treat these woods with a preservative like penta-chlorophenol ("penta," "Wood-Life," etc.). Where wood is in contact with the ground, pressure-treated creosote is the best preservative. If unavailable, soak the wood overnight in creosote solution.

* When preserving wood, dip the ends in the preservative before application. This is much more effective than painting the preservative on after the structure is complete. If the boards are too long for dipping, soak the ends and paint the centers before assembling.

* When painting wood, use at least one coat of primer, then two coats of good house paint (preferably by the same manufacturer). Use sash and trim paint for bright colors. All knots should be coated with shellac or an exterior sealer before priming so that the knots will not "bleed" through the paint. Wood should be repainted every three to five years, with all loose or blistered paint removed by thorough scraping.

* Plywood edges should be coated with surfacing putty to cover defects, allowed to dry, then coated with sealer. All edge grain should be given an extra coat of finishing material because of its extra absorbency. Exterior hardboard should be "conditioned" as explained on p. 00.

* Dimension lumber is always smaller than the stated size (except for length). A 6-ft 2×4, will be six feet long, but only 1-½"×3-½" in width and thickness, for example. This difference is a result of the "dressing" (planing) and natural shrinkage of lumber after drying. When you build anything of wood, check all actual dimensions and make sure that your plans do not employ "old wood" dimensions for 2×4s. (Originally 2×4's were 1-⅝" by 3-¾" in measure, for instance.) This is sometimes a problem, sometimes not. If the plan doesn't seem to work, this may be the reason.

* When sawing any material, particularly closely laid out plywood panels, be sure to allow for saw kerfs (the width of the cutting edge of the saw). Kerfs are rarely more than 1/32" for hand saws, 1/16" for power equipment, but measure if in doubt.

* When setting posts in the ground, always provide drainage at the bottom. A foot of gravel under the post bottom is advisable, even when using concrete. And slope the concrete surface away from the posts to drain water away from the wood.

* Most lumber sizes are given in "linear feet" (lin. ft.). Where a large quantity is ordered, the term "board feet" is sometimes used. A board foot is a stack of wood one inch high, twelve inches wide and twelve feet long—actually, one cubic foot. Since a 2×12 is twice as thick as a 1×12, a board foot would be only six feet long; a 1×6 would be 24 linear feet, etc. You can figure out how many linear feet are in a board foot by multiplying height times width, then dividing into the length. Or save yourself all that math and let the lumber dealer do it. It's his business.

2:

Your Home & Its Setting

The average American has the bulk of his savings as equity in the house that is his home. It is his rightly treasured "jewel." Too often, however, it is in a setting that doesn't do it justice. Proper landscaping provides a fitting setting for a house, and it should be given the same care and planning as the house itself. Trees and shrubs should be planted with the knowledge of how big they will get, when they will bloom (if ever), exactly where they will be placed, and the rest. In short, before you buy a single *arborvitae*, establish a "grand design."

In modern landscape planning, the garden is an outdoor extension of indoor living space. This idea calls for organization of outdoor space to match uses of indoor space. Outdoor areas should be organized into work, play, and living space. Indoors, walls serve to separate living activities. Outdoors, shrubs, hedges, fences, and building walls offer privacy, separate activities, and create background for objects, both utilitarian and decorative.

In looking at your outdoor space, you must envision what you want to do with each area. If you have children, how much of the yard will they require as their play space? Do you need space for touch football, badminton, a swimming pool, or just a swing and sandbox? For yourself, do you want just a pleasant place to sit? Or do you want an outdoor grill and patio? Do you want a vegetable garden? How large? What views are good from the house? Do you need shrubs to frame the view or the house? Do you need trees to shade the roof of the house, the patio, or the lawn? Do you have a view or a service area that needs screening, either from the house or from the street?

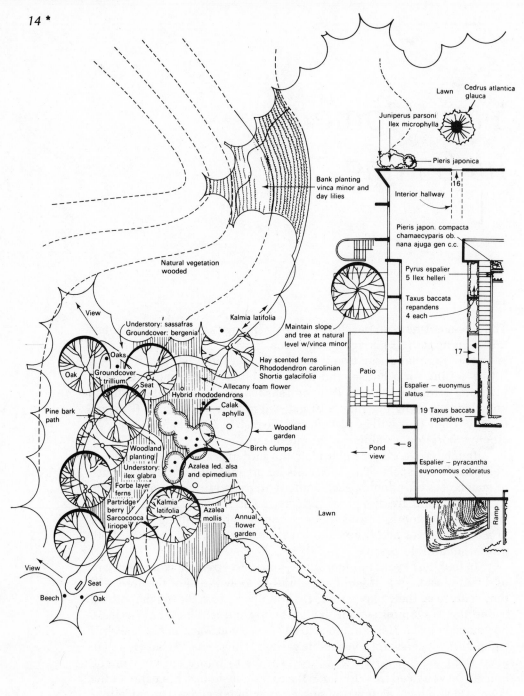

Figure 2-1: Designs can be as elaborate as this one planned for a sizeable Long Island estate.

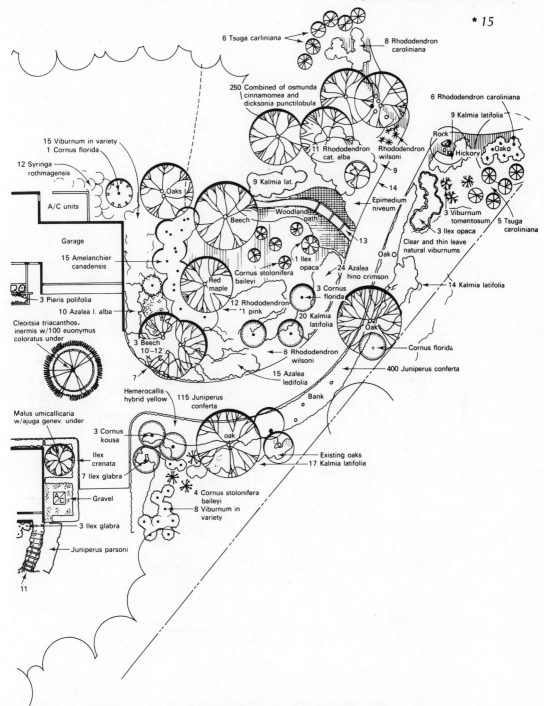

6 Tsuga carliniana

8 Rhododendron caroliniana

250 Combined of osmunda cinnamomea and dicksonia punctilobula

6 Rhododendron caroliniana

9 Kalmia latifolia

Rock

Hickory

Oako

11 Rhododendron cat. alba

Rhododendron wilsoni

9

14

Epimedium niveum

15 Viburnum in variety
1 Cornus florida

12 Syringa rothmagensis

A/C units

Oaks

9 Kalmia lat.

Beech

Woodland path

13

3 Viburnum tomentosum

3 Ilex opaca

5 Tsuga carliniana

Garage

15 Amelanchier canadensis

Red maple

Cornus stolonifera baileyi

1 Ilex opaca

24 Azalea hino crimson

Oak O

Clear and thin leave natural viburnums

3 Pieris polifolia

10 Azalea I. alba

12 Rhododendron *1 pink

3 Cornus florida

14 Kalmia latifolia

Cleoitsia triacanthos, inermis w/100 euonymus coloratus under

20 Kalmia latifolia

Oak

3 Beech 10'–12'

6 Rhododendron wilsoni

Cornus florida

7

15 Azalea ledifolia

400 Juniperus conferta

Hemerocallis hybrid yellow

115 Juniperus conferta

Bank

Malus umicallicaria w/ajuga genev. under

oak

3 Cornus kousa

Ilex crenata

7 Ilex glabra

Existing oaks

17 Kalmia latifolia

A/C

Gravel

4 Cornus stolonifera baileyi

8 Viburnum in variety

3 Ilex glabra

Juniperus parsoni

11

Figure 2-1 (continued): These drawings are adapted from the architect's plan (*courtesy of Panfield Nursery, New York*).

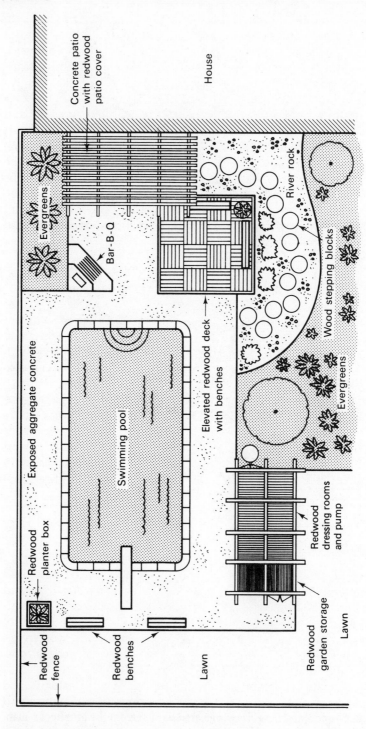

Figure 2-2: This relatively simple design shows a fenced-in swimming pool.

You will no doubt think of other questions that govern your own situation. Whether you are beginning homesite planting on a bare lot around a new house or want to give new life to a tired, uninspired yard, there are certain basic principles you need to follow: natural factors, family needs and preferences, and the plan itself.

When you start planning, the first step will be to analyze your natural assets and limitations. Set up a "ledger" for garden assets and liabilities, listing everything you know or can find out about the physical aspects of your property. This will include all elements of the environment: soils, climate, the orientation of the house on the land, the topography, existing trees and shrubs. In the environment there will be factors over which you may have little or no control—the weather, the subsoil, and exposure to sun. But you need to know about them in order to take advantage of favorable conditions and, in so far as possible, avoid trouble from the unfavorable ones.

Kinds of Soil

You need to know what kinds of soil you have and to what extent you can improve conditions if your soil is poor. A soil test will show whether your soil is acid or alkaline. Most areas have a county agricultural agent who can test your soil and tell you what minerals you need to add for the kinds of plants you expect to grow.

If your soil presents a problem—clay, hardpan, or too sandy—you may find it necessary to alter or replace it, at least in small areas where you want to garden or plant trees and shrubs, creating a soil environment in which your plants can survive. For lawns, a whole new bed of topsoil may be needed, providing a root zone that will allow the rain to soak in rather than run off or just stand in the hole and give your grass "wet feet."

Climate and Landscaping

You can't alter the weather, but you can allow for it. Take into account the temperature range for your area, with minimum lows and maximum highs. You can get help from the U.S. Department of Agriculture and your state agency. It would be well, too, to consult your county agent or local nurseryman. Their experience could help you avoid choice of plants that would not tolerate your local weather conditions, saving not only money but also growing time.

Find out about local temperature ranges, the average rainfall, and its distribution throughout the year if you are new to the community. If your area suffers from prolonged dry seasons, be sure to provide adequate facilities for watering your garden, favorite trees and shrubs. If strong winds are your local hazard, you may want to plant windbreaks or use walls or fences to shelter vulnerable plants.

ORIENTATION

The placement of your house on the lot and its relation to the sun and prevailing wind are important too. If you have a voice in the placement of a new house, well and good. You will want to see that it meets zoning requirements with regard to lot lines and that it is placed to best suit the climate (especially with regard to exposure to the sun) and to satisfy your need for privacy

If your house is already built, you may want to think of plants to provide shade for areas that otherwise would be overexposed to intense summer sun. It is said that properly placed shade trees can reduce the summer room temperature of a frame house in an arid climate by as much as 20 degrees. This can be translated into dollars if you are paying for air conditioning—and comfort, of course.

TOPOGRAPHY

The lay of the land will influence your landscape design and your choice of plant materials. Usually, natural formations can break the monotony and help you develop a yard of distinction. For instance, you may have a residual stream bed, a depressed marshy spot, or even an outcropping of rocks. Perhaps you can capitalize on such seeming disadvantages to add excitement and interest to your overall plan. The stream bed might be screened with shrubs and used as a natural play area for the children. The depressed, marshy spot might be lined to make a little pool and used for water plants. An outcropping of rocks is a "natural" for a rock garden with succulent and exotic or alpine plants.

One of the most common problems, especially in some housing developments, is a sloping bank, which is often steep and troublesome to mow. These can be planted with trees, shrubs, or groundcovers, or terraces can be built and used for other planting. If such natural features are in the wrong place or simply don't fit in with your own needs and preferences, you may have to resort to grading and fill to achieve the yard you want.

EXISTING TREES AND SHRUBS

In your analysis of the natural factors to be considered, make careful note of any trees or shrubs that are already on the lot. You may want to make a special checklist, entering them by species, number, and other characteristics that would influence your decisions on what to

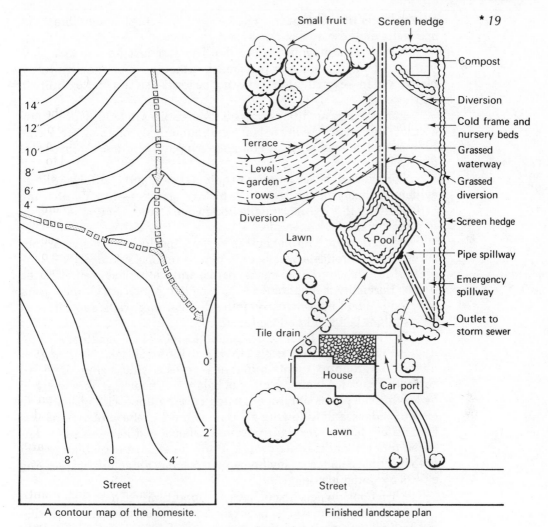

A contour map of the homesite.

Finished landscape plan

Figure 2-3: A contour map (*detail at left*) can be of great help in planning the overall landscaping design, particularly when the land has more than the usual gentle slope with subsequent drainage problems.

keep or eliminate. Mark the ones you want to save. If you don't want to save any, or if your building plans require removal of some, keep a record of the kinds native to that environment. This natural association will help you in buying new plant materials. Try to combine plants that originated under the same or similar conditions of light, shade, moisture, and soil. Getting plants that are compatible will help you achieve unity and make a more successful garden.

20 *   *Planning Your Garden*

You don't want your garden, like Topsy, to just grow. With a plan, you can plant all at once or piecemeal, if that is more attractive financially. A plan—even though it may not be ideal—allows for flexibility in its execution.

Landscaping architects suggest three choices in landscape design: a formal design, where the balance is symmetrical; informal, where the balance is achieved without complete symmetry; or a combination of the two.

Formal design was popular in colonial days and is still beautifully evident in many of the country's historic gardens—Mt. Vernon and Williamsburg in Virginia, and the Longwood Gardens at Kennet Square in Pennsylvania, for example.

If you do want a formal design, draw a line down the center of your garden area. Duplicate whatever is placed on one side exactly on the other side. This applies to rocks, paths, and statuary as well as to the plants. Formality is heightened by seeing that plants are clipped, lines are straight, and edges clearly defined. Retaining walls and different levels might be used to add interest.

In the informal balance design, both sides of an imaginary center line are in balance with each other, but informal balance is accomplished by grouping plants differently on each side, using sizes and colors of plants to obtain a feeling of balance. A natural look is retained by leaving the plants unclipped, using curving lines with obscure and merging edges, and following natural contours in the garden. Japanese gardens are famous for their informal balance and have greatly influenced today's landscaping design. Don't be afraid to combine formal with informal balance. Many homeowners today are achieving pleasing effects by doing just that.

Most homeowners do not have the opportunity to plan their houses and gardens together. If you are buying a new house, the chances are that the builder has provided a minimal, so-called foundation planting, leaving the personal landscaping to you. Even if you are living in a home with an established yard, you can put your own imprint on the grounds just as you would with your own choices of furniture and color scheme inside the house.

In addition to the symmetry and balance already mentioned, other considerations help make a garden a delight to the senses. Scale, color, outline, texture, and even fragrance need to be considered.

Scale in Landscaping

Scale means the relationships in height and width between your house and the plants on your grounds. This relationship concerns the

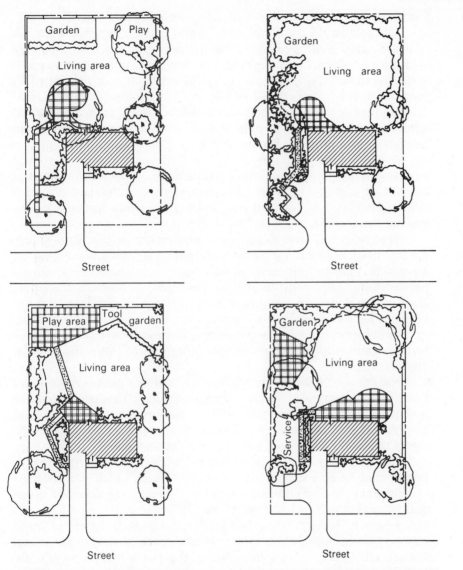

Figure 2-4: Once you have your new house and site selected, try one or more general plans to see which works best for your situation; then carefully work out the scale, color, and special effects you want.

ultimate height and spread a plant will attain, of course, not its size at the time of purchase. By your choices, you can create various illusions and effects. For instance, if you live in a small one-story house, your natural solution for a tree as the main accent to the house would be a medium-sized tree that grows to about thirty feet. That would be in scale. If you wanted your house to appear larger than it really is, you might choose a tree that grows to about fifteen feet. On the other hand, a tree that grows 120-feet high would dwarf your house and make it look like a toy. Of course, it takes many years for a tree to reach such a height; if you are planting a young tree, you might find that for the length of time you will live there, the taller-growing tree might be satisfactory. Whatever effect you wish to achieve, it should be planned, not accidental. Consider all the plantings, from the tallest shade tree down to the grass and ground cover. Careful choices will help you avoid monotony and insure an interesting, attractive, and natural-looking planting.

Decide on the large tree to complement your building. It should serve to join the garden and the sky sympathetically. Depending on your area and lot, you might choose a tulip tree, pin oak, or a plane tree for this role. In the Plains States your choices might include spruce, pine, or some of the poplars.

Next, you will want to plant an "understory" tree or large shrub, one that has horizontal, rather than upright or drooping branch habits, and one that grows well under other trees. Possible selections include the flowering dogwood, doublefile viburnum, or western dogwood. The Chinese dogwood is not so common, but it blooms later and has attractive leaves. If you live in a community where you must forego the tall shade tree and the understory tree, consider an overhead arbor or trellis as a substitute. It will contribute to the desired three-dimensional effect.

Near and below the understory tree, you can plant evergreen or broad-leaved evergreen shrubs, such as azaleas, rhododendrons, or leucothoe. In the West, buckthorn, lilac, cotoneaster, spirea, and honeysuckle offer possibilities. For a more pleasing effect, group three to five of the same shrubs together; don't plant just one.

And last, use a layer of ground cover, such as ivy or myrtle, to give the finishing touch and unify the whole. With such a plan you will have four different levels to attract the eye as well as differing shades of green and textures of leaf (more about texture below).

Where builders provide the foundation planting, they tend to use only evergreens. Many homeowners also prefer them next to the house. But in making choices for the garden, the home landscaper should consider those deciduous plants which lose their leaves in winter, because of the beauty of their seasonal flowers, fruit, and leaf color. Many of these plants are lovely and interesting not only when they are in leaf or flower, but for their structure. They can contribute beauty of shape and outline in winter. Further, deciduous trees provide welcome shade in summer, but let the warm sun through in winter.

For dramatic effect, combine the conifers, or needled evergreens, with deciduous plants and broadleaved evergreens. The conifers usually are dark green but at times become blue- or yellow-green. Perhaps because of their silhouette or because the needles absorb rather than reflect light, they strongly accent the garden. Choose them wisely.

Figure 2-5: A small, ornamental tree gives welcome color and a cheery greeting in this entrance planting.

COLOR AND TEXTURE OF PLANTINGS

You have been dealing so far in the various shades of green. Now consider the addition of color through the use of flowering or fruiting trees and shrubs.

The flowering dogwood, which blooms in spring, is colorful in the fall with its brilliant red berries and is attractive in winter for its branch and twig patterns. Viburnums, hollies, and pyracantha offer varying shades of yellow to red in their fall fruits. Pyracantha and viburnums are especially attractive espaliered along side walls or fences, as are roses and some fruit trees.

Many homeowners emphasize trees and shrubs that flower in the spring and forget that many others provide bloom in mid- and later-summer. Crapemyrtle, mimosa, Chinese dogwood and goldenrain can extend your flowering season. The goldenrain tree also offers a change

24 *   from the pinks and whites of most flowering trees to yellow—a relatively rare color among flowering trees (two other trees with yellow blossoms are cornelian cherry and the goldenchain). But highly-colored plants and those with variegated foliage should be used with restraint, particularly near the house.

Look for differences in texture, too. Texture may be fine, medium, or coarse with gradations in each. Plant texture of a deciduous shrub or tree may appear heavy and coarse in winter when its branches and twigs are bare. But in summer, when it is covered with medium-sized leaves, it may have a medium texture and fine texture in spring if the blossoms are small. Using a variety of leaf and branch texture is good and prevents monotony.

FLOWERS FOR DISPLAY & FOR CUTTING

Flowers are a fragile element of landscape design, but they offer much-desired color through the spring and summer and into the fall. They should be used with background structure. Just as a chest in the living room needs the strong structural background of a wall to complement its color and shape, so flowers need the support of a wall, fence, shrubs, or trees.

Choose flowers not only for color and fragrance but to supply interest through the changing seasons. Be careful, for instance, not to concentrate on flowers that bloom early and are gone; try to have several different kinds that will bloom from early spring to fall.

Keep in mind the purpose you want the flowers to serve. If, in addition to providing garden color and relief from monotony, you also want to have cut flowers to take indoors, choose some varieties that have long-lasting bloom after cutting. If you plan extensive cutting of blooms, try to have a cut-flower garden away from your display areas so that cutting will not deplete your "show" places.

Fragrance may be an incidental consideration. But some people think so highly of the delicate fragrance of lilac or the nighttime sweetness of honeysuckle that they especially want them in their plantings. These may be ruled out by the allergy-conscious. But, if you want fragrance, consider it in the light of the other contributions your favorite plants would make to your garden.

RESTRAINT AND REPETITION IN LANDSCAPING

Two other general rules—restraint and repetition—are good to follow. They seem almost to contradict each other but are wise and valuable guidelines, expecially for the home landscape gardener.

Exercise restraint in the selection of types of materials, using as few different types as possible. One reason for restraint is that you are dealing with living, growing, everchanging materials. They need room to develop. It is better to use too few materials than too many. Restraint will help unify your garden by making it harmonious.

Coupled with restraint is repetition. It is wise to repeat the same texture, the same color, or various tones of the same color, in different parts of the garden. This repetition also makes a contribution toward unity and keeps the garden from being "too busy."

Don't carry either restraint or repetition too far. Avoid having all your plants a uniform size, texture, and color. Vary their heights and try to use at least three textures and either two complementary or two contrasting colors and their tones.

Be a good neighbor. Don't plant a tree that will be a pest to your neighbor. Don't plant a tree or large shrub too close to the lot line. If you do, you may be the loser. In many states, the law provides that a neighbor may trim off all branches that hang over the line on his side. This could leave you with an unbalanced and unsightly tree as well as a hostile neighbor.

Don't forget that living things require food, water, and tender, loving care. Plants have their likes and dislikes just as they have their own characteristics and life-spans. It takes time to make a garden. The most important precept of all is patience.

Foundation Plantings

A fundamental element in landscaping is the foundation planting. It is here that your home begins to blend with its surroundings. A house with a high foundation wall exposed above the soil line requires more planting around its base than one with a low foundation wall. A house with poor architectural lines may use large masses of plants to screen these imperfections. Large-growing shade trees placed from 20 to 30 feet from the corner of a house minimize the unattractively high appearance of tall, narrow houses. Near a house of this type, narrow upright evergreens in the base planting will increase the visual height of the house, while horizontal lines will diminish it. Plants that branch horizontally will reduce the apparent height, as will structural devices—window boxes, window blinds, and two-tone painting.

CHOICE OF PLANTS

Some homeowners want only evergreens in the front planting in order to have green foliage in winter. Others prefer deciduous flowering shrubs (those that drop their leaves in winter) to have an informal effect and flowers in spring and summer. To obtain both effects, plant a combination of evergreens and flowering shrubs. In suitable situations, broadleaved evergreens such as mountain laurel and rhododendron can be used. These bear green leaves year-round, and flower in spring or summer.

RELATIONSHIP TO HOUSE DESIGN

For the planting to be in keeping with older homes, traditional shrubs may well be used. Some examples are flowering almond, snowberry, snowhill hydrangea, sweetshrub, kerria, flowering quince, weigela, forsythia, lilac, and mockorange.

Other types of hardy landscape plants that blend better with simplified architectural lines may be used with contemporary homes (ranch style, split level, raised ranch). Some examples are rockspray cotoneaster, bayberry, slender deutzia, dwarf flowering quince, juniper (spreading types), dwarf or semi-dwarf rhododendrons, mountain laurel, Japanese hollies and viburnums. Existing climatic and other site conditions as well as personal preference will determine which of these (or similar type) plants to use.

MATURE SIZE OF PLANTINGS

The mature size of each plant is a basic consideration in selecting it for any given location. After the size requirement is determined, the selection of the plant to be used in each place is a matter of personal choice.

It makes a noticeable difference in the ultimate appearance of the landscaping whether a plant grows to be three, five, eight or 15 feet in height. It is a mistake to use a plant that will mature at eight feet where a dwarf plant would be more suitable. The large shrub would have to be pruned severely to keep it down to a proper shape for that location, and such pruning often ruins natural shape and usually eliminates flower production.

Most persons buy small plants because they are less expensive than large ones of the same variety. Space these small plants to allow for several years' growth. The sparse appearance of a new planting of this kind may be disappointing. However, planting ground cover between the shrubs will partly overcome this disadvantage. The best way to obtain an immediate effect is to purchase nearly mature plants of suitable kinds. Because large plants are more expensive than small ones of the same kind, the size chosen will be determined by balancing a willingness to wait for the plants to mature against the cost of large plants.

Another method and probably the least practical, is to "plant thick and thin quick." This involves using several small plants in the area that one plant will occupy in a few years. The immediate effect is fairly good, but the procedure is impractical. Some of the plants will have to be removed and probably discarded. Although each plant is relatively inexpensive, the total cost of several small ones can be as

| New planting | 5 years later | 15 years later |

Figure 2-6: Always consider the mature size of your plantings. Small bushes purchased from the nursery may someday overwhelm the house if not properly selected and pruned.

much or more than the amount spent on a single large plant. Another argument against close planting of small-sized shrubs is that each succeeding year the annual growth causes the plants to become more and more crowded and misshaped. Each loses its characteristic shape and individuality. In spite of this fact, most people will not remove the plants that are detrimental to the rest of the group. Leaving all of the original plants in the group always results in a planting that should be replaced sooner or later.

IMPROVING OLDER PLANTINGS

Old, badly planned plantings should be managed differently, depending upon how much out of line they are or will become in a few years. Shrubs that are only slightly large for their positions may be modified by removing some of the older branches at the base. If any of the shrubs, either evergreen or deciduous, are much too large, it is best to remove them. A very large shrub that is still well shaped and in good condition may be transplanted to a more suitable position, such as the corner of a building, a large wall space, or a border planting.

If the plant, especially an evergreen, is not in good condition, it might better be discarded. Old, ill-shaped diciduous plants usually can be transformed into well-shaped plants by cutting them back severely. This forces new shoots to come up from the base and produces a new and lower-growing plant. In this way, old, badly-planned plantings can look almost like new plantings.

Important Planting Rules

Do not plant:
* Tall-growing trees in the foundation planting.
* A straight row of one variety entirely around the house.
* Tall-growing shrubs in front of windows. They darken the room and block the view.
* Too great a variety of plants. Such plantings may seem to be competing with one another for attention. Plants with brightly-colored foliage should be used with caution.

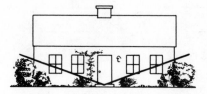 

Figure 2-7: Plants should be lower near the entrance and under windows, higher at the corners. Think of the foundation plantings as an elongated "V" and plant accordingly.

Do plant:
* Lower-growing shrubs at the entrance, higher ones at corners.
* Low-growing shrubs beneath windows, or ground covers; or space may be left unplanted except for lawn extending to the foundation wall.
* Low-growing shrubs around porches unless porch is also a living area, then taller plants are needed for privacy. (Part of a large porch may be shaded by a vine or a tree-form shrub.)
* Dwarf plants at the sides of small entrances and steps; may be supplemented by a vine at the side of a doorway. Such an entrance planting usually is better than a narrow, upright evergreen at each side of the doorway.
* Medium to tall shrubs at the corner of the house except where a driveway or walk is close to the side of a house or a vine instead of a tall shrub. Dwarf shrubs may be used if windows are at the corners or a tree-form shrub may be planted to shade the window.
* Medium-sized shrubs or vines in spaces along the foundation where the windows are far apart.
* Vines on a chimney unless the chimney is small. A shrub also may be used near a chimney.
* Duplicate plants to avoid the appearance of a botanical collection.

Steps in Planning Growing Areas

In planning each area decide where plants should be located, and how large a plant will be suitable for each place. Consider the spacing between the plants, from the foundation, and from the walk or drive, and select a plant from the proper size group for each place. See Table 2-1.

Table 2-1: Plant Groups

Group 1: Vines	Group 4: Medium Shrubs
a: evergreen	Group 5: Large Shrubs
b: deciduous	Group 6: Very Large Shrubs
Group 2: Ground Covers	Group 7: Ornamental Trees
Group 3: Small Shrubs	Group 8: Large Trees

A good way to plan the foundation planting is to photograph each side of the house and have an 8x10 inch enlargement made. Placing a piece of transparent paper over the enlargement, trace the outline of the house, including the windows, doorways, and porches. A fairly accurate scale drawing can be substituted for the photograph. Draw in the foliage masses that will provide the effect you wish. Select the plants from the proper size group for each place.

ENTRANCE PLANTINGS

Entrance plantings should give a feeling of easy access to the house. Low-growing plants at the side of the steps give this effect. Tall plants frequently encroach on the entrance and can make access uninviting and difficult. When planting for a larger entrance platform, more plants are needed on each side. Sometimes the windows are rather widely spaced, so a plant from Group 4 is selected. If the windows are closer to the doorway, in a position where a four- to five-foot plant would grow over the window, use one from Group 3.

A similar situation occurs when one window is near the entrance and the other window is farther away. A plant from Group 4 fills part of this larger wall space, and a vine on the other side of the doorway provides balance.

Frequently doorways are near the corner of a house. Here the corner planting for the house is also part of the entrance planting. Provided

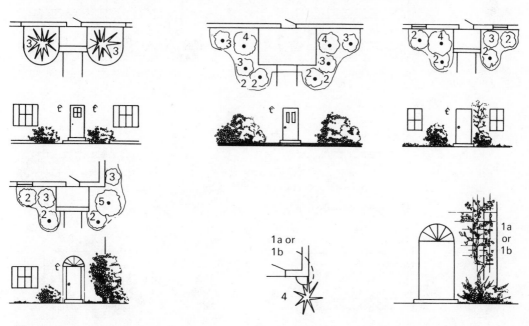

Figure 2-8.

30 *

there is enough width, a medium-to-large-sized shrub may be used at the house corner. If a window, sidewalk, or driveway is so close to this corner that a large-growing shrub would be undesirable in this position, a vine may be used at the corner.

PLANTING AROUND LARGE PORCHES

Most of the plants used around a porch should be low-growing varieties. Proportionately larger growing shrubs should be used near porches with a solid-wall railing and near porches that are higher from the ground. The main purpose of a vine growing on a porch is to shade or give privacy to the portion of the porch where the furniture is placed. Near very large porches, a tree-form shrub sometimes is used instead of a vine. This arrangement not only provides shade and privacy, but also an interesting variation.

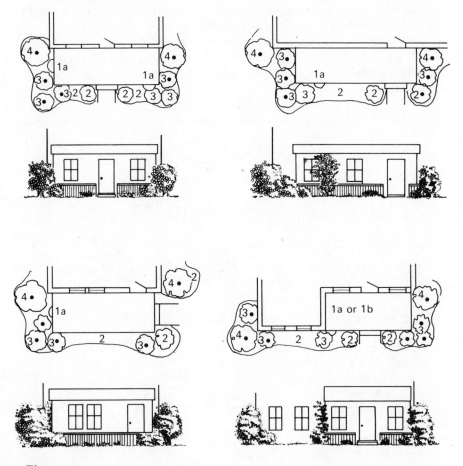

Figure 2-9.

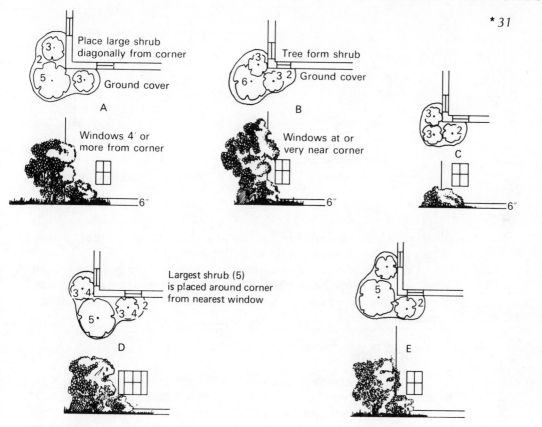

Figure 2-10.

CORNER PLANTINGS

A simple corner planting consists of three shrubs and some ground cover. When the windows of both walls are some distance from the corner, a tall shrub is placed at the corner where it will not grow up in front of either window. When both windows are near the corner, plant a tall tree-form shrub or a small tree in a position to shade these windows somewhat but not cut out too much light, or use a group of low-growing shrubs. Some people prefer to have no planting at this kind of corner.

When the window on the side wall is nearer the corner than the window on the front wall, place the large shrub on a line with the side wall, bringing it approximately midway between the two windows. Lower-growing plants are placed beneath the windows. This type of tall shrub inside the corner decreases the apparent length of the house. The reverse condition is when the front window is near the corner and the side window is several feet away. Again, the large plant is placed in a position where it will not grow in front of either window. This type of

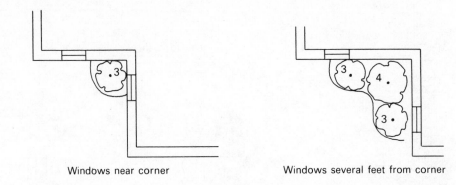

| Windows near corner | Windows several feet from corner |

Figure 2-11.

planting, with the tall shrub placed outside the front corner, may be used to increase the apparent width of the house.

For inside corners, the length of the angle and the positions of the windows determine the number and size of the plants to use. If the inside corner is small, the planting may be combined with one of the outside corner plantings.

WALL PLANTINGS

These six diagrams for wall plantings represent situations common to most homes. Your home undoubtedly has some variation of one or more of these conditions; nevertheless, you may need to make some changes to correspond with the actual positions of windows or the size and shape of the chimney.

A: A suitable planting for a wall space between windows that are several feet apart could be a symmetrical planting, with one shrub placed midway between the two windows. A nonsymmetrical planting, however, is more interesting, with low-growing plants set beneath the windows. Some possibilities are ground covers, annuals, or perennials. These plants also may be used along a foundation wall between the shrubs. Plants with vividly-colored flowers should be used with caution.

B: You may encounter the same window arrangement, but with less width because of proximity to a sidewalk, driveway, or property line. Here a vine will provide foliage height without width.

C: Shrubs at each side of the picture window areaway can be selected from the same size group, but a less symmetrical planting is probably more interesting. Ground covers planted in front of the areaway will not block the light.

D: Low-growing shrubs may be planted beneath bay windows. This not only improves the appearance of the wall space but hides the open area beneath the bay. If some shade is desired, a taller shrub may be used beside the window, even taller than illustrated in this plan.

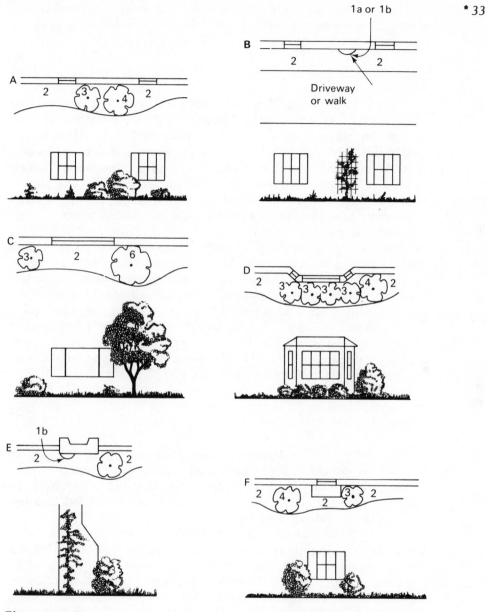

Figure 2-12.

E: A chimney looks good with a vine selected from Group 1. A shrub placed at one corner of the chimney adds to the interest of the planting. If the chimney is small, it may be best to use a tall shrub instead of a vine.

F: Where there is a high foundation wall with a basement window without an areaway, use ground covers in front of the window unless light from the window is not essential. If light is needed, plant dwarf shrubs on each side of the window but not directly in front of it. The shrub on each side may be tied back when it is necessary to open the window to put fuel or other materials into the basement.

USE OF VINES

Vines to ornament the walls and porches of homes should be selected with regard to the type of construction and the space they are to occupy. Twining vines should be used on homes with wood siding and may be used on stone or brick if proper support is provided. Clinging vines are more often used on stone or brick walls. Vines such as bittersweet and Boston ivy cover large wall spaces; clematis and akebia, which are not so rank in growth, are better suited to smaller areas. Thorny vines such as climbing roses may be troublesome near doorways or other passageways.

Most clinging vines require artificial support only until they attach themselves to a wall, although heavy clinging vines, such as bigleaf wintercreeper and trumpet creeper sometimes need extra support. A strap laid across the stem and nailed to the wall usually keeps them secure. Twining vines must have a trellis or other support. Most trellis designs should be simple and constructed to fit the space they occupy. Some areas require only a rectangular support. Occasionally two vines are used, one on each side of a window or doorway, and an overhead support is provided to frame the opening.

Planting Trees

No part of the landscaping scheme is so abused as large trees. The builder, in most cases, treats them as an obstacle to construction, to be slammed into oblivion by the bulldozer so that the driver won't be inconvenienced. A hundred years of growth are sacrificed to a few minutes of a bulldozer operator's time.

Lucky is the man who buys a home with large trees already part of the landscape. A study reported by the American Museum of Natural History has shown that mature trees add as much as $10,000 to the value of a medium-priced home. Trees soften the harsh, stark lines of buildings, add beauty and interest, and supply valuable shade—which saves on air-conditioning dollars and provides an agreeable place to sit and cool off on a summer's day.

But trees are often purchased on a very short-sighted basis. A good, mature tree is expensive, but it adds considerably to a home's value. Strategically placed, it can recoup its original cost with a few years' of saving on the cost of air-conditioning. Yet people often buy cheap, skinny trees which take decades to reach a useful size, are subject to disease and early death and cause excessive lawn litter.

Figure 2-13: At one time, the American elm arched over many town and city streets in lovely cathedral fashion. Now, the elms are either gone or going, victims of Dutch elm disease.

Sometimes even foresighted gardeners are defeated by the forces of Nature. In many of our large cities graceful elms were planted which in time formed beautiful archways along the streets. The Dutch elm beetle was unknown then, but its dirty work is all too familiar now. Many a charming old neighborhood has been reduced to ugly nakedness by Dutch elm disease. Similar problems exist with the gypsy moth in the East and the tussock moth in the western forests. Oaks, chestnuts, and many others have seen various blights come and go, decimating their ranks.

So, it pays to choose your trees wisely. Weigh the cost of a large tree against the benefits to be gained. Most nurserymen will guarantee trees planted by them, and this seems to be worthwhile insurance. Some of the factors to be taken into consideration are:

* **Hardiness:** Find out what trees are resistant to weather, disease, and insects in your particular area and try to get one of these.
* **Form:** Select the tree best shaped for your particular use.
* **Size:** See the growth rate and longevity charts and determine which is best for you.
* **Undesirable characteristics:** Disease-prone species and those with certain nuisance features, such as large seed pods or sticky fruits.
* **Availability:** No tree is worth considering if it just isn't for sale in your area.

Figure 2-14: The form of a tree should fit its site and use as much as is practical. This low-spreading tree is fine overhanging a small patio.

HARDINESS

Start with a list of trees that are hardy enough for the environment. Consider the total environment: the climate, the soil type, the available moisture, the contaminants in the atmosphere, and competition from the activities of human society.

When you consider hardiness to the climate of your area, remember the summer's heat as well as the winter's cold. Trees native to northern climates easily withstand southern winters but may be scorched beyond use by heat of a southern summer.

And be sure trees are reliably hardy in your area. Trees planted north of their adapted range may grow satisfactorily through a series of milder-than-normal winters, but when an especially severe winter comes along, they will be killed. Then the person who planted them will have lost money and labor and—most precious of all—time.

Soils in the city tend to be mechanically compacted and poorly drained. If you are selecting trees for city planting, therefore, you must either select trees that are tolerant of such compaction or be prepared to invest time and labor in overriding these conditions.

Available moisture, too, can limit a tree's usefulness. In park plantings or specimen plantings in a yard, trees native to the area are not likely to suffer from lack of water during periods of normal rainfall. Near a street, however, trees can never receive their fair share of water. Rain flows off into gutters and storm drains and is carried away. For the city select trees that can grow in reasonably dry soil, then see that they get enough water to keep them growing until their root systems adjust to the continuous subnormal soil moisture.

City air is filled with smoke and fumes, dust, and soot. Some trees can grow successfully in this environment, others cannot. For example, gingko and London plane trees do well in downtown fumes and dirt; sugar maple does not.

Trees planted in the open—in parks or large yards—usually have less competition from the activities of humans than street trees do. But many city trees must compete with automobiles, foot traffic, and lawn-mowers, with sewer lines underground and utility lines overhead. To deal with human society successfully, a tree must be tough.

FORM

Consider whether the mature form of a tree is appropriate for its intended use. A broad-spreading, low-hanging tree may be ideal as a park or yard tree, but it would be unsatisfactory along a driveway. A slim, upright tree may be perfect for lining driveways, but of little use for shading a patio. If you are not familiar with the mature form of trees under consideration, study illustrations of them in books or nursery catalogs.

Figure 2-15: Here a tall, slim tree gives interest to a bare brick wall without overwhelming it.

APPROXIMATE SIZE OF FULL-GROWN PLANTS

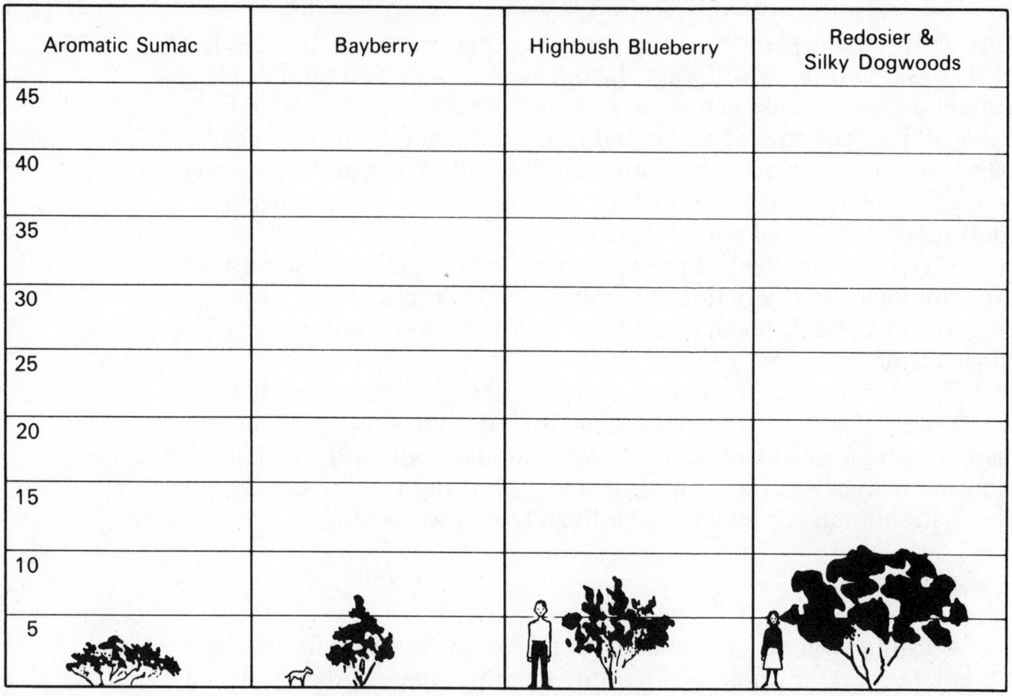
Aromatic Sumac
Bayberry
Highbush Blueberry
Redosier & Silky Dogwoods
45
40
35
30
25
20
15
10
5

APPROXIMATE SIZE OF FULL-GROWN PLANTS

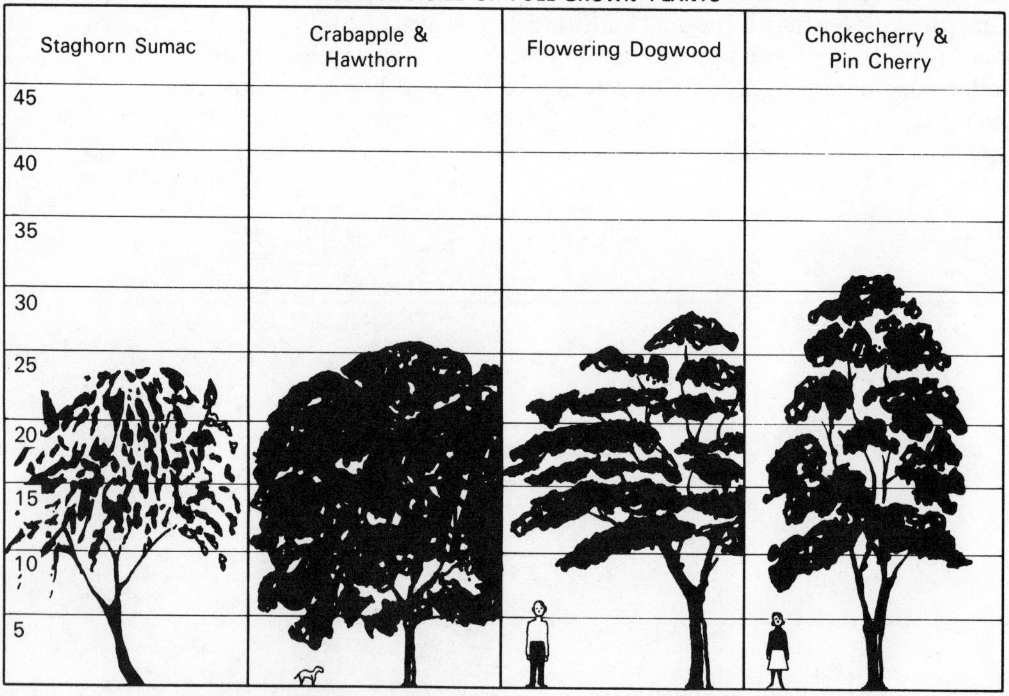
Staghorn Sumac
Crabapple & Hawthorn
Flowering Dogwood
Chokecherry & Pin Cherry
45
40
35
30
25
20
15
10
5

Figure 2-16: The ultimate size of any trees that you plant should be of some concern, even though they may not reach full growth for many years.

APPROXIMATE SIZE OF FULL-GROWN PLANTS

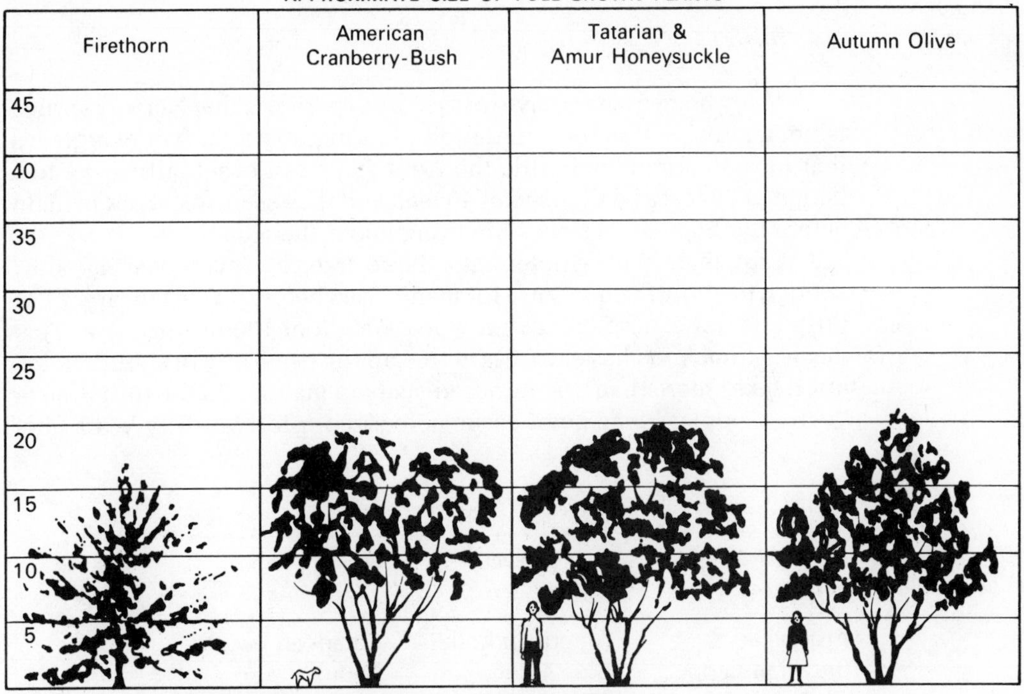
Firethorn
American Cranberry-Bush
Tatarian & Amur Honeysuckle
Autumn Olive
45
40
35
30
25
20
15
10
5

APPROXIMATE SIZE OF FULL-GROWN PLANTS

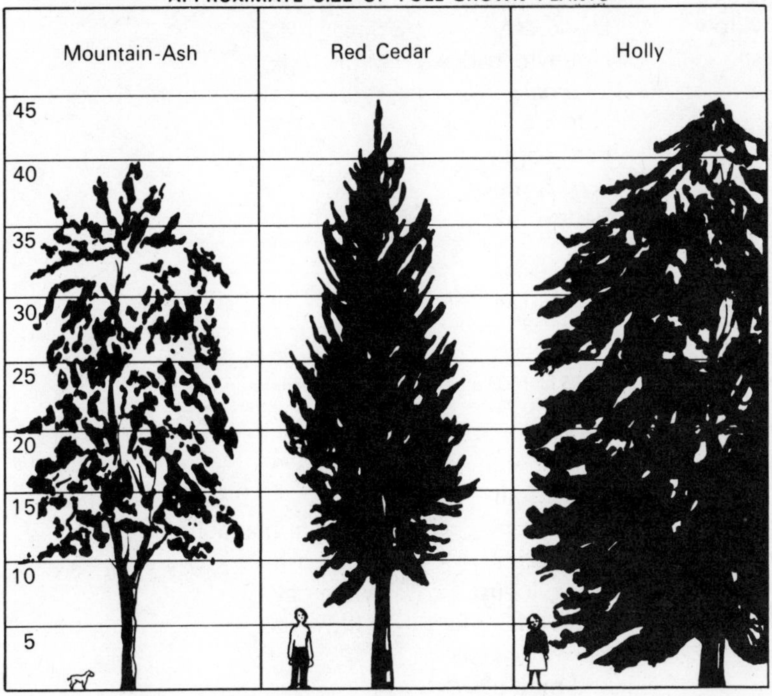
Mountain-Ash
Red Cedar
Holly
45
40
35
30
25
20
15
10
5

Figure 2-16 (continued): These drawings show the scale of the full-grown familiar trees most favored by birds on this continent.

Many homeowners have learned by experience that Norway spruce is not a suitable tree for foundation plantings. The six-foot evergreens that look so attractive beside the front steps can eventually grow to a height of 70 feet and a spread of 40 feet, and they seem to get out of hand before the homeowner does anything about the situation.

Growth rate of a potentially large tree, however, may be slow enough to allow the tree's use for many years before it gets too large. The tulip tree, for example, may grow to a height of 100 feet or more. That makes it much too large for a yard tree on the usual city or suburban lot, but it takes more than one hundred years to mature. So the tulip tree or "yellow poplar" may be of acceptable size for forty or fifty years after

Table 2-2: Size of Full-grown Trees

Small (up to 40 feet)	Medium (40 to 75 feet)	Large (more than 75 feet)
Arborvitae	American holly	American beech
Brazilian pepper	Blue spruce	Pecan
Cherry laurel	Goldenrain	Southern magnolia
Desert willow	Hackberry	Sugar maple
Green ash	Honeylocust	White oak
Hemlock	Live oak	Willow oak
Jacaranda	Norway maple	
Mimosa	Red maple	
Wax	Scotch pine	
	Valley oak	

Table 2-3: Average Life Span of Trees

Short (to 50 years)	Medium (to 75 or 100 years)	Long (100 or more years)
Arborvitae	American holly	American beech
Brazilian pepper	Blue spruce	Live oak
Desert willow	Goldenrain	Pecan
Mimosa	Green ash	Southern magnolia
Redbud	Hackberry	White ash
Sydney wattle	Honeylocust	White oak
Umbrella tree	Jacaranda	Willow oak
	Norway maple	
	Red maple	
	Scotch pine	
	Valley oak	

planting. You must decide if you care what happens forty years hence.

Longevity also is a matter for thought. Some trees grow rapidly, giving shade and screening soon after they are planted. They reach maturity quickly, then decline. How soon will they decline? Will their decline—and need for removal—affect you? If, when you are 23 years old, you plant a tree with a 40-year life expectancy, you may have to cut it down just as you are planning to spend some of your retirement time sitting under it. But if you plant the same tree when you are 45, you can sit under it in retirement years not caring when it begins to decline. You have to decide whether you are planting trees for posterity or for yourself.

UNDESIRABLE CHARACTERISTICS

It is difficult to find a tree that has no undesirable characteristics, but some make a tree unsuitable for residential plantings. For example, the American elm has been so ravaged by Dutch elm disease that it is a poor risk almost anywhere. Thornless honeylocust is subject to attack by the mimosa web worm—a pest that ruins the appearance of the tree unless it is sprayed every year. White mulberry and the female ginkgo produce what are generally considered objectionable fruits. Other trees have traits that are tolerable nuisances. Oaks, hickorys, horse chestnuts, crabapples—all produce fruits that attract children who may use them for missiles. Sweetgum fruits (gum balls) are covered with thorny protuberances that make them a nuisance in lawns. Poplars and mimosa produce an abundance of seeds that sprout in lawns and flowerbeds. If you like these trees otherwise, you may choose to overlook their undesirable characteristics. Some trees have characteristics that are intolerable in one situation but not in another. Some maples, for example, have a tendency to raise and crack pavement with their roots. If they are planted where there is no nearby pavement, this is no problem. Some trees—red and silver maples, elm, willow and poplar—are notorious sewer cloggers. If they are planted away from sewer lines, again this is no problem. Match the tree's characteristics with its intended use and decide if they are compatible.

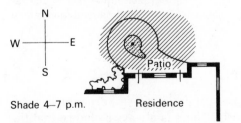

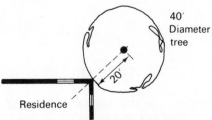

Figure 2-17: Locate trees to provide shade during the hours that outdoor living areas will be used most.

Figure 2-18: Plant trees no closer to a house than one-half the diameter of the full-grown tree.

42 *

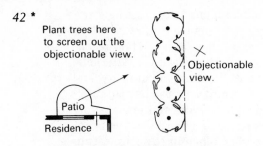

Plant trees here
to screen out the
objectionable view.

Objectionable
view.

Patio

Residence

Figure 2-19: Neighbor's unsightly trash cans bother you? Screen them and other objectionable views by planting a row of trees near the property line.

Figure 2-20: What about a view you really like? Locate trees to create a natural picture frame—perhaps something like this.

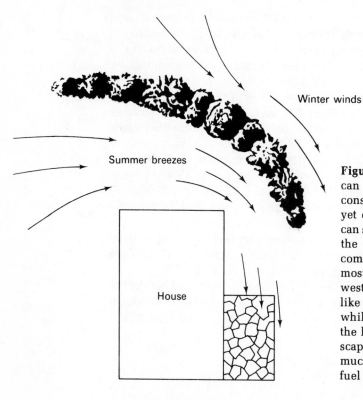

Winter winds

Summer breezes

House

Figure 2-21: Curved, high hedges can be planted carefully so as to conserve heating fuel in the winter, yet catch the cooling breezes that can supplement air conditioning in the summer. Since winter winds come from northerly directions in most areas, and from the south or west in warmer months, a design like this helps ward off cold winds while directing welcome breezes to the house and patio. Such a landscaping technique has saved as much as 22.9 percent on annual fuel costs.

AVAILABILITY OF SPECIES

When you have narrowed your list down to a few acceptable trees, find out which are available locally. There is always a chance that the best tree for the purpose may be in such demand that it is not available locally. Then you must either settle for second-best or shop around by mail to find the tree you want.

Figure 2-22: Where house sites are crowded, a tall hedge of privet, arborvitae, hemlock or—as illustrated—pine can effectively create a little island of privacy for outdoor living.

Many reputable nurseries do business by mail. You can usually feel secure in dealing with any of the old-line firms. But beware of companies that make fantastic claims for their nursery stock or promote common trees by giving them unusual names.

PLANTING

The key to good tree planting is generosity. Be generous in digging a planting hole, in replacing poor soil with good, in expending energy to do the job right. And plan carefully so the trees fit into your grand design.

The right way to do the job depends on how good the soil is on the planting site:

In good soil:
* Dig planting holes for bare-root trees large enough to receive the roots when they are spread in a natural position.
* Dig planting holes for balled-and-burlapped trees two feet wider than the rootball.
* Dig holes deep enough so you can set the trees at the same level at which they grew in the nursery.

In poor soil:
* Dig holes for all trees as wide and deep as you can conveniently make them.

* Replace the poor soil from the hole with good soil when you fill in around the newly set tree, or mix the old soil with an equal amount of peat moss.

In soil with poor drainage:

* Take all practical measures to improve drainage.
* Limit tree selection to species having a mature height less than 50 feet.
* Set the rootball in a shallow depression in the soil.
* Fill in around the rootball with a good soil, forming a slightly concave bed extending out as far from the trunk as you can manage. Topsoil is often removed in building operations. Subsoil is commonly unfavorable for trees. In such cases, the best procedure is to use as much topsoil as practicable in the planting hole.

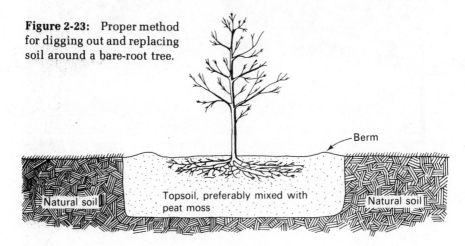

Figure 2-23: Proper method for digging out and replacing soil around a bare-root tree.

Berm

Natural soil

Topsoil, preferably mixed with peat moss

Natural soil

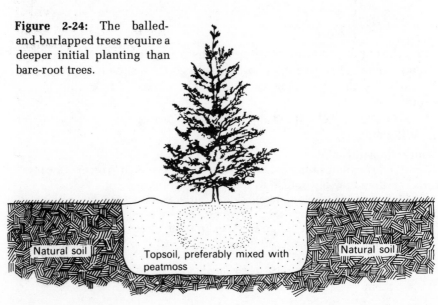

Figure 2-24: The balled-and-burlapped trees require a deeper initial planting than bare-root trees.

Natural soil

Topsoil, preferably mixed with peatmoss

Natural soil

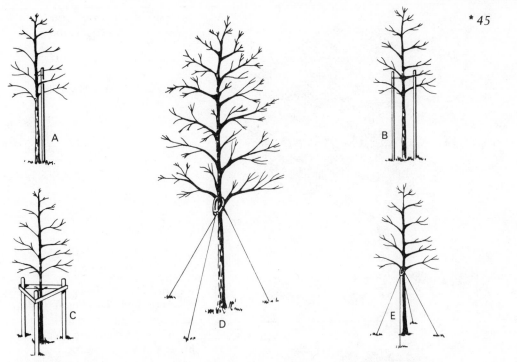

Figure 2-25: Effective methods of staking and guying young trees: (**A**) single stake; (**B**) double stakes; (**C**) triple stakes; (**D**) three-way guy wires; and (**E**) four-way guys.

Pack soil under the newly set tree until it sets at the level at which it grew in the nursery. Before filling around the rootball, stake or guy the tree. If the trunk diameter of the tree is three inches or less, use one or two six-foot poles or steel fenceposts to stake the tree. Set the poles vertically into the soil next to the rootball. Fasten the trunk to the poles with a loop of wire enclosed in a section of old garden hose to prevent cutting the bark.

If the tree trunk is larger than three inches in diameter, support it with three hose-covered guy wires. Loop the wires around the trunk about two-thirds up the main stem or trunk. Stake one guy wire to the ground in the direction of the prevailing wind. Stake the other two wires to the ground to form an equilateral triangle.

After the tree is set and the hole is filled with good soil, settle the soil around the roots by watering thoroughly. Then wrap the trunk with burlap or creped kraft paper to prevent sunscald. Start wrapping at the top and wrap toward the ground. Tie the wrapping material with stout cord, knotting it about every 18 inches. The wrapping should remain for one to two years.

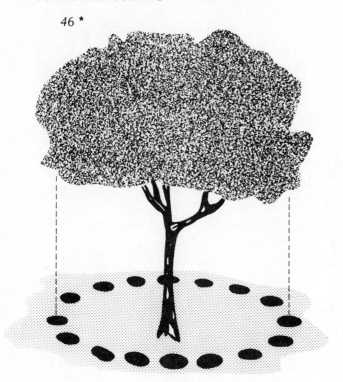

Figure 2-26: Best way to fertilize a tree is to dig holes around its drip-line (*18 to 24 inches apart and 15 to 24 inches deep*); insert fertilizer in holes and fill with earth, sand and peat.

FERTILIZING

If you use plenty of good soil for backfilling newly planted trees, the trees are not likely to need fertilizer for the first year after planting. However, street trees planted in the narrow parking between sidewalk and curb may need earlier feeding.

If you think your trees need fertilizer—if the leaves are paler than normal and if growth is slower than normal—you can apply it in spring this way:

* Measure the diameter of the trunk three feet above the ground; use two pounds of 5-10-5 for each inch of the diameter (a one-pound coffee can holds about two pounds of fertilizer).
* Using a soil auger, if one is available, or a crowbar or a posthole digger, make holes 15 to 24 inches deep and about 18 to 24 inches apart around the drip line of the tree (the area beneath the ends of the longest branches).
* Distribute the fertilizer equally among the holes, then fill the holes with good soil. A mixture of equal parts topsoil, sand, and peat moss is good for filling the holes; it provides aeration and water access as well as filling the space.

Many trees grow in places where the area of soil exposed to rainfall is small. Lawn trees have to compete with grass and other plants for water. City trees often get too little water too since drainpipes honeycomb cities and remove thousands of gallons of water every day. Trees can become conditioned to this constantly low amount of water, but they have to be kept alive until they can adjust.

Water trees for the first two seasons after planting them. Water about once a week and let the water run for several hours. If you have one of the special needles that attaches to a garden hose for injecting water and water-soluble fertilizer into the root zone, you will find it to be useful, particularly for watering curbside trees. If the soil in your area is tight clay or is underlain with hardpan, be careful that you do not overwater. Excess water will kill some kinds of trees faster than drought.

MULCHING METHODS

In the forest, decaying fallen leaves provide a protective mulch that conserves natural moisture, tempers summer's heat and winter's cold, and adds organic matter to the soil. In most city or suburban yards, however, fallen leaves beneath lawn trees are more likely to be considered litter than mulch and are usually removed. And fallen leaves

Figure 2-27: Shrubs and trees, like most growing things, benefit from a protective mulch.

48 * along curbs do clog gutters and drains, make streets slippery, and are fire hazards, so they must be removed. But in consequence, the soil becomes depleted of organic matter.

Yard trees can be mulched with material more attractive than rotting leaves—such as pine bark, tanbark, ground corncobs, or peanut hulls. They then receive the organic matter they need. Or trees can be fertilized with soil organic matter also. The holes for the application also help to keep the soil moist, aerated, and well drained.

EFFICIENT PRUNING

Inspect your shade trees regularly and prune them when needed. This way, you can improve their appearance, guard their health, and make them stronger by pruning them. As soon as the need becomes apparent, you can easily correct defects that would require major surgery if ignored. When you do this pruning, try to eliminate undesirable branches or shoots while they are small. Drastic, difficult, or expensive pruning may be avoided by early corrective action.

Figure 2-28: Weak V-crotches should be lopped off when a tree is still young (*courtesy of Seymour Smith & Son*).

Here is a list of things to look for and prune:

* **Dead or dying branches:** These and other unsightly parts of trees.
* **Sprouts:** Growing at or near the base of the tree trunk.
* **Center branches:** Those that grow toward the center of the tree.
* **Crossed branches:** That cross and rub together; disease and decay fungi can enter the tree through such abraded parts.
* **V-crotches:** If it is possible to do so without ruining the appearance of the tree, remove one of the members forming a V-crotch since they split easily; their removal helps to prevent storm damage to the tree.
* **Multiple leaders:** If several leaders develop on a tree that normally has only a single stem and you wish the tree to develop its typical shape, cut out all but one leader. This restores dominance to the remaining stem.
* **"Nuisance" growth:** Cut off branches that are likely to interfere with electric or telephone wires; remove branches that shade street lights or block the view so as to constitute a traffic hazard. Prune branches that shut off breezes. Cut off lower limbs that shade the lawn excessively.

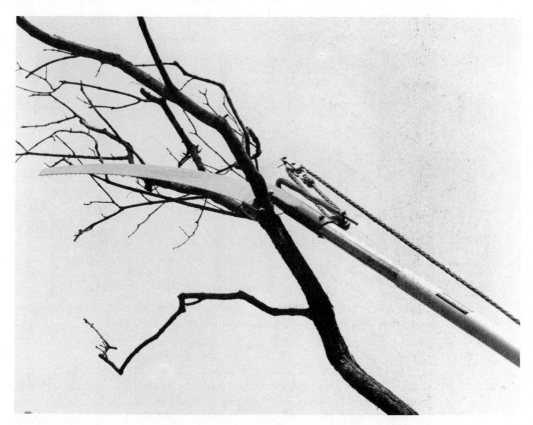

Figure 2-29: To cut off nuisance growth in inaccessible places, use a long-handled pruner (*courtesy of Seymour Smith & Son*).

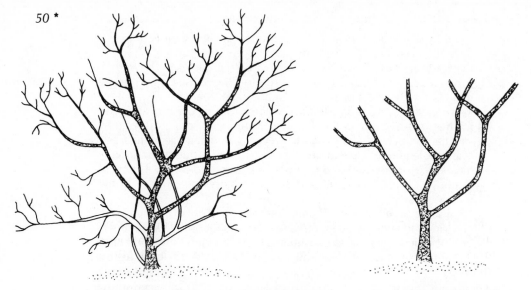

Figure 2-30: There are various techniques for pruning hedges and trees. Here the drawing shows a good way to prune dead wood from old bushes.

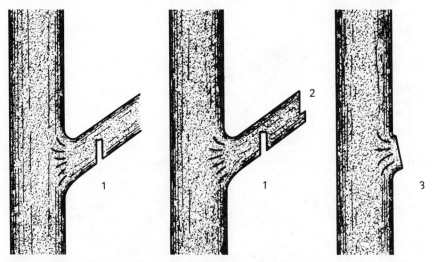

Figure 2-31: Here the illustration shows a series of cuts that will remove large unwanted branch without leaving a ragged stump on a tree.

Do not leave stubs when you prune. They usually die and are points at which decay fungi can enter the tree. Small pruning cuts heal quickly. Large cuts—more than one inch in diameter—should be treated with antiseptic tree dressing to prevent entrance of decay or disease while the wound is healing.

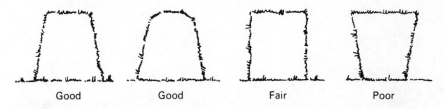

| Good | Good | Fair | Poor |

Figure 2-32: Two good and two not-so-good methods of trimming hedges and bushes.

TREE PROTECTION

Most insects and diseases can be controlled by spraying. Your county agricultural agent, extension landscape specialist, or state agricultural experiment station can tell you what spray schedules to follow in protecting your trees from insects and diseases. When trees are small, you can spray them yourself. As they grow larger, however, spraying becomes a job for professional arborists who have the equipment and knowledge required to do a thorough job.

Danger of injury to persons on foot or using lawnmowers and bicycles is reduced by stakes and guy wires around trees. Tree boxes can also be made from snow fencing and placed around trees if more conspicuous protection is needed—or wanted.

Table 2-4: Trees Immune to the Gypsy Moth

Ash	Dogwood	Locust
Butternut	Fir, Balsam	Poplar, Yellow
Catalpa	Hemlock	Sycamore
Cedar, Red	Holly	Walnut, Black

Figure 3-1: A good lawn not only enhances the beauty of one's home; it also provides a nice, soft spot for sunning and thinking.

3:

Care of Lawn & Garden

After you have established the grand design for your outdoor space, it is time to get to work on the individual components. Foundation plantings and large trees are essentials to every landscape, but there are other plantings that are a part of the setting, too. Some of these are more vital than others, and at least some of them are important for every home-owner.

If you are used to city or suburban living, you automatically think of a large, expansive lawn. Grass has always been, and will always be, a part of most homesites. But it is not a necessity and, indeed, in some cases it is not even possible. Beach homes and other vacation houses often do very well without a lawn at all, and some suburban settings do with little or no grass whatever. On hilly, rocky, or sandy soil, ground covers or other plantings take the place of a lawn.

Still, most homes look their best when viewed across an expanse of green, level lawn. Stretching out under a cool tree on a bed of soft grass is one of the most luxurious feelings in the world. Achieving this ultimate in tactile sensation is not always an easy task, particularly in hard or barren soil, but it can be accomplished anywhere by almost anyone—if he perseveres.

Planting a Sturdy Lawn

Knowing when to plant new grass is as important as how. Winter, in most areas, is obviously a poor time (although you can sow seed on late winter snow), as are the hot, dry months of summer. The best time to

54 * plant most lawns is in the fall; but for many grasses, particularly in the warmer regions, spring is fine, too. Even with those grasses that are better started in the fall, like the bluegrasses, fescues, and bent grasses, spring plantings can be successful if nurtured carefully enough. Indeed, if you have nothing but sod or mud for a lawn, anything that grows will be an improvement.

The actual selection of a hardy turfgrass depends on geography, temperature, moisture, soil properties, degree of shade and personal preference. Temperature is the most important.

COOL-SEASON GRASSES

The so-called "cool season" grasses grow best during the cooler parts of the year: spring and fall in the northern regions; late fall, winter and early spring in the southern United States. Although they stay green, these grasses are semi-dormant and grow very slowly during the summer.

Kentucky bluegrass is one of the most widely used of the cool-season grasses. Red fescue and chewings fescue are the next most popular in cool humid regions. Colonial bent grass has proved successful in New England, Washington and Oregon when used alone. In mixtures it is used throughout the northern United States and southern Canada.

Figure 3-2: Merion Kentucky bluegrass gives a healthy, deep-rooted turf that holds up well to rough wear and bad weather.

Figure 3-3: Bent grass is the Cadillac of American grasses, but it is expensive and difficult to maintain. Much used for golf greens, this grass can give your lawn that same such look and velvety feel if you work at it (*courtesy of The Lawn Institute*).

The cool-season grasses, if planted as a mixture, will produce a very satisfactory lawn under most conditions. The formula is fairly standard in areas where there are no shade problems:

* Colonial bent grass; less than 10 percent.
* Fescues; 20 to 40 percent.
* Kentucky bluegrass; the remainder (50 to 70 percent).

The above grasses require only routine maintenance and will withstand considerable traffic. Their percentages will sometimes have to be varied because of local conditions. Local seed dealers will usually provide such information.

For damp northern areas, include substantial portions of poa trivailis. Sandy soils may do better with some of the newer, improved rye grasses. In the southern limits of the cool weather zone, some Kentucky bluegrass may adapt to shady areas.

WARM-SEASON GRASSES

Warm-season grasses are those which reach maximum growth during late spring, summer, and early fall. Most of these grasses do not flourish during the winter in northern areas. With few exceptions, they turn brown with the first frost.

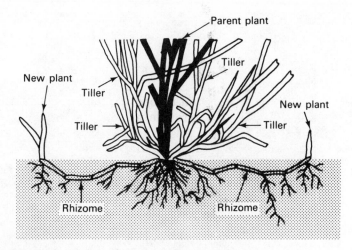

Figure 3-4: Drawing shows how a quality grass of the rhizomatous type reproduces and fills in a lawn by sending out rhizomes from the plant roots which, in turn, produce new grass plants (*courtesy of O. M. Scotts & Sons*).

Bermuda grass is by far the most popular of the warm-season grasses for open, sunny areas in the South. A trailing grass, it is vigorous and withstands a heavy and continuous traffic if properly managed. Its chief disadvantage is that it invades adjacent walks and flower and shrub beds unless periodically edged and trimmed. One variety, U-3, has been grown successfully as far north as the Philadelphia, St. Louis and Richmond areas.

Under limited shade in the South, zoysia will provide a sturdy although slow-growing turf. For heavy shade, St. Augustine grass is the number one choice in the southernmost states.

Other warm-season grasses are centipede grass, carpet grass and, under special conditions for the Great Plains areas, buffalo grass.

For winter color in the South, warm-season grasses are over-seeded with ryegrass or some other cool-season grass. Ryegrass is the most popular choice because the seed is readily available because it is easily established. As a matter of fact, some new, improved, perennial ryegrass varieties are being used as a permanent turfgrass in all areas, especially where the soil is of poor quality. No combination of cool- and warm-season grasses has thus far proved entirely satisfactory for maintaining a year-round green turf.

Whether the lawn is planted with a mixture of grasses or a single species, it is of paramount importance that only quality seeds or planting material of permanent turf species are selected. The inferior lawn seed mixtures frequently contain orchardgrass, timothy, or an undue amount of ryegrass. At best, they will produce coarse-textured tufts and give the lawn a ragged, unkempt look. Federal and state laws require that the analysis tags on seed containers give the percentage of each grass seed included, the purity and germination, and the date of test.

PREPARING THE SEEDBED

What are the requirements of a good seedbed? Ideally, the area should be properly graded to provide adequate drainage. A good seedbed should have a firm, but not compact surface and be free of all refuse and large clods. The seedbed should also contain an abundant supply of well-decomposed organic matter and ample fertilizer. It should be free of all depressions and have adequate internal and surface drainage.

Follow these basic steps in order to establish such a seedbed:

* If the site is new, remove the top four to six inches of soil before house construction begins. This can be used as the topsoil of the new lawn seedbed once the building and subsoil grading operations are completed.
* Remove all building debris from the site. Do not bury such material in the subsoil.
* Plan the lawn to avoid a terrace or a system of terraces if possible. Terraces are hard to maintain. But in areas where the land slopes steeply, build retaining walls.
* A slope of one foot every 40 to 50 feet is an adequate grade to insure good surface drainage. Certainly the fall should not exceed one foot in every 16 linear feet. Make certain that the soil slopes gradually away from the house, walks, and driveways so that no standing pools of water are created. If natural drainage does not take care of excess water, or if the water table is near the surface, you may have to install tile drains or dry wells.
* Where large trees are present in the future lawn area, it may be necessary to protect them if the new lawn is to be either higher or lower than the existing level. When the new level is higher, build a well of brick or stone around the tree; when lower, build a retaining wall.

DETERMINING SOIL QUALITIES

Once the grading of the new lawn is established and proper drainage assured, it is time to determine soil properties. The ideal soil is high in organic matter and has the proper amount of lime, potash, phosphorous and nitrogen. Soil tests are made by commercial firms in most areas. Some state universities provide this service. There are some excellent do-it-yourself kits as well.

To sandy or gravelly soils add peat, well-rotted manure, spent mushroom soil, or well-decomposed sawdust. Some clay may also be added if the soil is light; and the texture of heavy clay soil can be modified by adding sand, perlite, vermiculite, scoria, or peat.

Lime plays an important part in the mineral nutrition of plants. Its major role is to reduce soil acidity, but it also promotes soil granulation and aids in making soil and fertilizer nutrients more readily available to the plants. Dolomitic ground limestone, containing both magnesium and calcium, should be used if the soil is low in magnesium. A soil test will determine how much lime, if any, is needed.

Nitrogen is the most important element, and its correct use is the key to satisfactory lawn growth. It provides the basis of the fertilization program while phosphorous and potash are necessary for deep root development. Soil tests will help determine the amount of each element to use.

Spread the topsoil over the subgrade and incorporate "reserve" fertilizer (phosphorous and potash that is worked four to six inches into the soil). If additional lime is needed after the topsoil is spread, apply it at the time the soil is being worked.

Additives must be incorporated into the soil thoroughly. Failure to do so will create layers in the soil that will cause serious maintenance problems in later years. Layers of sand or gravel often stop water movement and prevent the development of deep grass roots. Layers of organic matter often remain saturated with water. This prevents penetration of the layers by the roots because such layers lack oxygen.

It is important that all tillage operations be performed when moisture conditions are normal. Do not work the soil when it is saturated. Plowing or spading, followed by discing and hand raking are the best methods of preparing the soil for planting. Excessive rototilling is not recommended because it tends to "float" the finer particles of soil to the surface. The beating action of the tiller may destroy some of the soil structure. Hand raking is necessary to level the soil and to prevent the formation of depressions and hollows where water might concentrate.

The seedbed should be allowed to settle. If there has been no rain, the area should be sprinkled thoroughly. Any depressions or high spots can then be smoothed out by raking.

STARTER FERTILIZER

The purpose in adding a "starter" fertilizer to the topsoil is to provide the new seedings with an immediate supply of available nutrients. If soil has not been sterilized, weeds will grow faster than grass. If weed control chemicals have been used (only after final grading) the starter fertilizer may be applied at time of seeding. If no weed control measures have been taken, the fertilizer applications may be delayed until a few weeks after final grading. In the latter case, it will be necessary to rake again at the time. This offers the added advantage of providing an opportunity to destroy by raking any weeds that might have sprouted since the final grading.

Table 3-1: Sowing Rates for Seeded Grasses

Grass Seed	Pounds per 1,000 sq ft	Time for seeding
Bahia grass	2–3	Spring
Bermuda grass	2–3	Spring
Blue grama grass (unhulled)	1–1½	Spring
Buffalo grass (treated)	½–1	Spring
Canada bluegrass	2–3	Fall
Carpet grass (Louisiana)	3–4	Spring
Centipede grass	2–3	Spring
Chewings fescue	3–5	Fall
Colonial bent grass (Highland, Astoria)	1–2	Fall
Creeping bent grass (Seaside)	1–2	Fall
Crested wheatgrass	1–2	Fall
Japanese lawn grass (hulled)	1–2	Spring
Kentucky bluegrass, common	2–3	Fall
Kentucky bluegrass, Merion	1–2	Fall
Red fescue	3–5	Fall
Redtop	1–2	Fall
Rough bluegrass	3–5	Fall
Ryegrass (domestic and perennial)	4–6	Spring-Fall
Tall fescue (Alta, Ky. 31)	4–6	Fall
Velvet bent grass	1–2	Fall
Mixture for sunny areas: 75% bluegrass, 25% red fescue	2–4	Fall
Mixture for shady areas: 25% bluegrass, 75% red fescue	2–4	Fall

SEEDING

Seed may be planted by hand or with a mechanical seeder. To obtain uniform distribution, the seed is mixed with small amounts of a carrier such as topsoil or sand. Divide the mixed material into two equal parts and sow one part in one direction and the other crosswise to the first sowing. Cover the seed lightly by hand raking, then firm the seeded area by rolling with a light roller.

Mulching with a light covering of weed-free straw or hay will help hold moisture and prevent the seed from washing away during watering or rainfall. Mulches applied evenly and lightly need not be removed. On terraced areas or on sloping banks, cheesecloth, open-mesh sacking, or commercial mulching cloth will help hold moisture and seeds in place.

60 * Grass will grow through such mulching material which may be left to rot.

New seedings should be kept moist until well established. Once seeds have begun to germinate, they must not dry out or they will die. Light and frequent watering during early stages of establishment may be required. But avoid saturating the soil, for excessive moisture will favor the development of "damping off," a fungus disease.

SODDING, PLUGGING, SPRIGGING, ETC.

Seed for many grasses is not available or does not produce plants that are true to type. Such grasses must be planted by vegetative methods such as sodding, plugging, strip sodding, sprigging, or stolonizing. Grasses planted by these methods include the zoysias, improved strains of Bermuda grass, St. Augustine grass, centipede grass, and creeping bent grass.

Unless good quality sod is available and complete coverage is needed immediately, the expense of sodding is seldom justified except on steep slopes or terraces. To sod, prepare and fertilize the seedbed in the same manner as for seeding. Firm the seedbed with a roller after final hand raking. Sod cut at a ¾-inch thickness will knit to the underlying soil faster than a thicker sod. The sod strips should be laid like brick and fitted tightly together in a running bond (see p. 168). After laying the first strip, use a broad board for kneeling during the rest of the sodding operation. This eliminates tramping on the prepared seedbed. Once the sod is laid, tamp it lightly and top dress with a thoroughly mixed and screened mixture of topsoil, sand, and organic matter. The sod should be watered regularly.

In spot sodding, small plugs or blocks of sod are planted at measured intervals, generally one foot apart. The plugs should be fitted tightly into prepared holes and tamped firmly into place.

Strip sodding means that strips of sod, two to four inches wide, are planted end to end, in rows at measured intervals. Firm contact with surrounding soil is necessary.

Sprigging is the planting of individual plants, runners, cuttings or stolons at spaced intervals. Sprigs or runners are obtained by tearing apart or shredding solid pieces of established sod. The space interval is governed by the spread rate of the grass, how fast coverage is desired, and the amount of planting material available. Sprigs or runners may also be planted end to end in rows rather than at spaced intervals.

Large Bermuda grass areas may be established by spreading shredded stolons with a manure spreader and discing lightly to firm them into the soil. This method requires 90 to 120 bushels of stolons per acre, and is used for large areas.

Whatever the method, the newly-planted grass must be kept moist until it is well established. During the first year, light applications of a

Table 3-2: Planting Rates for Vegetative Grasses

Grass	Amount of planting material per 1,000 square feet	Time for planting
Bermuda grass	10 square feet of nursery sod or 1 bushel of stolons	Spring-Summer
Buffalo grass	25–50 square feet of sod	Spring
Carpet grass	8–10 square feet of sod	Spring-Summer
Centipede grass	8–10 square feet of sod	Spring-Summer
Creeping bent grass	80–100 square feet of nursery sod or 10 bushels of stolons	Fall
Velvet bent grass	80–100 square feet of nursery sod or 10 bushels of stolons	Fall
Zoysia	30 square feet of sod when plugging; 6 square feet of sod when sprigging	Spring-Summer

nitrogeneous fertilizer every two to four weeks during the growing season will help speed the spread of the plants.

Lawn Maintenance

In a sense, grass was made to be cut. Unlike trees, bushes, and most other plants, grass grows up from the lower part of the stem rather than from the tips. Cutting stimulates growth by allowing more sunlight to reach the growing area. It also stimulates the grass to thicken at the base. That helps crowd out weeds. In fact, good grass growth is the best weed killer you can have.

MOWING GRASS

Each type of grass has an optimum cutting height. Cutting the grass too low can stunt growth and can cause disease to take hold. Grass should be cut less or "higher" during extremely high temperatures and during drought conditions. It's a good idea to check locally since there may be problems peculiar to your area. And indiscriminate cutting is always bad, of course.

Timing of the cutting is important too. Check the height of your grass and cut it only when you can cut one-half to one inch at a time. This may vary from several times a week early in the growing season to once a month in a dry spell, but it is important for good growth and for attractiveness to cut it promptly when required.

What about clippings? There are two opposing views: one that every single clipping should be picked up for a more attractive lawn; the other that clippings should remain on the ground as mulch and protection. Actually both are partly right. A lawn does look better without a

Figure 3-5: Mowing enhances the looks of your lawn, and keeps the grass vigorous and healthy. And, if you don't like hand work, you can do it the easy way with a riding mower. Use electric grass shears for edging and the difficult corners. Some cordless models with detachable handles can be used for both the upright and "stoop" work.

layer of clippings, but there is some value in letting clippings decompose on the lawn. Too many clippings, however, will choke off the air. That is bad for grass. Use your common sense, strike a happy medium.

It is also wise to vary the cutting pattern. Go back and forth in one direction for one cutting, then back and forth in the cross direction the next time. Cut diagonally sometimes. Continual cutting in the same way tends to slant the grass in that direction.

There are also right and wrong ways to guide your mower over the lawn. Most mowers "throw" the clippings either to the left or right. Try to discharge the clippings onto the lawn and away from walks to save sweeping up. A still easier way is to use a grass-catcher attachment with your mower or use a mulching mower that shreds the clippings and returns them to the grass. For edging and difficult corners, cordless electric grass shears are very useful. Some models even have detachable handles so they can be used either for hand or upright work.

A beautiful lawn can be yours if you plan ahead and take a little care. Modern lawn equipment can make pleasant exercise out of what was once a difficult chore.

Correct Cutting Heights

Bent grasses	¼ to ½ inch*
Bermuda grass	1 to 1-¼ inch
Zoysia	1-¼ to 1-½ inches
Merion Bluegrass	1-½ to 2 inches
Kentucky Bluegrass	2 to 2-½ inches
Others	1-½ to 2-½ inches

*Special type of mower required to cut grass at this height.

WATERING GRASS

One thing your lawn needs, especially during its siesta months, is water. Unhappily, summer is also the period when rain becomes infrequent or falls in great bursts only to run off into the sewers. The sun-parched grass rarely gets enough on its own, so you have to help it along. To solve this problem, the lucky people in this world install automatic sprinkler systems with computerized controls to water the grass at certain intervals. Some even have sensors which tell the controls when

Figure 3-6: If you like a nice, well-watered lawn and can spare a few hundred dollars, an automatic sprinkling system is an excellent investment (*courtesy of Rain Jet*).

64 * the grass is dry and needs a drink. The rest of the world has to settle for the garden hose or, better, a non-automatic sprinkler. How you water the grass is as important as when you do it. You should soak the lawn thoroughly every few days or even just once a week, with the key word being "soak." If you use a sprinkler, leave it in the same spot for at least a couple of hours, especially if the soil is sandy. If you want to be really scientific, check the depths of the water with a sharp instrument stuck into the soil. The ground should be wet at least five or six inches below the surface. Or set out a coffee can to serve as a makeshift water gauge. One or two inches is the proper volume per watering.

Established grass does not need frequent waterings, even during the summer, as long as you water it well when you do water. New grass, however, is a different matter. For new grass, water frequently and lightly. (There's no point in soaking below the roots.) In an emergency, even light watering is better for thirsty grass than no water at all, but it does encourage the growth of weeds and crabgrass.

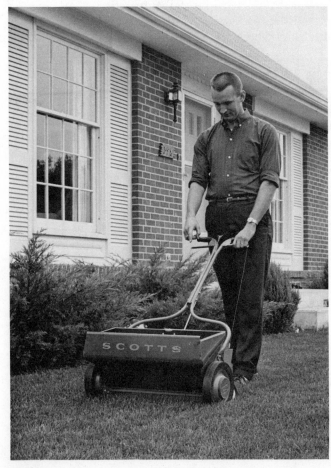

Figure 3-7: Apply fertilizer in the spring and fall, not in the summer; and for even coverage of the lawn, use a spreader.

FERTILIZER

The one thing the panicky homeowner tends to do when his lawn turns brown is douse it with fertilizer. Nothing could be less helpful. It is water that the grass is crying for when it turns brown (unless it is suffering from "brownpatch" or a similar disease).

Grass should be well fertilized in early and late spring, and again in the fall, but avoid summer fertilizing unless you did not do it in the spring. If you do decide to fertilize in the summer, be sure to use an organic fertilizer. This type releases its nutrient more slowly and reduces the chances of "burning" the grass. Better still, wait until fall if you can. Then give the lawn a double dose of fertilizer.

CRABGRASS, WEEDS, ETC.

Crabgrass must be stopped in its infancy, or it spreads millions of seeds over the entire area, incurring the wrath of your neighbors as well as your family. The best crabgrass-stopper is the pre-emergence type, which is spread in the spring, usually with fertilizer. But it's too late for that once the grass begins to sprout. Make a vow to use the pre-emergence next spring, but meanwhile, "DSMA" is the emergency treatment of choice. A consistent problem with crabgrass means poor watering.

To kill summer weeds, many good formulas are commercially available. Since most require dry weather, it is a good idea to water your lawn thoroughly and let it dry off on top before you apply the weed-killer.

There are many diseases which can attack your lawn. For these, it is best to take a sample of turf to your nurseryman and let him advise you of the best method of dealing with the problem.

Chinch bugs can be a particular problem in the hot months, and it takes a great deal of patience to get rid of them. These tiny bugs suck the juices out of grass blades and multiply rapidly in the summer. Proper control involves dusting each bug individually since the insecticide must make direct contact to be effective. Several sprays are available. For the best control, dust or spray three to five times annually, starting in late June and carrying through into September.

Perennials in Your Garden

Perennial flowers are like old friends. No matter how we treat them, they come back every year for more punishment. Although their tops die off, in most cases, their roots live from year to year. Usually, they flower only once each year, but the bloom lasts for a relatively long period of time.

Figure 3-8: One of the best perennials is the peony. Plants or seeds can be bought at nurseries or from mail-order houses like Stark Brothers, which cultivates this giant field in Louisiana, Mo.

Perennials give color to the garden in a shady spot and in front of shrubs in spring and throughout the growing season. Some perennials flower the first year. Usually perennials will not flower, however, unless they develop to a certain size and are exposed to low temperatures for a number of weeks, then to increasing day lengths and temperatures. Their flowering is the result of this sequence of day length and temperature.

Although perennials require constant care, they do well in most parts of the United States. You can grow them as annuals and eliminate the problem of protecting them in the winter. Among the more popular of the garden perennials are delphinium, peony, hollyhock, columbine, candytuft, carnation, and primrose.

Figure 3-9: The chrysanthemum is another favorite, though late-blooming, perennial. These two Yellow Eldorado (*left*) and Orange Magician (*right*) are both available from George J. Ball, Inc.

PREPARING THE SOIL

Soil preparation is extremely important to perennials. Annuals can grow and flower in poorly prepared soil, but perennials seldom survive more than one year if the soil is not properly prepared.

Properly prepared soil will have good drainage, protection from drying winds, and adequate water in the summer. If you prepare beds carefully—by spading deeply, providing adequate drainage, and lightening heavy soil with sand and organic matter—the flowers grown there are almost certain to be outstanding. When water can enter soil easily, seeds germinate readily and the plants grow deep, healthy roots, strong stems, and large abundant flowers. The benefits of careful soil preparation carry over from season to season. It is better to grow a small bed of flowers in well-prepared soil than to attempt to grow great masses of flowers in poorly prepared soil. For new beds, begin preparing the soil in the fall before planting time. To improve drainage, bed up the soil. Dig furrows along the sides of the bed and add the soil from the furrows to the bed. This raises the level of the bed above the general level of the soil so that excess water can seep from the bed into the furrows.

You may find gullies in raised beds after heavy rains. You can prevent gullying by surrounding the beds with wooden or masonry walls making, in effect, raised planters of the beds. Raised beds dry out more quickly than flat beds since little moisture moves up into the bed from the soil below, so be sure to water beds frequently during the summer.

After forming the beds, or determining that drainage is satisfactory

Figure 3-10: The ground should be turned over many times to prepare the soil for a perennial bed. A rotary tiller is very helpful for this chore (*courtesy of Gilson Bros.*).

without bedding, spade the soil to a depth of eight to ten inches. Turn the soil over completely. In this spading, remove boards, large stones, and building trash, but turn under all leaves, grass, stems, roots, and anything else that will decay quickly. Respade three or four times at weekly intervals. If the soil tends to dry between spadings, water it. If weeds grow, pull them before they set seed.

In spring, just before planting, spade again. At this spading, work peat moss, sand, fertilizer, and lime into the soil. For ordinary garden soil, use a one- to two-inch layer of peat moss and a one-inch layer of unwashed sand. If your soil is heavy clay, use twice this amount of peat and sand. By adding peat and sand each time you reset the plants, you can eventually make good garden soil from poor subsoil.

Have your soil tested as recommended earlier. Add a complete fertilizer such as 5-10-5 at the last spading at a rate of one and one-half pounds (three rounded cups) per 100 square feet. Add ground limestone at a rate of five pounds (seven rounded cups) per 100 square feet, unless testing shows that lime is not needed.

Rake the surface smooth; after raking, the soil is ready for seeding or planting with started plants. Add organic matter to the beds each year, either peat moss or compost.

SELECTING PERENNIALS

Select perennials for your particular area. Notice what grows well in local gardens, consult nurserymen, check with your state experimental station, and choose those that are most attractive to you. You can plant perennials as flowering edging plants, for accents in an evergreen planting, to give flower masses by covering a single area with one species, as rock garden specimens, or to provide a screen of color.

Observe the flowering times of perennials in your area. That way you will be able to choose plants that will flower together and plants that will flower when nothing else is in bloom. The flowering time may vary as much as six weeks from year to year, but plants of the same kind ordinarily flower together.

BUYING PLANTS OR SEED

It is best to buy perennials from your local nursery or garden shop. They usually are in bloom when offered for sale, which allows you to select the colors you want for your garden. Buy perennial plants that are compact and dark green. Plants held in warm shopping areas are seldom vigorous and should be avoided. You can detect those held in warm areas too long by the thin pale yellow stems and leaves.

Many perennials do not grow true to type from seed and must be taken from cuttings or clump divisions. If you do plant seed, off-colors and defective forms can be produced. You can sow perennial seeds directly in the beds where the plants are to bloom or you can start early plants indoors and set them out in beds after the weather warms.

Some perennials are best grown from seed each year. Many of the so-called biennials—plants that flower the second year—are grown only from seed; columbine, foxglove, canterbury bells, sweet william, and delphinium are among these.

To get a good start toward raising vigorous plants, buy good fresh seed. Do not buy it too far in advance of planting time; for best results allow no more than a 3-month interval before planting. When buying

70 *   **WHEN** —

Flowers
are small

Stems fall over easily
(have little vigour)

Old stems from
previous season

Root center is
hollow and dead

Root has many
underdeveloped
shoots

Root center
is hollow
and dead

Bottom foliage
is scant
and poor

Lateral vegetative shoots are pale green
or almost white when they start to develop

HOW —

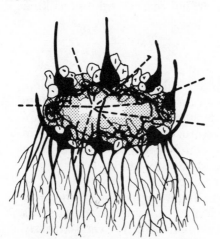

Lift plant. Wash most soil from root system.
Select divisions.

Pull or cut apart separate divisions.
Each division contains old stem, vegetative lateral shoot, and root system.

Plant divisions that have several
vegetative lateral shoots and
vigorous root systems.

Discard these or plant
several together.

Figure 3-11: **When** the right conditions prevail, it is time to divide your
perennials. **How** to divide perennials is illustrated step-by-step.

Figure 3-12: This garden contains Blue Mist Ageratum with a backdrop of seed-grown Carefree White Geranium (*courtesy of Pan-American Seed Company*).

seed, look for new varieties listed as F_1 hybrids—widely available in annuals and beginning to show up in perennials. Seed for these hybrids costs more than the seed of the usual inbred varieties, but its superiority makes it worth the extra price. These F_1 hybrids, produced by crossing selected inbred parents, are more uniform in size and more vigorous than plants of inbred varieties and they produce more flowers.

SETTING PLANTS OUTDOORS

Whether you buy plants from a nursery or start your own indoors, set them out the same way. When the time comes to set plants in the garden, remove them from flats by slicing downward in the soil between the plants. Lift out each plant with a block of soil surrounding its roots and set the soil block in a planting hole.

If the plants are in fiber pots, remove the paper from the outside of the root mass and set the plant in a prepared planting hole. When setting out plants in peat pots, remove the top edge of the pot to keep rain from collecting around the plant. Thoroughly moisten the pot and its contents to help the roots develop properly.

Drench the soil around the planting hole with a liquid fertilizer. Set the plant in the hole and press the soil up around it. Allow plenty of space between plants because perennials need room to develop. Perennials usually show up best when planted in clumps of the same variety.

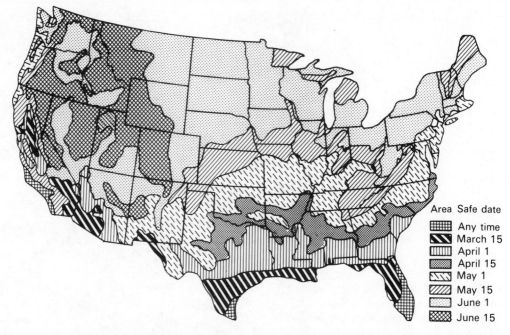

Area	Safe date
	Any time
	March 15
	April 1
	April 15
	May 1
	May 15
	June 1
	June 15

Figure 3-13: This map plots safe dates for sowing most seeds outdoors in the continental United States.

Figure 3-14: Peat pellets like these expand with water and can be sewed indoors for early starts. Later they can be planted outdoors, without disturbing the young plants.

Once safely planted in the ground, perennials are easy to care for. Water at regular intervals during the growing season, particularly during dry weather. Moisten the entire bed thoroughly, but not so heavily that the soil becomes soggy. A soaker hose is best, but a sprinkler will also do the job. Figure on four hours of watering for each perennial bed.

A good mulch will give an orderly look to the garden, keep weeds down, and add organic matter to the soil. Mulch materials are buckwheat hulls, peat moss, salt hay, pine bark, and wood chips. Winter mulch should be used only on newly planted or unhardy perennials.

Fertilizers should be used regularly but sparingly on perennials. Put little rings of 5-10-5 around each plant in March. Peonies like a little bone meal once a year. Water right away so that the fertilizer does not lay on the plant itself and burn it. This watering also delivers the food to the plant roots right away.

Most perennials are top heavy and need staking. Stake new plants when you first put them out. Do the same for old plants when they get to about half their final size. Remember to make the stakes high enough to hold up the plant when it reaches full size.

Growing Annuals

People grow flowers for a variety of reasons. Usually it's simply because they like them. If color is your particular interest, then your garden should be replete with annuals. As the name indicates, annuals are grown each year from new seed. Nevertheless, beginning gardeners are often surprised to find that their annuals have "reappeared" the next year. Actually, some annuals do reseed themselves and come up the next year with no help from man. The majority, however, must be planted anew each year. The cost of the seed is amazingly inexpensive, and if you treat the seed right, it will provide benefits far in excess of its modest cost per packet.

STARTING PLANTS

The best seed in the world costs very little per package, so don't skimp. Buy fresh seed each year and don't "save money" by planting seed left over from last year. It just won't grow right. The newer F_1 hybrids cost a little more but are well worth the extra price. If you're planting seed directly in the garden, follow instructions on the package. Be careful about sowing before the frost is over.

It costs a little more, but for those who want a guaranteed garden in the color they want, buy plants already started in a nursery. These come in flats divided into 12 to 24 plants per flat. Buy as many as you need,

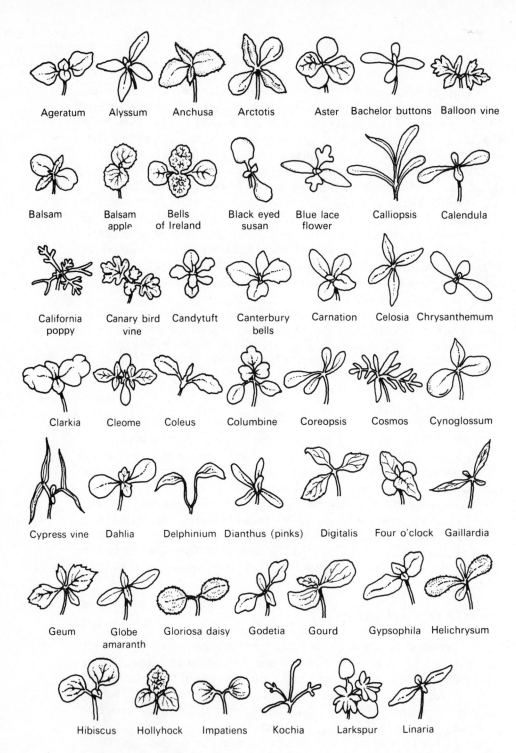

Figure 3-15: Flower and vine seedlings can be confused either with other plants or with weeds.

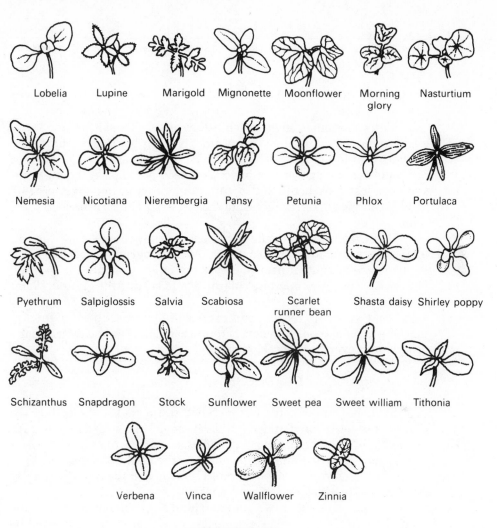

Lobelia | Lupine | Marigold | Mignonette | Moonflower | Morning glory | Nasturtium

Nemesia | Nicotiana | Nierembergia | Pansy | Petunia | Phlox | Portulaca

Pyethrum | Salpiglossis | Salvia | Scabiosa | Scarlet runner bean | Shasta daisy | Shirley poppy

Schizanthus | Snapdragon | Stock | Sunflower | Sweet pea | Sweet william | Tithonia

Verbena | Vinca | Wallflower | Zinnia

13 HERB SEEDLINGS

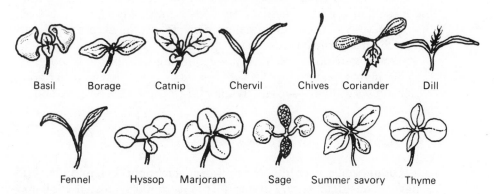

Basil | Borage | Catnip | Chervil | Chives | Coriander | Dill

Fennel | Hyssop | Marjoram | Sage | Summer savory | Thyme

Figure 3-15 (continued): Referring to these drawings will help you to distinguish the annuals and herbs from the chaff (*courtesy of Northrup King*).

76 *   plus another 10 percent or so, since some plants will not make the transplantation.

PREPARING FLOWER BEDS

Many gardeners give lavish attention to the soil around rose-bushes, evergreens, or almost every other type of planting, but just throw annuals into the ground as they arrive. Annuals are plants, too, and respond to care much as people do. You need not make elaborate preparations. Just loosen the soil a little and provide drainage, organic material and fertilizer. Soils east of the Mississippi may also need some lime.

Don't rush into planting either seed or new plants until the soil temperature is up to about 60 degrees and all danger of frost is long past. If plants are bought in peat pots, set the entire pot into the ground. Otherwise, cut plants apart with a trowel and set into the ground. Water immediately.

Many nurseries recommend the use of liquid fertilizer. If you use this type of plant food, pour some around each plant as you set it into the ground and every two weeks thereafter.

SOWING SEED OUTDOORS

Some beginning gardeners merely throw a packet of seed into the ground and let it come up (or not) as it may. This is certainly an easy method (and it sometimes works) but for best results, dig tiny furrows in the ground, fill with vermiculite, and sow the seed in the furrow. Usually a shallow furrow is needed, but it depends on the type of seed. Do read the instructions on the seed packet.

Virtually all seed-grown annuals should be thinned out. As soon as each plant grows two leaves, the weaker or excess seedlings should be pulled up and transplanted elsewhere. Be very careful about transplanting these delicate little plants. Handle as if they were new plants from the nursery. Even if you don't have a place to put the excess seedlings, uproot them anyway if you want plants that remain strong and vigorous.

Water your plants often in the beginning but not too heavily. As they get bigger, water more heavily but less frequently. A soaker hose, which allows water to seep slowly into the ground, is the best method for annuals.

STARTING PLANTS INDOORS

Unless you are willing to invest in special lighting equipment and to devote considerable care to starting plants indoors, it usually is better to buy plants or to sow seed directly in the garden. Home-started plants are seldom as satisfactory as those bought from nurserymen and rarely grow as well or bloom as profusely as those planted directly in the garden.

Home-started seedlings frequently are attacked by a fungus disease called damping-off. Those seedlings that escape the disease usually are weak and spindly and never become good garden plants; conditions of light, temperature, and humidity normally found in the average home are not favorable for plant growth.

Remember, if you do start your own seeds, the best soil is loose, well drained, finely textured, and low in nutrients. To prepare a starting soil having these properties, mix equal parts of garden soil, sand, and sphagnum peat moss.

Sow seed in flats at the depth and in the amount recommended on the seed packet. If you are growing large-seeded plants in peat pots, sow two to four seeds in each pot. After you have sowed the seeds, cover all furrows with a thin layer of vermiculite, then water with a fine mist. Secure a sheet of polyethylene plastic over the seeded containers and set them in the basement or some other location where the temperature ranges between 60° and 75°F. The containers need no further water until after the seeds have germinated. Nor do they need light. Under no circumstances should the plastic-covered containers be placed in sunlight; heat buildup under the plastic could kill emerging seedlings.

RAISING SEEDLINGS

As soon as the seed has germinated, remove the plastic sheeting and place the seedlings in the light. Many gardeners supply light to the seedlings by placing the containers on a window sill. This practice usually is unsatisfactory. Light on a window sill usually is diffused, coming from only one direction, and the period of strong daylight varies from day to day. In addition, the air surrounding plants on a window sill is too dry and the temperature too high.

For best results, seedlings should be raised under lighting conditions that can be closely controlled as to intensity and duration. Use a fluorescent tube and, for proper intensity, place the containers six inches below it. Control the duration of lighting by connecting the fluorescent fixture to a timer such as is used for controlling refrigerators or air conditioners.

After the plastic is removed from the container, the new plants must be watered frequently and fertilized. You can do both of these jobs at one time by using a solution of one tablespoon of soluble fertilizer per gallon of water.

When seedlings develop two true leaves, thin to one seedling per pot. Those in flats should be transplanted to other flats. Using a knife or spatula, dig deeply under the seedlings in the flats, lifting a group of the

Figure 3-16:   Some of the many, many varieties of annuals that can be grown from seed include Burpee's Emperor Zinnia (*left*) and Empress Marigold (*center*) Pan-American's Elfin Impatiens (*right*). They all grow very well in shade. The two strikingly handsome petunias, Flamboyant (*left, below*) and Chiffon Cascade (*right, below*) are also annuals (*courtesy of Pan-American*).

seedlings. Let the group of seedlings fall apart and pick out individual plants from the group. Handle the seedlings as little as possible, and don't pinch them.

Set the seedlings in new flats that contain the same soil mixture you used for starting the seed. Space the seedlings about one and one-half inches apart in the flats, water thoroughly, and replace under the fluorescent lights. Continue watering and fertilizing the plants until time for setting them out.

Roses—Perennial Favorites

Roses are everyone's perennial favorites. Once you plant them, with care and luck, they'll give the whole family many years of satisfying beauty and fragrance.

Figure 3-17: The huge blooms of the hybrid tea rose, Taj Mahal, are compared to the size of the half-dollar (*courtesy of Armstrong Nurseries*).

Figure 3-18: A floribunda rose, like this orange-pink Bahia, has smaller flowers than the hybrid tea, but there are a great many more of them on the same bush. Bahia is a 1974 All-America Rose Selection (*courtesy of Armstrong Nurseries*).

All roses are perennials, but they are not all everblooming. Everblooming roses provide flowers several times during the warm months. If you have enough bushes, there will be roses for cutting all season long.

Most of today's roses are everblooming, but there are several older varieties which bloom only once or twice. Some are still unexcelled for beauty. One of these is the hybrid perpetual Frau Karl Druschki. This grows into a large bush and has magnificent white blooms in June and again in late summer. There are several other old-fashioned single bloomers, such as York, Lancaster and Cardinal de Richelieu, which are very hardy, require little care, and furnish an abundance of flowers in June.

The newer everblooming roses, however, have far surpassed their ancestors. You can buy everblooming varieties in almost every form. The types fall into five major groupings.

Hybrid Teas: These are low, bush-type roses which are grown mostly for individual blooms. Expert gardeners "disbud" extra buds on the canes so that each cane will produce one large, perfect flower (more about disbudding later). This is the type used for cut flowers.

Floribundas: These are grown for displays of color in the garden and not so much for individual cutting. Floribundas produce a profusion of flowers, but they are in clusters and are usually smaller than the hybrid tea blooms. Some varieties, such as Betty Prior, develop into huge bushes over the years. Floribundas are somewhat hardier than hybrid teas and require less pruning and other maintenance.

Grandifloras: Of comparatively recent vintage, they were developed to take advantage of the better qualities of both hybrid teas and floribundas. Grandifloras produce larger bushes and larger flowers than most floribundas. The flowers resemble tea roses, except that they are mostly in clusters. Occasionally, a single flower will be produced that is the equal of most hybrid teas. The bushes are quite hardy and make fine hedges.

Climbers: These are among the oldest roses, and one variety, Blaze, is still by far the most popular. There are certain everblooming climbers, but most of these are hybrid teas that have been adapted as climbers and none are as rugged or as profuse as Blaze.

Tree Roses: These are hybrids grafted to a high trunk so that they grow several feet off the ground.

There are other minor rose groups such as polyanthas and miniatures, but the five groups listed earlier are the major ones. Most can be bought at your neighborhood nursery already growing in peat or paper containers. It is interesting to note that some of the older, non-patented varieties are often more highly ranked than their more expensive, patented brothers. Peace, highest-ranked of all, is one example, as are Crimson Glory and Charlotte Armstrong. The rose fancier will want all of them. Many gardeners prefer to order directly from long-established rose growers like Jackson & Perkins or Armstrong.

Figure 3-19: Climbing roses can transform any area, old or new, into a sea of beauty. This white Summer Snow is available from Jackson & Perkins.

Figure 3-20: A tree rose is a hybrid tea grafted onto a much longer stem. This variety is called Dr. Davis (*courtesy of Jackson & Perkins*).

82 *   Remove bare-root mail-order roses from the shipping package and place the roots in a container of clean, cool water for 24 hours or until proper planting weather. If a longer period than 24 hours is needed, keep roses in a sheltered area. This soaking period may be over a week if necessary. Soaking for 24 hours or longer will get your roses started quicker and make them grow faster.

Figure 3-21:   Steps to follow for planting a bare-root rose. First (*top, left*) dig a hole about two feet deep and wide enough to spread the roots naturally. Next (*top, right*), add a soil conditioner like peat moss or Redi-Earth and mix with dirt to form a mound. Spread roots over the mound (*bottom, left*). Then fill with more dirt and conditioner (*bottom, right*). Tamp down and water.

BEFORE PLANTING ROSES

Selecting a proper area for your roses will make them easier to care for and help produce flowers you will be proud to show. Major points to consider in selecting the planting site:

* The location should fit your landscape plan.
* It should have at least four hours of sun each day, preferably some morning sun to dry foliage and prevent mildew.

* The planting site should be close to a supply of water (if possible).
* The area should have a good soil with good drainage; wet spots are taboo.
* The location should be away from large trees or ornamentals that would deprive the roses of sun and nourishment.
* The area should have good air movement so that foliage does not remain wet, and the roses should be spaced to aid in air movement. Generally, 18 inches between plants is recommended; add a few more inches in the South and on the West Coast.
* The plantings should be away from eaves where falling ice and water would damage roses.

PREPARING AND PLANTING

First, remove the soil to make the bed or hole 24" deep. Dig the bed or hole wide enough so the roots will assume a natural position when planted. If the planting is a bed or hedge of roses, incorporate some crushed stone or gravel on the bottom to insure drainage.

Remove your roses from the water container they have been soaking in. Trim off roots or stems that are broken or unwanted. In the hole, build a mound of soil that will support the roots so that the bud union is at ground level (warm climates) or one to two inches below ground level (cold climates). If roses come in plantable peat pots, break off the pots to allow roots to expand. Fill the holes two-thirds full of soil mixed with one-third peat and tamp to remove air pockets. Then fill the remainder of the holes with about a gallon of water and let it soak in. Finally fill the holes with soil and firm the roses gently.

SPRAYING OR DUSTING

Spray or dust your roses immediately after removing the soil mound. The selection of spray or dust depends on your particular preference and any problem you may encounter with the roses.

* Read and follow label directions.
* Spray or dust every seven days under normal conditions.
* Spray in morning before temperatures are above 80°F.
* Always spray or dust for blackspot and other diseases before a rain if possible and within 24 hours after a rain.
* Maintain proper coverage as directed on the labels.

FERTILIZING AND WATERING

After roses are in full leaf, apply two tablespoons of rose food to each bush. Scatter this fertilizer over the surface, work it in, and water immediately. Water your roses thoroughly at least every seven days in dry weather. Soak the beds thoroughly without wetting the foliage. Be sure you have a well-drained soil so that roots are not constantly in water. Mulching with a two- to three-inch layer of compost, cocoa shells, ground corn cobs, peat moss, straw, or similar materials discourages weeds and retains moisture in the soil.

Cultivate roses as shallowly as possible. This will permit air to enter the soil and will not injure any roots growing in the upper soil layer. Never allow your soil to become hard at any time during the growing season.

WINTERIZING

To protect your tea roses through the winter, trim them back to 16 to 18 inches after the first killing frost. Be sure to dispose of the trimmings carefully since they may carry insects and diseases. Then apply a final spray or dust material to the canes and soil surface.

Cover the crown of each plant with a soil mound six to eight inches high to protect against frequent changing temperatures and extreme cold. Cover the entire plant and soil mound with hay, straw, or suitable protective material. This will help prevent the repeated freezing and thawing of the soil around the canes. In spring, remove the mounds and trim hybrid teas back to about six to eight inches.

CARE AND PRUNING OF CLIMBING ROSES

Climbing roses, depending on local conditions, may not bloom, climb, or repeat bloom for several years. This is natural for a climbing rose. Time is needed to produce these long, flowering canes. A complete rose food should be used at least three times a year.

Some climbers bloom only on second-year or older wood; therefore, you must preserve this wood when you prune. Shorten the light wood and remove only the dead and injured wood in early spring. When everblooming climbers have finished original bloom, the flowers only should be plucked off; no foliage should be removed as the reblooming occurs from the top leaves, immediately below the flower clusters.

ENJOY YOUR ROSES TWICE

There are many ways of using roses both in the house and in the garden. When they have developed into half-open buds, you can bring roses into the house where their color and fragrance can be fully enjoyed for many days. Regardless of whether you have a single bud or a dozen in full bloom, roses are easy to arrange in attractive, graceful bouquets.

Cut your roses with a sharp scissors or knife, just when the outside petals first start to unfold. Always leave at least two sets of five leaves remaining on the stems. The next flowers will develop from these eyes. Unless you need long stems, do not cut any more foliage than necessary.

Figure 3-22: Two of the many enjoyable ways to arrange and display roses (*courtesy of Jackson & Perkins*).

For prize-winning roses, disbudding will guarantee large blooms on each stem. Check your hybrid teas as the buds develop. If more than one bud appears on a stem, pinch off the side buds, leaving only the one in the center. In this manner, all the strength goes into the one flower, causing it to grow larger and more vigorous than if all flowers were allowed to remain.

FOR AN IDEAL ROSE GARDEN

Rose fanciers may obtain a complete listing of all the roses available in the United States. Send 10 cents in coin and a stamped, self-addressed envelope to The American Rose Society, P.O. Box 30000, Shreveport, Louisiana 71130 for "A Handbook for Selecting Roses." The booklet gives a description and performance rating for these easy to grow and relatively inexpensive roses.

Vegetables in the Kitchen Garden

There is nothing like a flower garden for beauty, but for practicality you can't beat vegetables. They are inexpensive, easy to grow, and the harvest is well worth the attention and labor. You can't eat flowers, but have you ever tasted anything as good as fresh picked corn? A single hardy tomato plant can yield several bushels of the ripe, red delicacy. Indeed, a few square feet of garden space will keep the average family

Figure 3-23: Growing your own food in a large vegetable garden is one way to soften the blow of inflation (*courtesy of Burpee Seeds*).

supplied with vegetables for a year—with some to spare for proud donations to relatives or neighbors.

Vegetables thrive in full sunlight and need at least five or six hours during the middle of the day. Excessive shading results in rank, spindly plants and poor yields. If possible, the garden should be reasonably near the house so that you can work in it at free moments. It should be an area that is or can be fenced conveniently to protect it from livestock, wood chucks, rabbits and children.

THE RIGHT SOIL

Soils for vegetables should be friable and porous for quick water drainage, crop root penetration, and good aeration. A deep, fine, sandy loam or silt loam is best. But the home gardener who has little choice of site can still grow many vegetables in relatively poor soils if he conditions them properly.

An area which is composed of "fill dirt" is difficult to reclaim for a vegetable garden. A fill area usually consists of a high percentage of bottom subsoil (clay), stones, and debris. Low and wet spots should also be avoided. If, after a moderate shower, water remains in puddles on the soil surface for several hours, the site should not be used for vegetables. Very few vegetables can stand "wet feet" for long periods.

Sandy soils are quite satisfactory for vegetables in years with average rainfall, but supplemental irrigation may be necessary in dry periods. Organic matter added to these soils will improve their water-holding capacity.

Lime and pH: A pH test may be necessary if the garden is in a new location. Most vegetables grow best in a slightly acid soil where the pH is between 6.0 and 6.8. Lime should be used on the garden only when a test has been made and the soil is too acid. If the pH is between 5.5 and 6.0, use three pounds of ground limestone to each 100 square feet of garden on sandy soils or five pounds on heavy soils. The application may be made before or after plowing or spading. If the pH is between 5.0 and 5.5, apply the amounts given above before plowing and make another application of the same amount after plowing but before raking or harrowing. If the pH is 4.9 or below, double the recommendation for the 5.0 to 5.5 range.

Commercial Fertilizers: Commercial fertilizers are applied to increase the nitrogen, phosphorus, and potash content of the soil. A 5-10-10 fertilizer contains 5 percent nitrogen, 10 percent phosphorus acid, and 10 percent potash. A 5-10-5, 5-10-10 fertilizer, or one with a similar analysis should be used at the rate of four or five pounds to each 100 square feet of garden area. On soils that have been well fertilized for many years, one to two pounds of 5-10-10 or 10-10-10 may give the best results, if the pH is in the 6.0 to 6.8 range. On sandy soils fertilizer is likely to give best results if part of it is broadcast after plowing or spading and the remaining portion applied during the growing season. On loams and clays, results are likely to be best if one-half of the fertilizer is broadcast after plowing or applied in bands near the row or around such plants as tomatoes.

ORGANIC GARDENING

The revival of interest in organic farming as well as threatened shortages of petro-chemical commercial fertilizers has prompted many

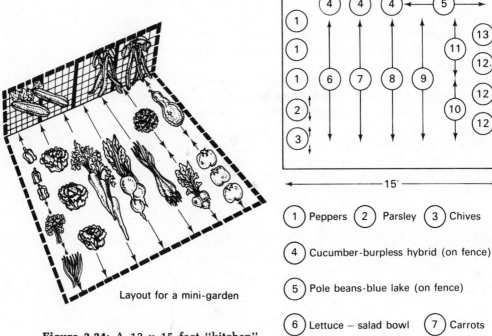

(Fence)

12'

15'

1 Peppers 2 Parsley 3 Chives

4 Cucumber-burpless hybrid (on fence)

5 Pole beans-blue lake (on fence)

6 Lettuce – salad bowl 7 Carrots

8 Beets 9 Onions 10 Chard

11 Endive 12 Tomatoes 13 Squash
                  (staked)   zucchini

Layout for a mini-garden

Figure 3-24: A 12 x 15 foot "kitchen" garden—as the French say—with the 13 vegetables recommended here should supply enough vegetables to feed the average family for an entire year (*courtesy of Northrup-King*).

gardeners to rely again on old-fashioned compost heaps. Once begun in a corner of the yard, such composting offers an ingenious way to dispose of foliage, cuttings, animal manure, and vegetable "waste." Careful gardeners can easily stack alternating layers of plant debris, manure, and soil so that a rich mixture of decayed organic matter is ready to add to the food growing site. Informative publications on the techniques can be purchased from the Rodale Farms (Emmaus, Penn.) and other organic farming stations.

CHOOSING THE CROPS

The home gardener should choose those vegetables which the family likes best. Some vegetables (celery is a good example) are difficult to grow. Usually, better celery can be purchased at the grocery store. The more perishable vegetables such as sweet corn, peas, snap beans, broccoli, and asparagus should receive first consideration in the home garden. These vegetables, when freshly harvested, have a flavor seldom found in a grocer's produce department.

Space is another consideration. A small space will provide vegetables for many meals if it is planted with such crops as tomatoes, snap beans, summer squash, broccoli, or cabbage. Corn, peas, winter squash, and melons require more space in relation to the amount of edibles produced.

The inexperienced gardener should grow fewer crops and select those which are easy to grow. Corn, snap beans, peas, tomatoes, and squash are good for beginners. Broccoli, cabbage, cucumbers, and melons are somewhat more difficult because of disease and insect control problems. The small-seeded crops, such as beets and carrots, are more difficult to get started.

The garden can be planted at one time, or the gardener can make a succession of plantings. One planting will give a long harvest of tomatoes, peppers, summer squash, beets, carrots, broccoli, and cucumbers. If sweet corn is planted at one time, it must include several varieties with a spread of maturity. Such crops as summer squash, broccoli, and cucumber must be kept picked or they will not continue to bear.

BUYING SEED

The quality of seed varies, but seed laws protect the gardener fairly well against poor seed and misrepresentation. The kind, variety, percentage of germination, and date of testing are marked on every package offered for sale. Buy enough seed at one time to last through the entire season.

Buy vegetable seeds and transplants by variety name. Varieties differ so much in time of maturity, quality, and disease resistance that success or failure in your garden may be determined by the choice of variety.

The best means of disease control in the home garden is through the use of disease- and insect-resistant varieties; these varieties should be bought whenever possible. Purchase your seed and transplants from a reputable firm.

GOOD TRANSPLANTS

A desirable transplant is stocky, medium-sized, relatively young, and free of disease or pests. For most vegetables, a good transplant has four to eight true leaves, and for fruit-type crops, such as tomatoes, it is better not to have flowers on the plant. For the vine crops, the two to three true-leaf stage is better than a later stage. Transplants of this group must have a block of soil with their roots. This can be assured by using bands or peat pots.

If suitable transplants are available from a local supply store or

Figure 3-25: The Beefeater, an improved F_1 hybrid Beefsteak, is one of many popular tomato varieties. The plants are easy to grow and provide an abundance of fruit (*courtesy of George J. Ball, Inc.*).

greenhouse, it is advisable for the home gardener to buy them. But if particular varieties are not available, he may be required to grow his own.

PLANTING AND CARE

Most home gardens can be planted over a period of three to four months, depending on the length of the growing season in your area. Spinach, peas, onions, and lettuce will do best if planted as early as the soil can be worked. Tomatoes and other tender plants should not be set out until the danger of frost is past. Planting of cabbage, cauliflower, broccoli, Chinese cabbage, turnips, and the like for fall harvest should be made in late June or early July.

Cover large seeds such as corn, peas, and beans with one to two inches of soil and all small seeds such as carrots and lettuce with one-quarter to one-half inch of soil. A good general rule is to plant shallow in early spring, especially in heavy soils. In warmer weather and in lighter soils, deeper seeding is usually advisable. In covering the seed, provide good contact between the soil and seed by gently firming the soil over the seed. Some additional loose soil can be pulled over the row to leave a slight ridge. In hot dry weather when the soil around the seed dries out quickly, frequent light watering will help germination. Another possibility is to shade the row until the young plants start to push through the soil. This may be done with boards or papers held in place with stones or soil.

Remove surplus plants before they can compete with those that are to remain. The total yield is likely to be much greater if thinning is done early.

Irrigation is sometimes needed in home gardens. Moisture will more likely be a limiting factor on sandy or shallow soils than on heavy or deep soils. Irrigation may prove beneficial when there has been no soaking rain (approximately one inch) for 10 to 14 days. If water must be carried in a pail, it may pay to water only recently transplanted vegetables. But a gardener who has a hose and adequate water pressure may find that it pays to water the entire garden once every week during dry periods.

Weeds can be the gardener's worst enemy. They compete for moisture and nutrients and may harbor insects and disease. They shade the plants and interfere with air circulation. Tall weeds may retard the evaporation of dew and rain from the foliage; thus, during periods of excess moisture, they may increase the incidence of infection by bacteria and fungi. Weeds can be controlled by hand pulling, cultivation, mulches, chemicals (herbicides), or a combination of these methods.

Figure 4-1: A handsome redwood fence provides privacy and distinction to an urban home.

4:

Walls & Fences and Your Land

"Mending Wall" by Robert Frost is often quoted by those who like to build barriers. "Good fences," they say, "make good neighbors." This was, however, only a line spoken by the "neighbor." The point of the poem is expressed better in the opening lines:

> Something there is that doesn't love a wall
> That sends the frozen-ground-swell under it
> And spills the upper boulders in the sun:

And later:

> Before I built a wall I'd ask to know
> What I was walling in or walling out

Frost's point is worth considering. How often do city folk flee to suburbia for the green, open spaces, and as their first proprietary act fence off that space with chain link? It's a hangover, perhaps, from the fear of crime and the crime that haunts urban America. Nonetheless, fence overkill is a frightening symbol of not very good times.

What's Good About Fences

But let's take a look at some of the good and cogent reasons for erecting a fence:

* **Boundaries:** A fence defines boundaries, establishing for once and all the limits of a given property. Surveys tend to confuse, with their "30.5" (meaning—30 feet, 6 inches); stakes get lost; and old residents tend to "squat" on undeveloped property and treat it as their own, even becoming resentful if the owner wants to use it.

94 *

* **Privacy:** A good fence or wall provides needed privacy. Every family has a right to a few moments without outsiders looking on, and a tall, solid fence is often the best way of maintaining such privacy. This is particularly true where houses are close together or where new houses may lack high trees and shrubs.

* **Safety:** Children, dogs, and swimming pools often require a closed-in area; a fence keeps your own in and others out. In fact, in most areas municipal statutes specify fencing around pools. Even if they do not, it is essential that the pool be fenced anyway, especially for the protection of small wandering feet.

* **Background:** Fences provide attractive backdrops (if intelligently selected and installed) and shelter for flowers, shrubs, ponds, and the like.

* **Shelter:** Fences provide shade and can turn harsh winds into cooling breezes; they can also hide garbage cans, work areas, or other offensive sights.

* **Space divisions:** A fence can simply serve as a "space divider" for outdoor living.

Figure 4-2: This little girl can play in complete safety behind this very attractive southern pine fencing.

Figure 4-3: Old-fashioned picket fence forms perfect backdrop for roses, yet protects them from wandering feet, both human and animal (*courtesy of Jackson & Perkins*).

Figure 4-4: Hilltop house is sheltered from winter winds by this reinforced plastic fence, which also provides shade on a treeless tract (*courtesy of Alsynite*).

Figure 4-5: The service area is screened off from the carport with a high cedar board fence that matches the house siding.

Figure 4-6: Here a redwood-and-plastic fence divides the terrace from the rest of the backyard.

Figure 4-7: Where lots are large and homes far apart, a frontyard fence is usually inappropriate; however, this fence provides private living space for the small yard and keeps kids safe from street traffic. Notice the attractive recesses for shrubs. Fir 1 x 8's with 1 x 2 battens are used in the construction (*courtesy of Western Wood Products Association*).

Planning Good Fences

If you have a good reason for putting up a fence, think first before you automatically fence off the entire property. Wouldn't the dog be better confined to one corner? Do you need privacy all around the house or just along the driveway where the neighbor's house is too close? Would shrubbery do the job just as well?

Many an attractive backyard setting has been ruined by an ugly fence or wall. The lawns and yards in front should be particularly inviting and warm-looking, of course. And fencing the front of property

Figure 4-8: Fencing can be constructed to suit varying personal needs. For example (*above, left*), a baffle screen of western red cedar wards off car headlights from an adjoining street, while the simple courtyard (*above, right*) is enhanced by a garden-grade redwood fence. The solid boards abutt to the neighbors' side and open strips at the side where privacy isn't the issue.

Figure 4-9: A low cedar fence (*above, left*) blocks out parking area and headlights but has friendly, warm look; while a Masonite "Ruf-X" fence (*above, right*) gives both privacy and protection yet allows ventilation through the textured panels alternating on both sides of the fence posts.

Figure 4-10: The basket-weave western pine fence is stepped up gradually to allow a view in the front and privacy in the back.

Figure 4-11: Pleasant and rustic looking, this popular old-fashioned split-rail is designed to keep people from trespassing without affront.

all the way to and along a suburban sidewalk is often offensive and unnecessary. But in congested cities, attractive frontyard fences can be a big improvement.

If you do have a good reason for using fencing, think of the others who also have to look at it. Remember, too, that it is an unwritten (and sometimes written) rule that the "ugly" side of the fence should face in. In any case, try to pick out fencing that is good-looking on both sides. Unfortunately, sectional fencing is expensive, so people are prone to buy the cheaper types, such as "stockade." They are even worse to look at from inside than out. You who are interested in fencing that is both attractive and utilitarian should carefully examine the types shown on these pages.

The hardest part of fence-building is setting the posts, but this is a do-it-yourself job even if you buy sectional fencing. After the posts are in, the rest is easy.

In spite of its obvious harsh look, chain link fencing is sometimes practical; for example, to fence in dogs on a small lot. Chain link fencing's big drawback is that it sets up hostile appearing barriers without adding anything to privacy. To overcome this somewhat you can thread aluminum or plastic strips between the links.

TYPES OF FENCES

The forms that a fence can take are as many and varied as its functions. It can consist of an open framework, a solid wall, louvers, latticework, or a combination of these. It can be made of boards, pickets, panels, rails, wire, brick, stone, or masonry units in any of an endless variety of shapes and patterns (see Chapters 6 and 7).

You can vary fence design largely to suit your needs and interests. Those shown next may serve as inspirations for adaptation or you may find one that exactly fits your tastes, your home, your lot, your budget, and local building ordinances. Before planning and buying, check zoning laws, which often include height and location restriction. Usually this checking can be done at a local building inspector's office.

The contour of your land—whether level or sloped and steeply or gently terraced, etc.—will have a great influence on the type of fence you choose. Its location, too, will affect your choice. You won't, for example, want to cut off the view from a patio, nor will you want to hide any of the desirable features of your home. And, if you're building next to a driveway, you will want to allow easy passage for the car as well as ample room for opening car doors.

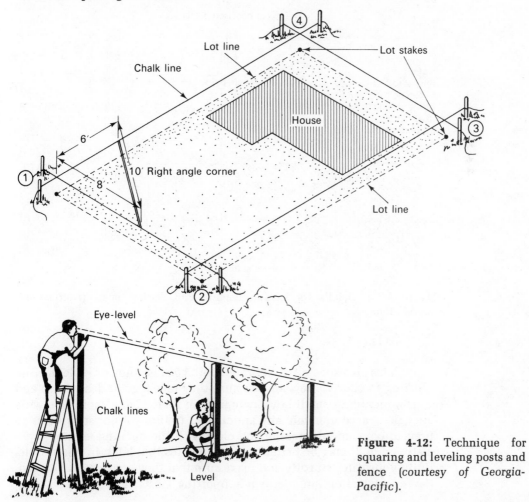

Figure 4-12: Technique for squaring and leveling posts and fence (*courtesy of Georgia-Pacific*).

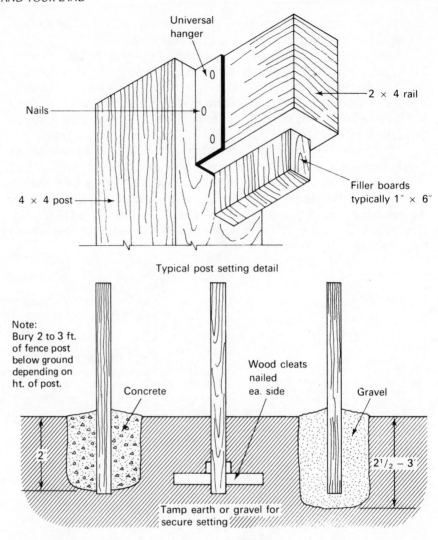

Figure 4-13: Details for joining fencing and setting posts (*courtesy of Georgia-Pacific*).

GATES

Gates are especially important, both because they provide the first greeting to your visitors and because they take a good deal of use and abuse, including small boys swinging on them. They should be wide enough to accommodate any anticipated traffic, yet not so wide as to prevent convenient opening and closing. If the opening is to be especially wide, it may be better to use two gates that latch in the middle. Build your gates sturdily and make sure that they are properly braced. Pay special attention to their supporting posts, using extra strong lumber and setting them well into their foundations so that they can't twist or be pulled out of plumb. Then hang the gates on strong hinges with long, heavy screws.

Redwood or incense cedar requires no preservative and is best for outdoor use. Treat other lumber that will be in contact with the ground, and all board ends, by soaking them for several hours in pentachlorophenol or other preservative solution—far more effective than brushing it on, by the way. Your lumber dealer can supply a preservative that you can paint over if you intend to so finish your fence.

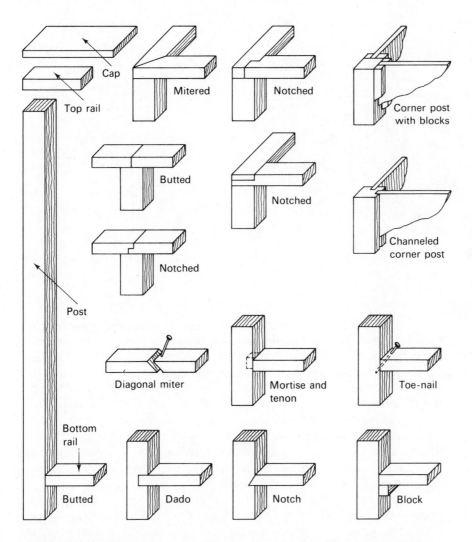

Figure 4-14: Examples of good fence "joinery," or the art of connecting wooden posts and rails.

102 *   SETTING THE POSTS

Make certain of property lines before you lay out your fence. Consult your survey for this. Then, with boundaries and set-backs accurately established, outline the fence with lines strung between stakes driven into the ground at corners. Measure along the lines with a steel tape to determine post locations and mark these by driving stakes into the ground. Posts are generally spaced on about eight-foot centers. Leave the line in position as a guideline for keeping the fence straight while you erect the posts.

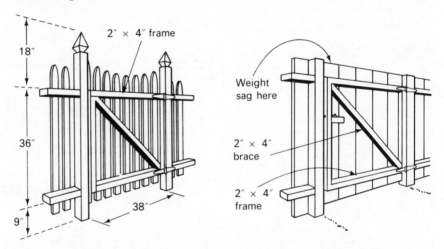

Figure 4-15: Typical gate construction. Be sure to use extra-heavy lumber for posts and set them solidly with good, strong hinges and long, heavy screws (*courtesy of California Redwood Association*).

Posts should be set into the ground approximately one-third of their height. A four-foot high post, for example, should be six feet long altogether, with two feet in the ground. (Gate-posts should be set a little bit deeper.) A post-hole digger (usually rentable) is most convenient for excavating. Dig the hole about four inches deeper than the post is to be buried. Pour gravel into the bottom of the excavation and set the bottom of the post in the gravel for proper drainage. Plumb the post with a spirit level, brace it temporarily in the plumb position, and dump earth into the hole, tamping it firmly in place and sloping it away from the post at the surface. When setting posts this way, nailing cleats or braces across the bottom of the post helps to anchor it firmly.

If you prefer, you may fill the hole around the post with concrete, again sloping away from the post at the surface. Before pouring, add at least a foot of gravel underneath for drainage. Let the concrete cure at least 48 hours before you proceed with construction. You may also simply fill the hole with gravel and tamp.

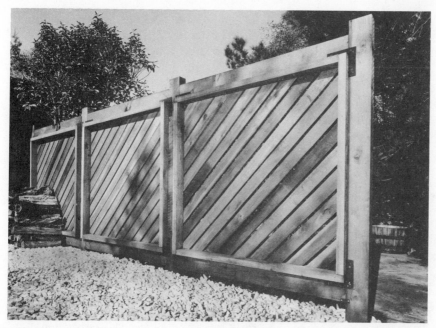

Figure 4-16: The photograph of this economical redwood fence shows how effectively such garden-grade lumber can be used.

Figure 4-17: Construction details for the fence illustrated in the previous figure. Galvanized 16d nails are used for all fastenings, except that toe-nailing is done with 8d galvanized nails.

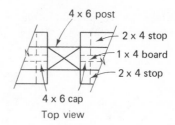

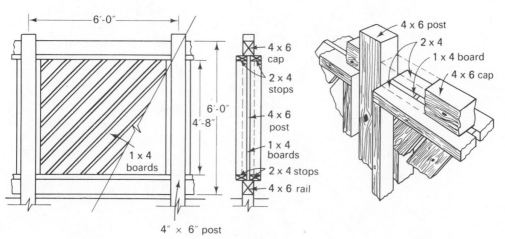

104 *   Fence rails may be fastened to the face of the post with a lap joint, or they may be simply butted on top of the post. Blocks are easy to use, or rails can be dadoed, notched or otherwise fastened to the post. Use only galvanized, stainless, or aluminum nails for fence construction—16d nails for nailing two-inch stock and 8d nails for one-inch stock.

Figure 4-18: Again garden-grade redwood makes a handsome fence (*courtesy of California Redwood Association*).

Figure 4-19: Construction details for the fence shown above.

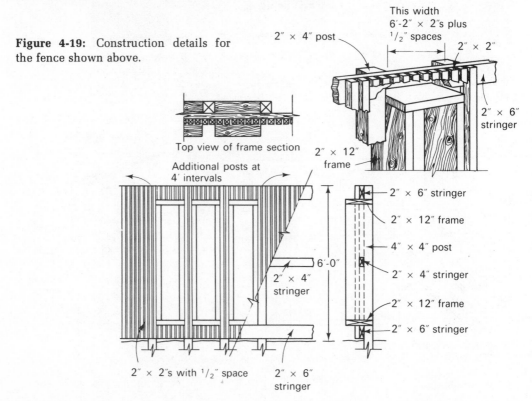

Figure 4-20: A high, sturdy fence also benefits from the liberal use of garden-grade redwood.

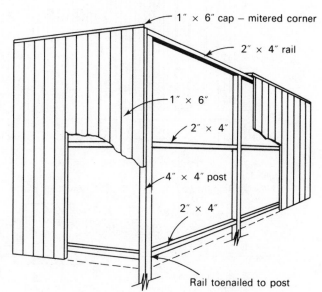

1″ × 6″ cap — mitered corner

2″ × 4″ rail

1″ × 6″

2″ × 4″

4″ × 4″ post

2″ × 4″

Rail toenailed to post

Figure 4-21: Construction details for the high fence shown above are simple.

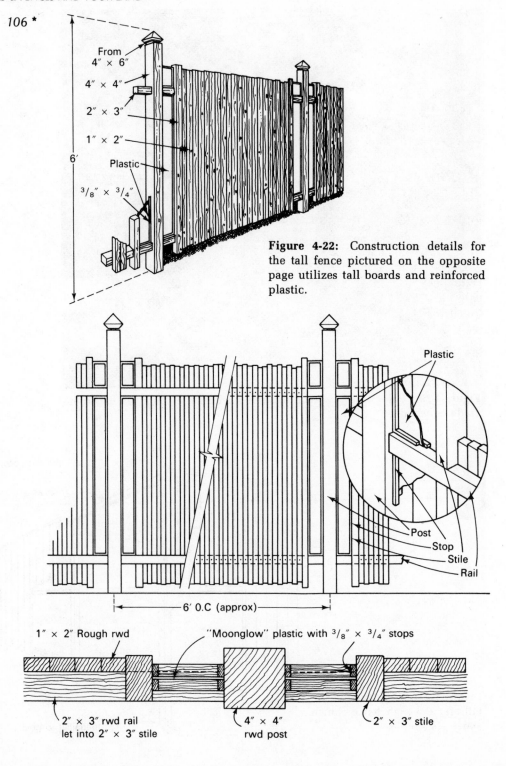

From
4″ × 6″

4″ × 4″

2″ × 3″

1″ × 2″

Plastic

³/₈″ × ³/₄″

6′

Figure 4-22: Construction details for the tall fence pictured on the opposite page utilizes tall boards and reinforced plastic.

Plastic

Post

Stop

Stile

Rail

6′ O.C (approx)

1″ × 2″ Rough rwd

"Moonglow" plastic with ³/₈″ × ³/₄″ stops

2″ × 3″ rwd rail
let into 2″ × 3″ stile

4″ × 4″
rwd post

2″ × 3″ stile

Figure 4-23: One of the attractive courtyard walls created from the California redwood and plastic specified in the plans on page 106 (*courtesy of WWPA and Malcom Lubliner*).

Figure 4-24: Resawn western cedar makes a handsome board fence that directs visitors from road to hillside house. Such a stepped fence is ideal for a slope, and is made of 1 x 4 boards attached to 2 x 4 stringers. Decorative 2 x 2's enclose the area under the rail.

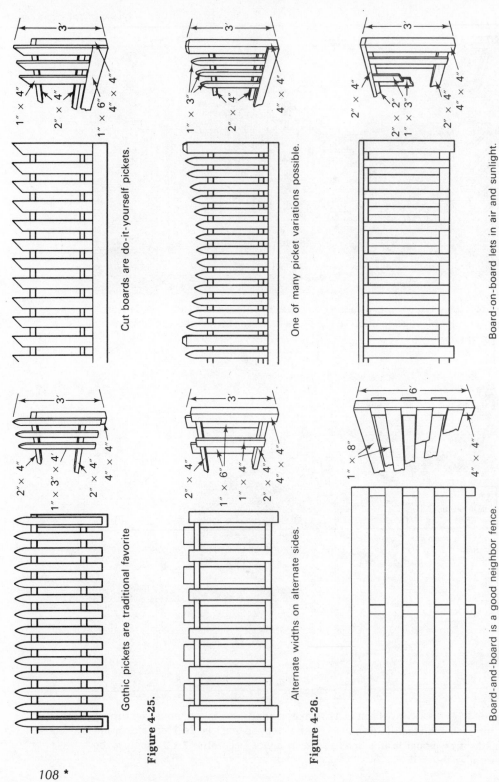

Cut boards are do-it-yourself pickets.

Figure 4-25.

Gothic pickets are traditional favorite

One of many picket variations possible.

Figure 4-26.

Alternate widths on alternate sides.

Board-on-board lets in air and sunlight.

Board-and-board is a good neighbor fence.

Figure 4-27.

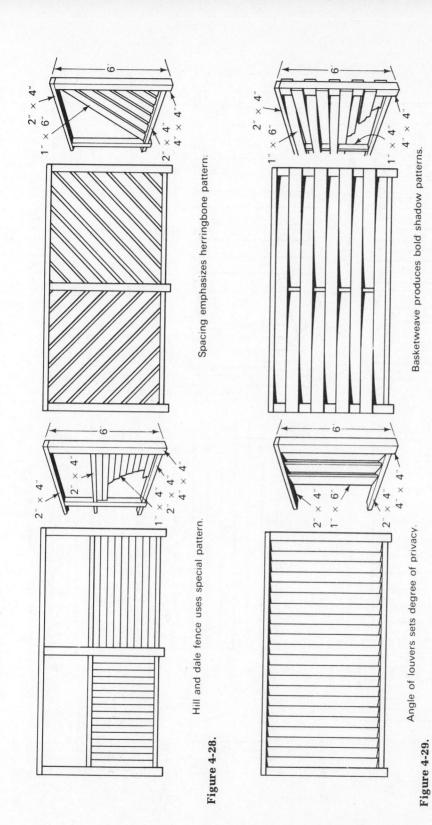

Spacing emphasizes herringbone pattern.

Basketweave produces bold shadow patterns.

Hill and dale fence uses special pattern.

Angle of louvers sets degree of privacy.

Figure 4-28.

Figure 4-29.

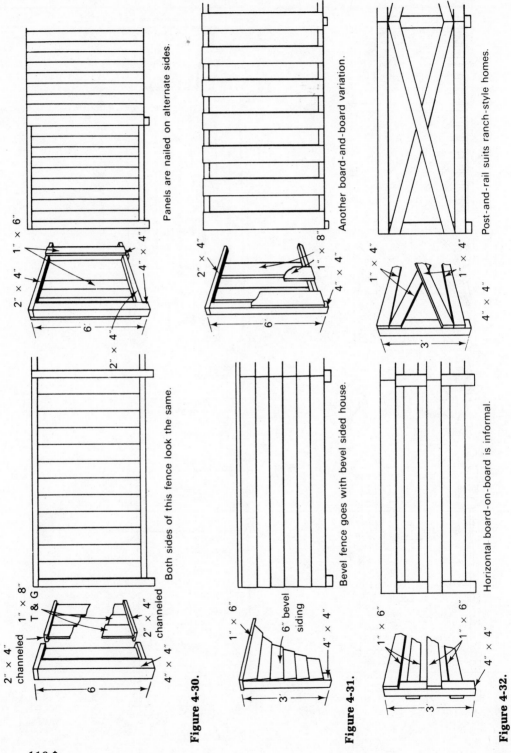

Panels are nailed on alternate sides.

Both sides of this fence look the same.

Figure 4-30.

Another board-and-board variation.

Bevel fence goes with bevel sided house.

Figure 4-31.

Post-and-rail suits ranch-style homes.

Horizontal board-on-board is informal.

Figure 4-32.

110 *

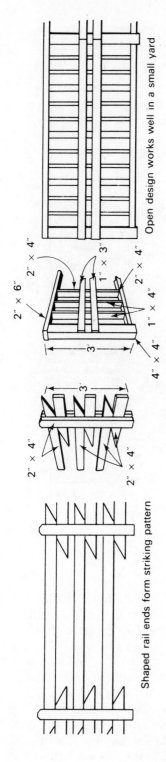

Open design works well in a small yard

Shaped rail ends form striking pattern

2" × 6"　2" × 4"

1" × 3"

2" × 4"

1" × 4"

4" × 4"

3'

2" × 4"

2" × 4"

3'

Figure 4-33.

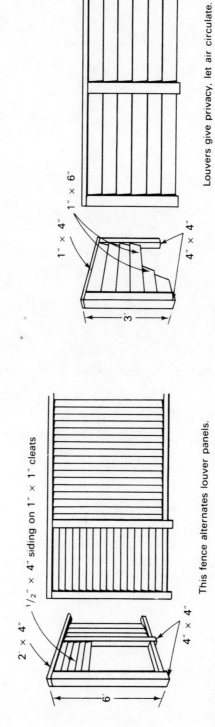

Louvers give privacy, let air circulate.

1" × 6"

1" × 4"

4" × 4"

3'

This fence alternates louver panels.

½" × 4" siding on 1" × 1" cleats

2" × 4"

4" × 4"

6'

Figure 4-34.

Figure 4-35: A particularly handsome way to adapt fencing to a staggered property line; here with durable garden-grade redwood.

Retaining Walls

A regular garden wall serves the same purposes as a fence. Actually, it is a fence, but we reserve that term ordinarily for fences made of wood. If you use stone, brick or something else, it is called a wall. Divider walls made of those materials are discussed in the appropriate chapters. A *retaining* wall is a completely different breed of cat. Its structural purpose is to hold back earth. Only the front of the wall is visible, while its back is covered to the top by soil. A primary reason for building a retaining wall is to institute different living levels on a building site. This may be necessary because of steeply sloping land or because a level area is wanted for a patio, for gardening, or for a swimming pool. Retaining walls also protect trees, shrubs, and the like from erosion. Or, the homeowner may simply decide that terracing will add interest to his property.

Figure 4-36: Wooden retaining walls can be dull if not dressed up. These 2 x 2 battens add texture to the tree-saver wall.

Every wall-building project is an individual one, and it's difficult to generalize about materials, types, and dimensions. Some people prefer concrete, some railroad ties, some stone or brick; some like them high, some like them low. Landscape architects advise not building any one wall more than three feet high. If this isn't high enough, several small walls (terracing) are preferable to one high wall.

When deciding upon which type of wall to build, the factors you will consider include height, strength, drainage, cost, ease of construction, and looks. Although "looks" is placed last, it is certainly not least. You don't want to plan a lovely garden and have the hill behind it held back by an ugly wall. On the other hand, a gorgeous wall isn't much help if it slides into the lily pond with the first rain.

It is theoretically possible to build a wall out of anything. Most people, however, choose conventional construction materials that will enhance the beauty of a house and its setting. The most common materials for retaining walls are concrete, brick, railroad ties, and stone.

Retaining walls can also be built of exterior plywood (reinforced by heavier timbers), concrete block and other handy, cheap materials. They are not recommended, however, because of their unattractive appearance. There is nothing wrong, however, with using these materials to form the main structure, with a veneer of brick or stone in front for looks.

114 *

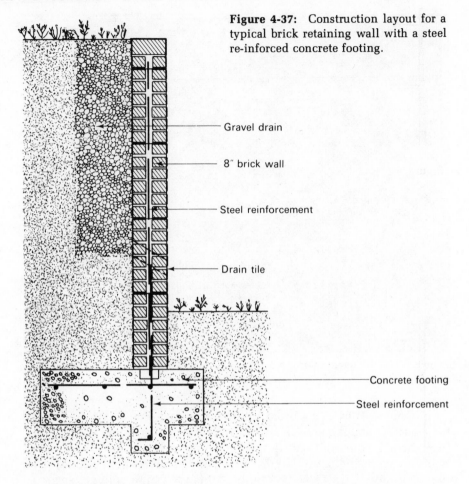

Figure 4-37: Construction layout for a typical brick retaining wall with a steel re-inforced concrete footing.

Gravel drain

8″ brick wall

Steel reinforcement

Drain tile

Concrete footing

Steel reinforcement

Or, you can use thick lumber of a decay-resistant wood such as all-heart redwood; but don't go over two feet without allowing for drainage and providing additional support.

If strength and utility is the main consideration, a concrete retaining wall is relatively easy to build. For those unfamiliar with concrete work, a contractor is advisable. A cracked concrete wall is worse than no wall at all. The pressure behind retaining walls after a rainfall is considerable, and the wall must be built quite exactly. Do-it-your-selfers interested in concrete work will be better off starting with projects that are less demanding (see Chapters 5 and 6).

If you like the look of brick—and it makes a very handsome retaining wall—the most efficient method is to lay brick veneer in front of a wall of concrete block (see Chapter 7 for details on working with both materials). You can build the wall entirely of brick if you prefer, but erect a double wall with steel reinforcing rods between, spaced every two feet.

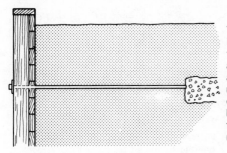

This wall uses 6 x 6 posts, and is similar in construction to those shown in Figures 4.38 and 4.39. Added stability is achieved by the use of "deadmen". Large redwood timbers or concrete blocks, they are buried in the fill and connected to the posts by steel tie rods.

Figure 4-38: Details for a retaining wall over 4 feet high.

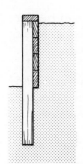

This is a simple method to build redwood retaining walls two feet high or less. The 4 x 4 posts, on 4-foot centers, are set in the earth to a depth equal to the height of the wall. Horizontal members 2" thick are then nailed on the earth-holding side of the wall, and a 2 x 6 cap is nailed along the top. The cap can be wider to serve as a seat.

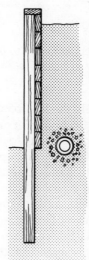

Here 4 x 4 posts are set in the earth approximately equal to the height of the wall (two to four feet) and on 3-foot centers. Horizontal members and caps are fastened as already described. A 6" drain tile runs along the base of the wall to drain off excess moisture. If seepage along the front of the wall is not objectionable, weep holes can be drilled along the wall's base instead of using drain tile. Drain tiles or weep holes are recommended for any wall over 2 feet high.

Figure 4-39: Details for a retaining wall up to 2 feet high.

Figure 4-40: Details for a retaining wall from 2 to 4 feet high.

Weep holes should be inserted every twenty-four inches, and concrete footings are a must below the frost line. Whether the average handyman should tackle this type of wall depends on how big it is and how good he is at bricklaying. Review Chapter 7 carefully.

Probably the most common type of retaining wall seen around single houses is the sort made of railroad ties. At one time this was a very inexpensive method since railroads were dismantling a lot of lines, and ties were dirt cheap. This is no longer true, but many people like the looks of the railroad-tie wall and find it a quick and easy method in spite of the increased cost.

You'll find that new "railroad ties" are just slightly more expensive than used ones and probably easier to find. Every other tie should be

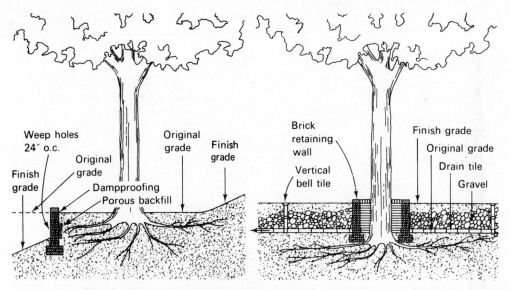

Figure 4-41: Two excellent ways to protect trees when you change the grade around them (*courtesy of Brick Institute of America*).

placed lengthwise into the hill for strength, but you can use half-ties for this if the wall isn't too high. For an interesting shadow effect, you can let these cross-ties extend four to six inches beyond the wall.

Ties are usually 6×8 inches and eight feet long. They can be somewhat difficult to handle, particularly used ties which have been pressure-treated with creosote. The creosote penetrates the tie, which is heavy enough by itself, and creates even more weight. You'll need a helper for ties with or without creosote.

For a small wall, ties can be toenailed together with a heavy hammer and very large galvanized spikes—at least 20d. If your wall is going to be large and hold back a substantial weight, it is best to drill holes in the ties and use reinforcing rods or long galvanized spikes to hold the ties together. Heavily creosoted ties, however, will take a heavy toll on drill bits—and saw blades. Try to work out your wall design so that ties do not have to be cut. It is an exhausting job, even with chain or power saws.

Probably the most interesting and attractive type of retaining wall is made of building stone. In many ways, it is the easiest, too, except for one vexing problem—cutting the stone. See Chapter 8 for the basics of stonework, including photos on how to build a stone retaining wall.

No matter what type of material is used, a high wall looks naked and obvious unless it is softened by landscaping. A row of shrubs, preferably evergreen, should run along the base. There should be plantings above, too, particularly hanging types which will spread over the top of the wall and blend it into the surroundings. On stone walls, plants can sometimes be planted in the niches like a rock garden, and vines may look nice growing over certain types of walls.

Figure 4-42: Railroad ties, whether new or old, make a rustic but goodlooking and easily constructed retaining wall.

Figure 4-43: Building stone makes a very attractive retaining wall, and one that a patient homeowner can put together. See Chapter 8 for details.

Figure 4-44: Brick retaining walls always look great. This one was built with concrete block backing the brick veneer (*See Chapter 7*). Be sure to provide weep holes for solid walls like this, so water pressure doesn't build up and break through.

5:

How To Build
Driveways & Walks

Driveways and walks are a large part of your landscape. Although their purpose is utilitarian—to direct vehicle and foot traffic—they do not have to look stark or ugly. Like other elements of your grand design, driveways and walkways should be blended as skillfully as possible into the overall scheme of things.

The most practical driveways and walks are made of concrete, although blacktop is cheaper and brick better looking. A driveway can be made of blacktop and a walk of brick, but the reverse doesn't hold true. Brick isn't very durable in driveways, and blacktop doesn't look very good as a sidewalk.

Good planning, formwork, and finishing are the essentials of quality concrete work. Also important is a substantial helping of muscle. In any concrete pour, a strong helper or two is a must. Yet concrete work is not all that difficult. It is well within the capability of the average do-it-yourselfer with a strong back. Although there are some differences in planning and formwork, walks, drives, patios, and other flat surfaces are essentially slabs and are built in the same way.

No matter what type of slab you are building, don't neglect to plan

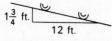

RIGHT: Maximum grade does not exceed 14% ($1\frac{3}{4}''$ per ft.) for good access.

Wrong: Grade too low, rear bumper of vehicle hits street.

Wrong: Grade too high, undercarriage of vehicle hits driveway.

Figure 5-1: The how and why of correct and incorrect driveway slope.

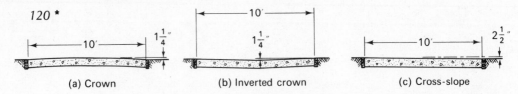

Figure 5-2: Three recommended ways to provide proper drainage for driveways.

for drainage. It's amazing how many handymen (and not a few builders) make driveways that drain either into the garage or into areas already subject to erosion.

Remember that flat impermeable areas, driveways in particular, act as conduits for heavy rains. Be sure that rain is properly directed so it will not damage the landscape.

Planning a Driveway

The best time to plan and build concrete projects is early in the construction season before the hot days of summer. There will be less chance of premature drying out from hot sun and winds plus cooler days for working.

Driveways for single-car garages or carports are usually 10 to 14 feet wide, with a 14-foot minimum width for curving drives. In any case, a driveway should be at least three feet wider than the widest vehicle it will serve. Long driveway approaches to two-car garages may be single-car width, but they must be widened near the garage to provide access to both stalls. Short driveways for two-car garages should be 16 to 24 feet wide all the way.

How thick a driveway slab should be depends primarily upon the weight of the vehicles that use it. For passenger cars, four inches is sufficient, but five or six inches is recommended if an occasional heavy vehicle such as an oil truck uses it.

If the garage is considerably above or below street level and is located near the street, the driveway grade may be critical. A grade of 14 percent (or a vertical rise of 1¾" for each running foot), is the maximum recommended by the Portland Cement Association. The change in grade should be gradual enough to avoid scraping the car's bumper or undercarriage. The most critical angle of travel occurs when a vehicle's rear wheels are in the gutter as it enters the driveway from the street.

The driveway should be built with a slight slope so that it will drain quickly after a rain or washing. A slope of ¼-inch per running foot is recommended in the direction of drain. The specific direction will depend on local conditions, but usually it should be toward the street. A crown or cross-slope may be used for drainage where the drive may be

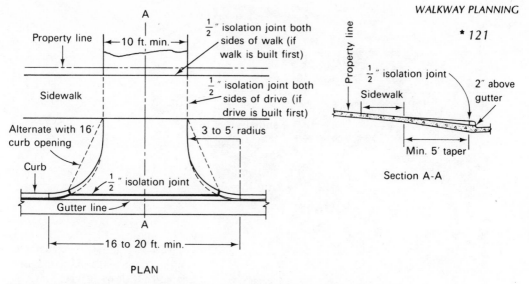

Figure 5-3: Construction details for a typical driveway entrance.

sloped toward the garage. If the drive must slope toward the garage, a dry well of adequate size should be built in front of the garage.

The part of the driveway between the street and the public sidewalk is usually controlled by the local municipality. The municipality should be consulted if a driveway is built after the street, curbs and public walks are in place. If curb and gutters have not been installed, it is advisable to end the driveway temporarily at the public sidewalk or property line. An entry of gravel or crushed stone can be used until curbs and gutters are built. At that time, the drive entrance can be completed to meet local zoning requirements.

While in the planning stage, consideration should be given to other elements that can make a driveway a beautiful approach to a home rather than just a pathway to the garage. Consider using exposed aggregate or other "fancy" concretes, offstreet parking, turnaround areas for safe head-on entry to the street, multi-use paved areas for games and the like.

Walkway Planning

Private walks leading to the front entrance of a home should be three to four feet wide. Service walks connecting to the back entrance need be only two to three feet wide. Public walks should be wide enough to allow two people walking abreast to pass a third person without crowding. The width will vary with the amount of pedestrian traffic on your street, with four to five feet advisable for quiet areas with single-family housing. A greater width is required near schools, churches, shopping centers, and other areas where walks are used by a great number of people. Walks serving apartment dwellers predominantly

Figure 5-4: Sidewalks need not be simple narrow slabs. With imagination and a little extra work, you can make a very attractive entranceway, like this exposed aggregate path with wood strips and plain concrete feature areas.

should be at least eight feet wide. Those in commercial shopping areas should be 12 feet wide. On the other hand, there is no need to exceed four feet in width along rural highways (if you need a sidewalk at all).

In areas where there is a frequent discharge of automobile passengers (such as homes near churches or restaurants), it may be wise to install a courtesy walk next to the curb. This not only accommodates people, but it saves grass. Such walks are usually from eighteen to thirty inches wide.

In some neighborhoods, all sidewalks are built adjacent to the street curb. This allows larger lawns and proper footing for people alighting from vehicles. Such sidewalks, however, give pedestrians less protection from street traffic than walks set back from the curb. A study of pedestrian and bicycle accidents in a suburban area found that the accident rate with five-foot walks next to the curbs was two and a half times the rate for areas with similar walks set back seven to fourteen feet.

Private residential walks should not be less than four inches thick. Walks in commercial or business areas are generally five to six inches thick. Your local building code may specify the width, depth, and so forth for public sidewalks.

SIDEWALK DRAINAGE

It is customary to slope walks a quarter-inch per foot of width for drainage. Where walks are next to curbs or buildings, the slope should be toward the curb and away from the building over the full width of the walk. In some areas where side drainage permits, walks built with a crown or slope from center to edge are desirable (see driveways above). Certain conditions may require other than the customary slope—for example, where a new walk meets an existing driveway or alley. In such cases, the cross-slope of the walk may be increased to a half-inch per foot.

For the convenience of pedestrians, sidewalk approaches at street intersections should be planned to eliminate steps by providing a gentle ramp from walk to street. This is ideal for cyclists, roller skaters, people with baby buggies or carts, and elderly or handicapped pedestrians.

Sidewalk design is closely linked with street, pavement, curb, and gutter design. Quite often all are constructed at the same time. By coordinating sidewalks with streets, curbs, and gutters, a pleasing effect can be obtained.

Public walks adjacent to private properties are generally controlled by the municipality. These walks perform a valuable service by enhancing the value of the private properties. Accordingly, it has been traditional for municipalities to charge abutting properties for all or part of the cost of construction and maintenance of such public walks.

Building Regulations

Before construction begins on a driveway, sidewalk, or anything else, it is advisable to check with the city or county building department. Most communities require a building permit to ensure that work is done in accordance with the building code. Laws regulating building methods vary with localities. Building permits are especially important for driveways and sidewalks that cross a public way (that strip of land on either side of a street extending from property line to curb and reserved for public sidewalks, grass and trees). Some cities also establish sidewalk grades when a sidewalk permit is obtained.

How To Make Concrete

Concrete is a mixture of Portland cement, water, and aggregate. Although some people incorrectly refer to the material as cement (a "cement" driveway), only from 7 to 14 percent of a good mixture is actually cement. The word "cement" is also used to identify various compounds which bind or hold other things together; for example, rubber cement. All the cement used in ordinary construction concrete is Portland cement, the soft, fine, grayish green powder usually packed in large bags of 94 pounds each. The term Portland was applied by a nineteenth-century Englishman named Joseph Aspdin who thought that

124 *   concrete made from it resembled "Portland stone," a widely-used building material in his day. Cement and water mixed together actually form a sort of adhesive which fills in space and binds the aggregate particles together. The cement-water mixture, called "cement paste" by masons, describes its function quite accurately.

Figure 5-5: Photos show various degrees of dampness in sand used with cement. "Wet" sand (*above left*) that forms a ball in the hand is right for concrete when it leaves no noticeable moisture on the palm. Sand (*right*) is too "dry" for concrete since it falls apart and (*left*) it is "too wet" since it leaves noticeable moisture behind and sticks to the hand.

Modern Portland cement is a finely pulverized material consisting principally of lime, silica, alumina and iron. It is manufactured from limestone and other ingredients such as clay, shale, or slag from blast furnaces. The materials are burned in a rotary kiln at a temperature of 2700 degrees Fahrenheit, which welds the materials into clinkers. The clinkers are cooled and then pulverized, with a small amount of gypsum added to regulate setting time.

Aggregate is inert and plays no part in the chemical process that takes place when concrete sets. Yet it is the real basis for its durability and strength and constitutes from 66 to 78 percent of its volume. In effect, the more aggregate, the richer the mix. Table 5-1 shows the correct proportions. Aggregate usually consists of crushed stone, gravel, sand, or blast furnace slag. The size of the particles of aggregate depends on the type of work, with the large jobs such as bridge pilings requiring the largest-sized aggregates. Some variation in size is desirable, even with sands, because the smaller pieces fill in between the big ones. A mix of aggregate sizes is usually cheaper as well.

Table 5-1: Recommended Mixes for Concrete Slabs

Total Ingredients	Proportion by Weight	Proportion by Volume
Cement	94 lbs.	1 part
Sand	215 lbs.	2 ¼ parts
Aggregate (coarse)	295 lbs.	3 parts
Water*	42 lbs. (approx.)	5 gals.

*Always figure five gallons of water per 94-lb. bag of cement (each gallon weighs 8.337 lbs per gallon at 15°C).

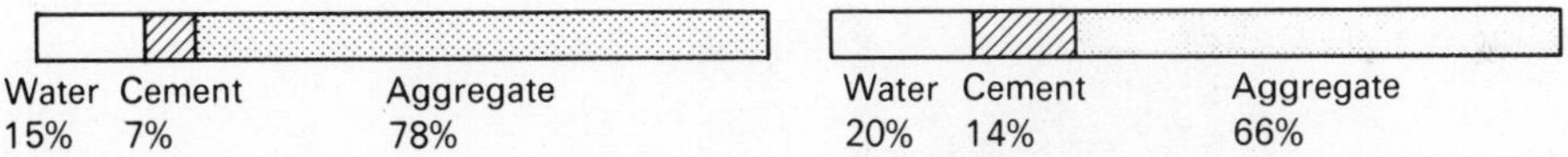

Water 15%	Cement 7%	Aggregate 78%	
Water 20%	Cement 14%	Aggregate 66%	

Figure 5-6: The proportion of ingredients for good concrete mixes are diagrammed above: in the first, 78% aggregate is used if the stones are large, along with lesser percentages of water and cement; in the second mix, the aggregate is smaller in diameter and the amount of water and cement increases. Most mixes are somewhere in between. The first or "lean" mix has a somewhat stiff consistency and the second or "rich" mix is liquid.

All aggregate should be clean and free of loam, clay, or vegetable matter, since these foreign particles prevent the cement paste from properly binding the aggregate together. Sand should be "wet" for most formulas. Concrete containing foreign matter will be porous and have low strength. That is not to say that you cannot use other solid materials such as bricks, old concrete, rocks and iron in your foundations or footings. Toss them into the bottom of the excavation—it's a good way to get rid of this stuff—but not, obviously, into the concrete mix itself.

THE MIX FOR SLABS & FOOTINGS

How do you know when you have the proper mix? For one thing, read the directions on the bag. Another way is to try troweling the

126 *   mixture. If there is insufficient cement paste, there will be a coarse, stiff surface, with large pieces of aggregate very visible. If the mixture is too "wet," there will be scarcely any aggregate apparent. Before it is troweled, the mixture will be soupy. The proper reaction is for the troweling to smooth the surface, but for the aggregate to be clearly visible where the mixture has not been troweled. The mix will have a stiff—but not dry—appearance.

PREPARING SUBGRADE AND FORMWORK

The first step in constructing a slab is to prepare the subgrade. All sod and vegetable matter should be removed, and any soft or mucky places must be dug out, filled with granular material, and thoroughly tamped. Exceptionally hard, compact spots must also be loosened and tamped so as to provide the same bearing power as the remainder of the subgrade.

When additional fill is required to bring the slab bed to the proper grade, this should also be of a granular material, thoroughly compacted in six-inch layers. It is best to extend the top of all subgrade fills at least one foot beyond the edges of the walk and to make the slope flat enough to prevent undercutting during rains.

Figure 5-7: Proper subgrade is essential for concrete work. Any loose material must be thoroughly tamped; soft or mucky soil should be replaced with granular material such as sand or gravel.

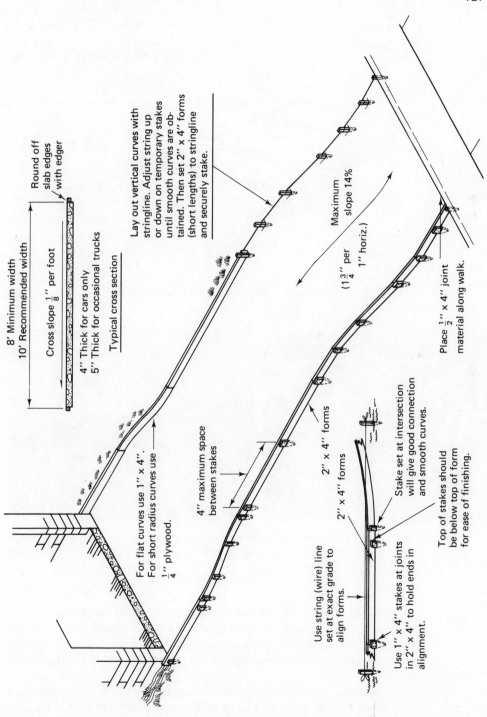

Round off slab edges with edger

8' Minimum width
10' Recommended width

Cross slope $\frac{1}{8}$" per foot

4" Thick for cars only
5" Thick for occasional trucks

Typical cross section

Lay out vertical curves with stringline. Adjust string up or down on temporary stakes until smooth curves are obtained. Then set 2" x 4" forms (short lengths) to stringline and securely stake.

Maximum slope 14%

($1\frac{3}{4}$" per 1" horiz.)

Place $\frac{1}{2}$" x 4" joint material along walk.

For flat curves use 1" x 4". For short radius curves use $\frac{1}{4}$" plywood.

4" maximum space between stakes

2" x 4" forms

2" x 4" forms

Stake set at intersection will give good connection and smooth curves.

Top of stakes should be below top of form for ease of finishing.

Use string (wire) line set at exact grade to align forms.

Use 1" x 4" stakes at joints in 2" x 4" to hold ends in alignment.

Figure 5-8: Layout for formwork used to pour a typical driveway slab.

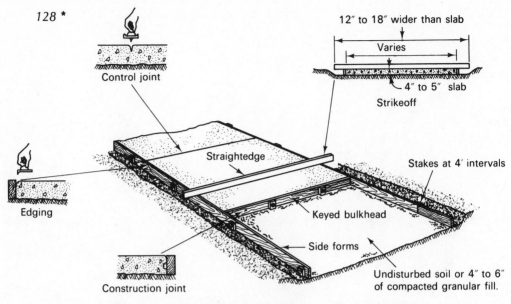

Figure 5-9: Construction details for a concrete sidewalk.

Figure 5-10: Techniques for strengthening wooden forms: note extra bracing (*left foreground*) where extra stress is anticipated; steel stakes (*right*) make good braces, too, and are easy to set.

A well-compacted, well-drained subgrade does not require a specially prepared subbase. Subgrades which are water-soaked much of the time should be provided with a six-inch subbase of sand, gravel, crushed stone, or cinders. Subbases must be drained to prevent the collection of water.

Sidewalk and driveway forms may be made of either wood or metal. They must be staked so that line and grade are held true. The upper edge of the forms should be level with the finished grade of walk, and the forms should be oiled before the concrete is poured. For wide-radius form curves, 1×4 lumber with closer staking is recommended. For short-radius curves, use ¼" plywood or straight runs with stakes a maximum of four feet apart.

Ready-mix Concrete

If the job is big enough, it may pay you to have ready-mixed concrete brought in a truck; this can be poured quickly and easily from a chute. Look in the yellow pages under "Concrete—Ready Mixed" for a supplier and tell him how much you want. To determine that, use the following table (all computations are for four-inch thickness):

Area in Square Feet	Concrete in Cubic Yards	Area in Square Feet	Concrete in Cubic Yards
10	0.12	100	1.23
25	0.31	200	2.47
50	0.62	300	3.70

For a 6×20-foot walk, for example, multiply the two dimensions to get 120 square feet. To 1.23 cubic yards for the first 100 square feet, add .31 for the 25 square feet, for a total of 1.58. If you have measured and dug exactly right, one and one-half yards should be enough. Play safe, however, and order the next highest amount the supplier will sell you (probably two cubic yards).

As long as you are ordering, make sure you get the right concrete for the job. Here are some of the specifications for your supplier:

* Specify the amount of cubic yards, remembering to make allowances for uneven grades, spillage, etc. It is far better to have a little left over than to run short.
* Specify at least six sacks of cement per cubic yard to ensure a good bond.
* Ask for not more than a four-inch slump to insure the proper type of mix. (Slump is a measurement of consistency.) Four-inch slump will give you a good, workable mix. Stiffer mixes are harder to finish by hand. Mixes that are wet and soupy will not produce durable concrete.
* Specify a coarse gravel aggregate from ¾" and 1-½" in size (a one-inch maximum is ideal).
* Ask for 6% "air entrainment" (plus or minus one percent) to obtain good durability—particularly in colder climates. Air entraining re-

130 *

duces damage by frost and salt because it develops minute, well-distributed air bubbles in the concrete.
* Specify where and when to deliver the concrete, and, if possible, place your concrete order at least one day ahead of time.

PLACING THE MIX

Before the concrete is poured—either by you or by your supplier—wet the surrounding earth, the subgrade, and the forms themselves with a garden hose. This wetting helps prevent water from leaching from the mix into dryer areas around it. Have a wheelbarrow handy for both ready- and home-made mix. (If there is much hauling to be done, add still another person to the two or three recommended earlier.)

Have the concrete poured in the forms to their full depth, spading along the sides to complete filling. Try to load it as close as possible to its final position without too much dragging and spading. This will not only save your strength, but will prevent overworking of the mix. Use a square-end short-handled shovel and/or a concrete rake for this.

Do not pour too large a portion of the concrete for your slab at one time. Once placed, the mix should be bull-floated as quickly as possible. After placing, strike off the surface with a 2×4 straightedge, working it in a sawlike motion across the top of the form boards. This "screeding"

Figure 5-11: When concrete is poured, spade it as quickly as possible into position, working it along the sides of the forms with your shovel to ensure complete filling.

Figure 5-12: Level and "strike off" the concrete with a piece of 2 x 4 or a specially-made straightedge like this one—an eight-foot length of 1 x 4 with a ½" x 2" shoe strip attached to the bottom. The hand grip is a 4-foot length of ¾" half-round molding.

Figure 5-13: Immediately after striking off, work over the surface of the pour with a "bull" float as shown, or use a small wood or magnesium hand float.

smooths the surface and cuts the concrete off at the proper height. Go over the concrete twice in this manner to take out any bumps or fill in low spots. Tilt the straightedge slightly in the direction of travel to obtain a better cutting action during this strike-off.

Immediately after, rough-float the surface to smooth it and remove irregularities. Use the small wooden hand float for small or close work, and the large "bull" float (made of wood or steel) for larger areas. The "darby" is an excellent all-around tool that can be used as a straightedge as well as a float. The bull float is tilted slightly away from you as you push it forward, then flattened as it is pulled back. The darby is held flat against the surface of the slab and worked from side to side.

Do not overdo any of the smoothing motions. Overworking of concrete concentrates water excessively and makes the fine particles rise to the surface. That in turn makes the surface more prone to flaking and chipping.

Finishing Concrete Surfaces

If you use air-entrained concrete—and you should—finishing can usually follow immediately after floating. When the weather is cool and humid particularly, you should check the surface before you finish it. Begin by making sure that there is no water sheen on the surface; then test for stiffening with your foot. An indentation from your shoe should be no more than ¼" deep—otherwise proceed no further. You can help ensure that the surface is dry enough by taking a little time before finishing to cut the forms away from the concrete. Do this by working a pointed trowel along the forms to a depth of about an inch.

The first finishing step is edging, which should take place as soon as the surface is stiff enough to hold the shape of the edging tool. The edger is run between the form and the concrete with the body of the tool held flat on the concrete surface except for its leading edge which is tilted up slightly.

Control joints are desirable if the slab runs more than 10 feet in any direction. These joints help control large cracks. They are made with a "groover," which is similar to an edger except that it cuts down the middle. The tool should cut to a depth from one-fifth to one-fourth of the slab thickness. A portable circular saw can be equipped with a masonry-cutting blade to serve the same purpose as the groover.

Isolation joints are similar to control joints except that they are inserted before the concrete is placed. They are used wherever two surfaces with potential stress are jointed—such as those between a sidewalk and a driveway or building or those around manholes, poles, and similar obstructions. Half-inch thick fiber material is nailed to the forms about a quarter of an inch below the surface and left there.

One excellent way to control stress and have a decorative touch is to use redwood 2×4's at regular intervals. The redwood forms are left in as divider strips but are protected by masking tape while you work the concrete.

Finish floating is done with a wood hand float. This procedure eliminates any remaining imperfections—such as the marks from the edger and groover—and produces a smoother surface. The large aggregates are embedded and the mortar is consolidated at the top for further finish operations. If a rough, non-skid surface is desired, finish floating can be the final step.

Although the slightly rough surface created by floating is safer for walking, many people prefer the smooth finish created by troweling. For

Figure 5-14: Use an edger to finish along the sides, and a "groover" to put in expansion joints as shown. The piece of wood alongside helps guide the tool at right angles to the forms. Note the marks left by edger and groover; they are removed during finish floating.

Figure 5-15: The last smoothing step, finish floating, is done with a hand float or trowel, (shown) which produces a neater but more skid-prone sheen.

this purpose, rectangular, steel-bladed trowels are used. At least two passes are necessary. Even if an automatic trowel is used for the first step, it is always followed by hand troweling. The final troweling should produce a ringing sound as the blade traverses the hardened surfaces. (See page 135–39 for ways to make decorative finishes.)

HYDRATION AND CURING

The chemical reaction between water and cement is called hydration. This process must continue for several days to a week after the concrete is placed in order for the concrete to attain maximum durability. Hydration stops if too much water is lost by evaporation or if the temperature falls below 50°F.

Curing is also an essential process and is designed to keep water in the concrete for the right length of time. To stop evaporation, several methods are used, the best of which is simply keeping the surface moist. To do this, wash out some burlap bags with a hose to remove any foreign matter that can cause discoloration. Place the bags on top of the concrete and wet them down, keeping them wet during the entire curing period.

Another way of keeping the surface wet is by running a sprinkler or soaking hose continuously over the surface. For small jobs, try "ponding," or building dikes around the edges of the job to keep a pool of water on the slab.

An easier but less effective way to cure concrete is by spreading sheet plastic or waterproof paper over the entire surface. Such materials form a moisture barrier that prevents excessive evaporation. To do a proper job, however, the plastic or paper must be thoroughly sealed at joints and be laid perfectly flat to avoid discoloration.

Curing time can be as little as three days, but at least five days are recommended in warm weather and seven in cold weather. During very hot, dry weather, hydration may occur very rapidly, and precautions

Figure 5-16: The curing method being used above is fast and easy, but the covering must be laid on without creases or open spots; otherwise, discoloration results. See text for more conventional and safer curing procedures.

should be taken to prevent excess evaporation while working. Be sure to wet the area thoroughly before placing, and work as rapidly as possible. Try to work in some sort of shade, avoiding the hot hours of late morning and early afternoon. The cooler hours will be kinder to your body as well as the concrete.

DECORATIVE CONCRETE FINISHES

Many people are perfectly content with typical light gray, rough or smooth-surfaced concrete. There are, however, a variety of specialized concrete applications which have more eye appeal than plain concrete.

Coloring: If you have ever tried to paint concrete, you know that all too soon the paint wears or starts flaking off and becomes unsightly. Those who like colored concrete are well advised to pay the extra cost of having color worked into the concrete itself. If you want a nice white look instead of the usual concrete gray, simply order white Portland cement instead of regular. It costs a little more, but not much. No special methods are involved.

Other colors require the addition of a pigment. It is done in several ways. A coloring agent, a mineral oxide made especially for concrete, is added to the mix before it is poured. This can be done with ready-mix or in your own batch. White Portland cement provides brighter tints than the regular gray and should be used unless you're working with the darker pigments. Coloring agents are available from most of the same

Figure 5-17: Workmen here are troweling in black abrasive dry shake which creates a non-skid surface and changes the color.

sources as the cement. They should not exceed 10 percent of the cement by weight.

To save money on the fairly expensive pigment, pour the concrete in two courses, using the coloring agent only in the top course. If you do this, however, be sure to leave the surface of the first course very rough to provide a good "tooth" for the second. The top course need be only one-half to an inch thick.

If you prefer to use the quicker but more costly one-course method, make sure either to soak the ground thoroughly the night before or to put down a moisture barrier such as plastic sheeting under the slab. If you don't, some pigment may escape with the water and cause uneven coloring.

You can also color the concrete with dry shake compounds, applied by hand to the surface just before final floating. These abrasive grains have the additional merit of creating a non-skid surface. Two applications are necessary, and the surface must be floated, edged and grooved after each one.

Table 5-2: Guide to Coloring Compounds for Concrete

Color	Additive
White	White Portland cement, white sand
Blue	Cobalt oxide
Brown	Brown oxide of iron or burnt umber
Buff	Synthetic yellow oxide of iron or yellow ocher
Green	Chromium oxide
Red	Red oxide of iron
Pink	Red oxide of iron (in small amounts)
Dark Gray	Black oxide of iron

Exposed Aggregate: This popular terrazzo-like finish takes extra time, effort, and money, but the investment is worthwhile. The result is anti-skid and highly durable, as well as very attractive. For best results, use colorful, rounded pebbles of equal size. Adjust your usual concrete formula to provide a stiffer mix with more and larger aggregate.

The concrete mix is placed in the usual manner, except that it should be leveled off from ⅜" to ½" below the top of the forms to allow for the extra aggregate. Screed and float in the usual way, then spread your rounded stones evenly over the surface with your shovel. Fill in the bare spots by hand until the surface is completely covered with aggregate. If the first few stones sink to the bottom, wait a half-hour or so until the mix gets a little stiffer.

When you have a good, even stone cover, tap it into the surface of the concrete with a 2×4, darby or wood float. Then go over the entire surface with your wood hand float, working the stones down into the

Figure 5-18: To make an exposed aggregate surface, set stones all over the surface of floated concrete (*left*), then pat them in with a wood float, a 2 x 4, or a "darby" (*right*).

Figure 5-19: This attractive walk-way combines exposed aggregate with brick strips.

138 * concrete until they are entirely covered again by cement paste. The surface will look almost like it did before.

Wait for an hour or two, until the slab can bear the weight of a man on kneeboards without leaving an indentation. Then brush the surface lightly with a stiff nylon-bristle broom to remove the excess mortar.

The final and most difficult job is hard-brooming the surface while washing the stones with a fine spray. Either have a helper for this, or alternately spray and broom. But brush hard enough to dislodge as much cement film as you can. Ideally, all you should see are the pretty, colorful stones. If the surface is too dull, give it a bath with muriatic acid.

Textured and Novelty Finishes: The only prohibition when finishing concrete is an infertile imagination. Almost any pattern is acceptable as long as you can figure out a way of applying it.

A textured finish is one in which the regular floated or troweled surface is altered in some way. The most common—and easiest—pattern is a broomed finish. Simply work a stiff-bristle broom back and forth over a newly floated surface. Either a straight or wavy pattern provides a good-looking, skid-resistant surface. An attractive "swirl" finish is produced by making semi-circles with a hand float or trowel. To produce a uniform pattern, use your entire arm and keep the wrist rigid.

Figure 5-20: "Brooming" is easy to do and gives a good anti-skid surface. The broom can also be worked in semi-circles to make another good-looking wavy pattern.

Figure 5-21: This texture is obtained by first scattering rock salt over the surface after finishing "off" the new concrete, and then pressing it down into the plastic concrete. After it sets, the salt is washed out, leaving the random pit marks behind on the hardened concrete.

Another way to provide texture is to scatter rock salt over the slab top after you hand float or trowel the concrete. Press the salt firmly into the surface so that it is almost invisible. Then, when the concrete is hard, dissolve it out and you have an attractive pitted surface.

Geometric patterns can be pressed into concrete surfaces with a variety of tools or instruments. A piece of curved copper pipe, for example, can produce a random flagstone pattern. Scored lines, which look like recessed joints, are made after bull-floating and while the mix is still plastic. After hand-floating, the pipe should be run through again and the joints cleaned of burrs with a fine broom and a soft-bristled paint brush. You can also use empty cans of varied sizes to create circles or rent a device to create brick or other patterns.

Figure 5-22: "Brick-maker" forms like these can be rented from specialty houses. Often other patterns are also available for concrete work.

140 *   Concrete Repairs and Patches

If a section of driveway or sidewalk is heaved and broken by tree roots, the best cure is to break up that section with a sledgehammer, remove the concrete and chop off the root. A tree with roots that big and powerful is mature enough to survive, and you can simply replace the sidewalk section. Save the broken pieces, though, and use them as fill.

If the problem is flaking or other surface deterioration, you can probably do a quicker and easier job with vinyl patching cement. This type of patch can be "feathered" at the edges and will not wear like other cement compounds. Chip out the bad areas and apply the vinyl patch with a steel trowel.

When only certain areas are damaged, or if a large crack appears which should be filled, the deteriorated parts should be cut out with a cold chisel, undercutting the crack or edge so that the crack is narrower at the surface than the part underneath. Ordinary concrete, with finer aggregates, can be used for this type of patching, or premixed mortar or rubber patch can be purchased at the hardware store. The undercut edges should hold the patch in the same way your tooth holds a filling.

Figure 5-23: To fix cracked concrete, chisel out the crack in an inverted "V" so that the top is narrower than the bottom. Fill the widened crack with mix made from one of the patch materials available at most masonry or building supply houses (*courtesy of Hartline Products, Inc.*).

Laying Blacktop

A complete blacktop driveway is a job for professionals, since it should be applied hot and compacted by a roller. But laying small walks and patching can be performed by the homeowner. "Cold patch" can be purchased at asphalt plants in larger quanties, but for small jobs, bags of pre-mixed blacktop are ideal.

To repair blacktop, cut out all the broken material to a solid surface. All loose gravel should be removed to a depth of about two inches. If the hole is deeper than this, fill with fine gravel. Pour in a blacktop mix so that the patch projects about a half-inch above the surface. Pack the blacktop down thoroughly with an iron tamper, or make your own tool by nailing a piece of ¾" plywood to the end of a 2 × 2. For very small jobs, the back of a shovel or rake may suffice.

Not only *can* you drive over the patch right away, you *should* drive over it a couple of times. The car's tires will act similarly to the roller, and help compact the material. Drive smoothly, however, and don't skid or accelerate quickly.

To make a small walk, or extend your driveway, use the same general techniques as for patching. Dig down two inches farther, however, when you expect heavy traffic. Fill in the extra space with fine gravel. For large areas, tamp well and keep traffic off for a few days. Blacktop sealers prolong the life of driveways and help eliminate major repair bills. Sealer should be applied every two or three years.

6:

Patios, Steps, Etc. in Concrete

Previously we reviewed the basic techniques of concrete work as they are most frequently applied in constructing walks and driveways. But there are lots of other ways to put the low-maintenance, high strength, and great durability of concrete to work around the house. For these projects you will need all the know-how acquired from Chapter 5, plus a few more techniques.

Building a Patio

A concrete patio is simply a kind of slab. Use the same techniques as for making any four-inch slab. But you may need long-handled tools, especially if the patio is to be very large. Either buy them or lash regular tools to a long pole.

Something should be said early on, however, about the location of a patio. Do not just situate it anywhere impulsively. Later, when you want to put in a pool or run a gas line to a barbecue, you will value the "delay" used for planning. As always, it is essential.

PLANNING THE PATIO

The ideal location for your outdoor living room may be directly outside of, and connected by sliding glass doors to, the family room, kitchen, or living room. This convenience will pay off, especially if you entertain frequently, but the saving in steps means a lot even when the family is having a hot dog feast on the patio. It's also nice to be close to

Figure 6-1: A patio near the house makes it easy to keep an eye on a playing child. Note the interesting use of permanent redwood divider strips for this exposed aggregate finish slab.

the house to keep an eye on the children as well as for easy access to the refrigerator and those cooling summer drinks.

But this convenience is not the only factor to consider when deciding the location of your patio. Your home's design may not invite an attached patio, or you may prefer to locate it in a far corner of your lot, possibly for privacy or to take advantage of a view. Most important is the location of the patio in relation to the sun. Depending on where you live, you will want to orient the patio to take advantage of, or to block out, the sun. A patio that faces the south will almost surely need a roof and some sort of sun screen. An eastward-facing patio gets the morning sun (pleasant for Sunday breakfasts), while a westward-facing patio will get the hotter midday sun. An attached patio that faces north will be shaded by the house during most of the day. Prevailing breezes are yet another consideration in your planning.

As an extension of the home—although not necessarily a physical part of it—the patio should be planned to complement the home's architectural features. Shape and size must be considered in relation to the house and to the shape and size of your lot. In most cases, an outdoor living room should be larger than the rooms inside the house, with plenty of room for oversized lounging furniture (see Chapter 11). In some instances, however, a small, intimate patio is preferred outside a master bedroom or even a bathroom.

Concrete is a long-time favorite for patios, and it can be employed in a number of ways—small modules (easy for the home handyman to manage), a slab, alternate squares of plain and pebbled concrete, softly tinted concrete to offset glare, concrete patio blocks. Other materials well-liked by the exterior home decorator are brick, flagstone, and tile. Often a combination of two or more of these is employed to make a very attractive patio.

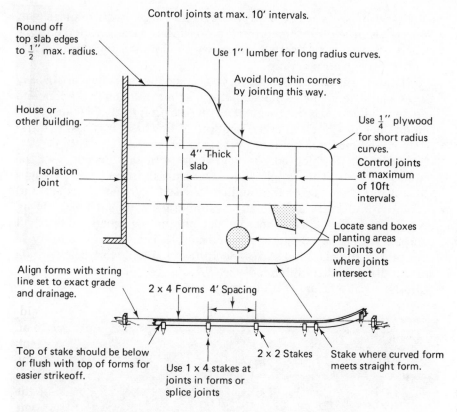

Control joints at max. 10' intervals.

Round off top slab edges to $\frac{1}{2}''$ max. radius.

Use 1'' lumber for long radius curves.

Avoid long thin corners by jointing this way.

House or other building.

Use $\frac{1}{4}''$ plywood for short radius curves.

4'' Thick slab

Isolation joint

Control joints at maximum of 10ft intervals

Locate sand boxes planting areas on joints or where joints intersect

Align forms with string line set to exact grade and drainage.

2 × 4 Forms 4' Spacing

Top of stake should be below or flush with top of forms for easier strikeoff.

2 × 2 Stakes

Stake where curved form meets straight form.

Use 1 × 4 stakes at joints in forms or splice joints

Figure 6-2: Typical plan for attached-to-the-house patio shows construction details.

CONCRETE PATIO SLABS

Carefree concrete makes a fine patio surface and, while many homeowners may prefer to leave this project to a contractor, there is no reason why willing and talented do-it-yourselfers who can invest some time and perspiration should not reap the reward of a considerable cost savings. Some variations of regular slab work are described here.

A gridwork of redwood lumber embedded in a concrete patio can give it a pleasing appearance. A grid also makes it easy for the weekend worker to do the job in stages. First excavate the area of the patio as necessary, and prepare the subgrade with gravel or cinder fill. Then construct the gridwork of 2×4 lumber, face-nailing it together with 8d galvanized nails. The grid can be of any reasonable dimensions that seem to look best for your patio and its surroundings—four-foot squares, rectangles, a random pattern, or whatever gives the best accent and pattern to the area.

To form wide radius curves, use 1×4 lumber. Form short radius

146 *   corners with hardboard or ¼" plywood. Hold the gridwork in place with 1×4 stakes driven into the ground around the perimeter. Stake forms closely at curves, and set all stakes well below the top edges of the lumber forms before nailing.

Once the gridwork is in place, you can do the concrete work in easy stages—just a few squares or rectangles at a time. Either mix the concrete and pour it by hand or rent a small mixer (see Chapter 5). Of course, you can do the entire patio in one operation; in this case, it is best to order ready-mixed concrete brought to the site by truck.

Strike off the poured concrete flush with the top edges of the redwood boards. Then apply the desired finish, (described on pages 132-39) and allow to cure thoroughly. Exposed aggregate, brushed, and decorative finishes are especially desirable for patio surfaces, adding textural interest. A checkerboard effect, alternating squares of brushed concrete with exposed-aggregate for example, is another possibility. It goes back to the planning stage—deciding what will work best with its surroundings and its intended use. (See pages 156-58 for details on building a patio of pre-cast blocks.)

Figure 6-3: Redwood divider strips make it easy to strike off the patio's new concrete.

Figure 6-4: A broomed finish (*left*) is anti-skid; so is exposed aggregate (*right*). The latter is durable and attractive as well. Review Chapter 5 for details on the techniques used to produce these finishes.

How To Make Concrete Steps

Concrete steps are more difficult to make than the slab projects previously described; however, they can be built well—with proper care. You should probably not attempt to build more than three stairs the first time, but after the experience gained from that, you should be able to tackle a bigger project.

Steps for residential entranceways, however, must conform with local building codes. These codes establish critical dimensions such as:

* Width of step.
* Height of flights without landings.
* Size of landings.
* Size of risers and treads.
* Relationship between riser and tread size.

Always check before building; steps for private homes are usually 48″ wide. Some codes allow 30″ and 36″ widths; steps, in any case, should be at least as wide as the door and walk.

A landing is recommended to divide flights of more than five feet. Landings should be no shorter than three feet and the top one no more than 7½″ below the door threshold.

For flights less than 30″ high, maximum step rise is usually 7½″ with an 11″ minimum tread width. For higher flights, step rise may be limited to six inches, with a minimum tread width of 12 inches. Choice of riser and tread size should depend on how steps are to be used. For esthetic reasons, steps with risers as low as 4 inches and treads as wide as

Figure 6-5-: Exceptionally handsome steps can be made with exposed-aggregate slabs used here on a gently sloping grade.

Figure 6-6: Plain concrete steps are utilitarian and economical.

19 inches are often built. Do not, however, make steps higher than 7½" or narrower than 11 inches. On long, sloping approaches, use a stepped ramp.

As a general rule, the closer the climbing steps come to the normal walking stride, the safer and easier it is for all ages. For safety's sake there should be no variation in the height of risers and width of treads in any one flight.

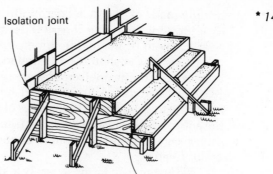

Isolation joint

Note: bevel on bottom permits
finishing of tread under riser form

Figure 6-7: Formwork for the typical entrance steps illustrated in
Figure 6-6.

FOUNDATIONS FOR STEPS

The footing or foundation for steps should be placed at least two
feet deep in firm, undisturbed soil and, in areas where freezing occurs,
six inches below the prevailing frost line. Steps with more than two
risers and two treads should be supported on unit masonry or concrete
walls or piers at least six inches thick, or should be cantilevered from the
main foundation walls. Steps should be securely tied to foundation
walls with anchor bolts or tie rods. On new construction, step footings
should be cast integrally with foundation walls.

When new steps are added to an existing building, the following
economical procedure will prevent their sinking. Two or more six- to
eight-inch-diameter postholes should be dug beneath the bottom tread
and filled with concrete. The holes should extend to the depth indicated
above. The top step or landing should be tied into the foundation wall
with two or more metal anchors.

FORMWORK FOR STEPS

There are two ways to make step forms. They depend on the
finishing technique you want to use. The formwork shown on page 149
makes simple steps. With the first finishing method, the forms are left in
place for several days after curing, but the landings and treads are
finished almost immediately after the concrete is placed. The rest of the
work is later. With the other finishing method, the riser forms are
stripped from half to several hours after placing or as soon as the
concrete begins to set. At this point, the steps should be strong enough to
support a man's weight. When you use this technique, make certain that
the riser forms can be removed easily without affecting the stability of
the sidewall forms. The sidewall forms are left in place until last.

All forms must be rigidly braced, since the volume of concrete
loaded behind them is greater than that of a simple slab. Forms are

usually made of one-inch boards, although sidewalls can be built of ¾" exterior plywood or hardboard if desired. When you use panels, cut the riser forms to fit the inside dimensions.

Riser forms should be installed from the top down to eliminate unnecessary traffic on risers already in place. Remember to allow at least ⅛" slope for drainage on each tread, but make sure that each riser is level from side to side. The bottom edges of riser forms are beveled in to allow the entire tread to be finished first (see diagram). You can tilt or "batter" each riser in toward the bottom about an inch, if you want, to provide wider treads.

To fasten riser forms securely to panel sidewalls, use wood cleats as shown in Figure 6-8. Brick, stone, broken concrete, or other solid material can be used as fill inside the formwork to reduce the amount of concrete needed. No fill material should be any closer than six inches to the face of any form.

Figure 6-8: When panel sidewalls are used, the forms must be securely braced. Wood cleats hold riser boards on each side.

PLACEMENT AND FINISHING

Mix the concrete in the way described in Chapter 5, except that the coarse aggregate should not exceed one inch in diameter, and a "three-inch slump" should be ordered with ready-mix. Forms should be wet with water if they will be removed the same day. Those to be left in place for several days should be oiled.

Begin placing concrete with the bottom step and work upward. The concrete should be spaded close in to the edges of the forms. Each tread should be struck off and floated as it is filled. When the top step or landing has been floated, finish the one below it, then the next, etc. Use knee boards to work on the upper treads. Under the first method discussed above the forms are left in place until the concrete is completely

Figure 6-9: The top landing of a newly-poured entrance is struck off and floated first.

set—usually a few days. After the forms are stripped, any projections are chipped off and holes are filled, then the whole surface is given a grout rubdown of one part cement to 1½ parts fine sand.

If forms are stripped the same day, wait for at least half an hour, then carefully remove the riser forms from the top down. Risers are floated and finished, using additional mortar if the surface is too stiff. When the risers are finished, sidewalls can be finished next, or left in place for a few days and finished with a grout rubdown as above. You must work fast with this method to avoid having the concrete set too hard. Steps must be cured in the same way as detailed in Chapter 5.

Figure 6-10: When riser forms are all stripped the same day, they are removed from the top down. Knee boards prevent the do-it-yourselfer from sinking into the lower treads.

Figure 6-11: The risers themselves are then floated and finished quickly—before the concrete sets too hard to work.

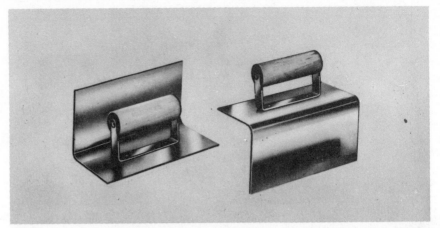

Figure 6-12: A pair of matched concrete edging tools like these are a must for inside and outside corners when you use the same-day method (*courtesy of Portland Cement Association*).

For a non-skid surface, work a damp brush across each tread. A more permanent nonslip tread can be obtained by using a dry shake of abrasive grains. Edges are finished with matching tools for inside and outside corners.

Concrete Castings for Yard & Garden

Concrete castings give you an easy way to achieve instant interest in your front or back yard. Large flower pots, bird baths and other standard units are available in masonry or building supply houses, nurseries or specialized casting suppliers. Many of the units are small and light enough to be handled by women or older children, so a project like a garden walk can be a family affair.

Figure 6-13: Templates for casting bowl section of concrete bird bath with forms are seen here in use (*courtesy of Portland Cement Association*).

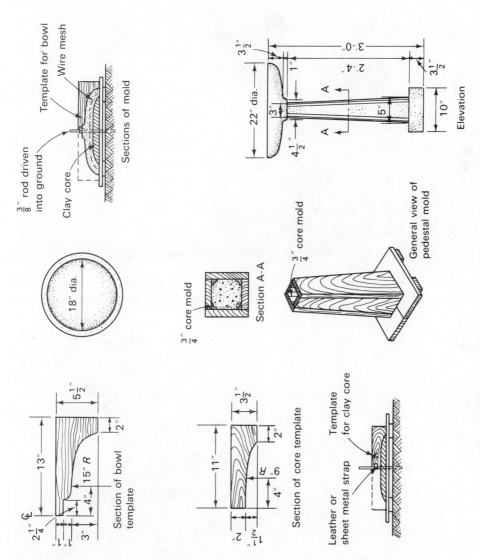

Figure 6-14: Details for constructing forms to cast a concrete bird-bath.

154 ＊   But you can make your own castings, too, by buying forms from such organizations as the Concrete Machinery Company. For further information about precision aluminum molds, write the company at P.O. Drawer 99, Hickory, North Carolina 28601.

Figure 6-15: When aluminum is used to cast concrete, you must coat the insides with oil both before and after use. Here an enthusiastic gardener takes steps to cast a large durable flower pot for outdoor use.

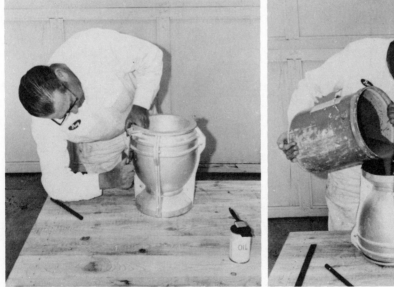

Figure 6-16: Next, the inside and outside sections are bolted together. Then a "wet" concrete mix is poured into the mold and allowed to settle.

Figure 6-17: Then the mix is "prodded" with a metal rod using a gentle up-and-down motion to ensure that it fills the form completely and without air pockets. Next, excess water is removed and any depressions are filled with additional mix. The top of the mold is struck off as with a slab. (The metal pipe left in the center makes an opening for a drain hole.)

Figure 6-18: When the concrete is stiff, the drain-hole pipe is pulled out. Then the forms are removed, the interior form first.

Figure 6-19: Finally the outside forms are removed and the flower pot is ready (*courtesy of Concrete Machinery Company*).

Pre-cast Paving Materials

An excellent way to build a walk or patio is to buy pre-cast concrete modules in manageable sizes, then lay them on a base of sand or well-compacted soil. The modules come in square, rectangular, and circular shapes. You can also pre-cast your own modules. If you do use pre-cast patio modules, be sure that you prepare an absolutely level sand base for them. Embed leveling boards to the exact grade wanted and then screed the sand firmly across them. When the leveling is finished, carefully remove these leveling boards and fill in their "sockets." (Details for estimating concrete needs, mixing, pouring, and curing are also included in the previous chapter.)

You can pre-cast the actual modules in your basement or garage during the off-season, then lay them when the warm weather arrives. To build a form for square or rectangular blocks, use 1×4, 2×4, and 4×4 lumber cut to size. Bolt them together and cut notches halfway through each form piece, then simply fit the pieces together. They come apart easily for re-use. For circular blocks, cut 2" wide strips out of ⅛" hardboard for blocks up to 12" diameter (3" strips for wider blocks). Cut them slightly more than three times longer than the intended diameter. (Remember the old formula: circumference = π (3.1416) × diameter.) Bend the strips into a circle with smooth sides turned inward. Where ends meet, wrap them securely with heavy duty tape, then wrap the outside of each circle with tape to make a sturdy form. Like the straight forms, these circular forms can be re-used. You need make only one, but you can cast a number of blocks at a time if you make several.

Grease the insides of the forms before use, then place them on tarpaper on the floor of the basement or garage or a similar flat surface. After you pour the concrete leave the forms in place for a few days. They

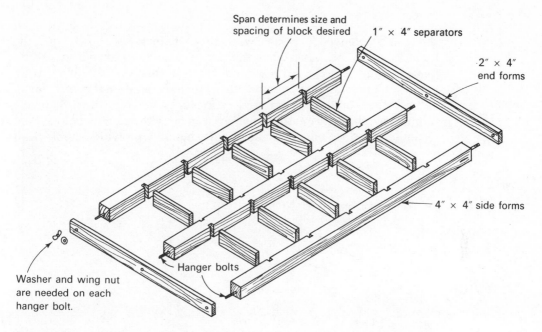

Figure 6-20: Make forms for your own pre-cast blocks with the layout shown in this diagram. Base the actual dimensions on the size wanted for the modules.

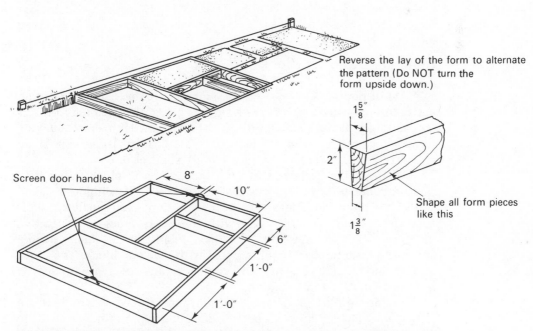

Figure 6-21: To cast patio blocks in place, make a portable form like this one and move it as you go along. Always remember to oil the forms before and after each use.

can then be removed for re-use, while the cast blocks are allowed to cure for at least a week. Later when the concrete modules have been set in place outside, you can fill the joints between them with sand. Or you may wish to plant grass or some other greenery between the units for a natural effect. In the case of round patio blocks, you can fill with gravel or pinebark chips. Very striking effects can be achieved with colors. For example, use deep blue or black circular blocks with white pebble fill.

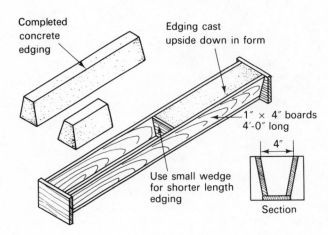

Completed concrete edging

Edging cast upside down in form

1″ × 4″ boards 4′-0″ long

Use small wedge for shorter length edging

4″

Section

Figure 6-22: Make attractive garden edging with this form. For colored concrete formulas see Table 5-2 on page 136.

Concrete Building Blocks

While poured concrete is the best for making slabs, stairs, and other easily-formed structures, concrete block is generally preferred for walls and buildings. It is easier to lay block on block than it is to erect elaborate forms. Once the technique is learned, a reasonably skilled handyman can put up concrete block in surprisingly short order.

Some of the projects that lend themselves to block rather than poured concrete are fireplaces, barbecue grills, retaining walls, and walls for garages and homes—including additions. You can build handsome fences and privacy walls with the many types of decorative masonry which are, in reality, glorified concrete blocks. Many people still build in-ground swimming pools with concrete block. The block alone is too rough and pourous of course, so it is covered with a vinyl liner or mortar "parge" coating.

In addition to the "glamor" masonry mentioned above, there are also special facings made to blend with other types of materials. One example, "stone-faced" block, is designed to blend with the stone foundation of older homes. Furthermore, most "brick" walls are really brick veneer, with concrete block providing the stability (see Chapter 7).

Remember, you must be very exact when you work with block. Depending on the needs of the project, it is wise to plan every dimension in multiples of eight inches. Standard concrete block is actually 7⅝" × 7⅝" × 15⅝", but well-laid joint mortar brings the building units to exactly 8×8×16 inches. Half-blocks (8" cubes) are used when 16 inches is too long. The closer you hold your design to 8" modules, the simpler and cheaper it will be.

FOOTINGS FOR CONCRETE BLOCK

Block is always laid on a poured concrete footing. The footing must be at least two feet below the surface or six inches below the frostline. Footings should be twice as wide as the wall, so the standard footing is 16" wide. The usual footing is also as deep as the wall is wide, in this case eight inches.

For extra strength, key the footing with a groove down the center, so that the mortar fills in and creates a firmer bond between the footing and the first course. An oiled 1×4 board embedded in the footing will hold open the space for such a key.

No special finish is necessary for footings, since they are not visible, but they must be as level as possible to provide a good start for the block. Retaining walls or other walls that will undergo a lot of stress should be braced through the block cores with steel reinforcing rods. They are embedded in the footings for maximum strength.

Figure 6-23: Footings for concrete block should be twice as wide as the wall and as deep as the block is thick. Note the centered groove in footing top. It serves as a keyway for the mortar used in the first course.

LAYING THE FIRST COURSE

The block you lay is only one part of the equation. Good mortar is the other part. Masonry cement for mortar comes in several sized bags, the most common holding a cubic foot. Follow manufacturers' instructions for the best mix. Usually it is one part masonry cement (Portland cement and lime) to three parts sand and just enough water to make the mix workable. A mud-like consistency is best. Pre-mixed mortar is easy to use and widely available. Simply add water as instructed.

For the first course, you will use a "full bed" of mortar, as opposed to "face-shell" bedding for the other courses. A full mortar bed simply means that the entire horizontal surface is covered with mortar instead of just the front and back. Footings should be wet down first to minimize absorption. (Never wet the block itself). The mortar bed should be laid down the center of the footing and furrowed down the middle with a pointed trowel, allowing the face shells of the block to absorb most of the mortar. Each block must be checked for level and plumb. Make sure that the mortar bed is ⅜" thick at every joint—or as near that as you can lay—evenly. Align all blocks correctly and work carefully, but not too slowly. All adjustments must be made before the mortar stiffens. Be sure to lay the block with the smaller ends of the core-holes up (to provide more space for mortar).

Figure 6-24: Concrete block is laid up from the corners and must be level, plumb and straight. Check each block with the level for true.

The vertical joints between each block should contain mortar at each edge of the block. Set the block on end before placing and "butter" the other end with mortar. Press the mortar down onto each edge so that it will not fall off, then lift the block into place. If you have used enough mortar, it will now ooze out of all the joints. Cut off the excess mortar with the trowel and return it to the mortar board.

Hopefully, you have planned your wall so that the last "closure" block will be 16 inches, counting its mortar. If so, butter the "ears" on both sides of the last block plus the edges of the blocks already in place. Lay the closure block in from the top, being as careful as you can not to knock off the mortar from any of the edges.

If the space for the closure block is not exactly 16⅜" (counting the joints on both sides), you will have to cut the block. Mark off the distance (subtracting ¾" for the mortar) on the closure block and cut it with a brick chisel. To avoid fitting problems, it is a good idea to make a "dry run" of the first row and make any adjustments before you mix the mortar.

SUCCEEDING COURSES

After the first course is in place, succeeding courses are laid up from the corners. It is particularly important that the corner blocks be accurate. Block is usually laid in a "running bond" in which the top block overlaps two bottom ones equally. Lay three or four courses in each corner before joining the bottom one. String a line from one corner to another to ensure accuracy.

After the first course, face-shell bedding is used. Mortar is spread along the front and back of each row instead of over the entire surface. Except for this difference, the succeeding rows are placed exactly as the first.

As you work, be careful not to spread the mortar too far ahead. Two or three blocks ahead is plenty for the beginner. If it starts to harden, apply fresh mortar. By the same token, double-check your work as you proceed, filling in any open joints or holes in the mortar while it is still plastic. Do not attempt to change the position of any block after the mortar has stiffened or you will break the bond. If a block must be shifted, remove it entirely, scrape off the old mortar, and relay it with fresh mortar.

Use special jamb blocks for doors and windows. Lintel blocks go across the opening. No special techniques are needed for laying these. Just make certain that you follow your plan exactly. Where a partition meets a wall in a "T" joint, metal ties may be needed. You can run electric wire through the cores of the blocks if you want, and heating ducts can be easily set into the wall by using 4" thick instead of 8" thick block. But use these only in non-load-bearing partitions.

If the exterior of the wall is to face the weather, tool the joints in a concave or V-joint pattern before they harden. You can buy special tools

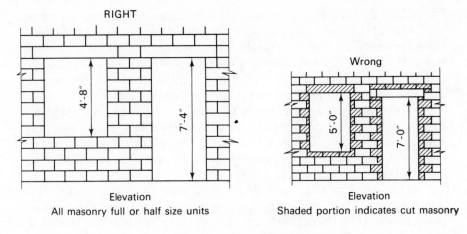

RIGHT

Wrong

Elevation
All masonry full or half size units

Elevation
Shaded portion indicates cut masonry

(Based on 8″ × 8″ × 16″ block)

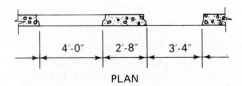

PLAN

Figure 6-25: Intelligent planning makes it easy to lay out doorways and windows and eliminate as much cutting as possible. Use special jamb blocks where indicated and lintel blocks across openings.

for this or use a piece of half-inch copper tubing. Do horizontal joints first, then the verticals.

It is difficult to clean mortar off concrete, so be careful not to spill too much. And wipe it off as soon as possible. If mortar does harden on the block, scrape it off neatly with a piece of broken block.

DECORATIVE BLOCK

See your masonry dealer for a review of the wide variety of decorative block. Some blocks are solid, others have holes of various shapes and can be laid so as to provide an open, airy effect. There are even pre-cast concrete louvers to use with them. They provide privacy, yet allow breezes to blow through.

The choice of block is, of course, up to you. Decorative block is laid in the same general way as standard block. Footings are required as always. Reinforcing rods or outside lintels may also be in order if the wall is not sturdy enough on its own. Your masonry dealer can best advise you on such details for your own particular project.

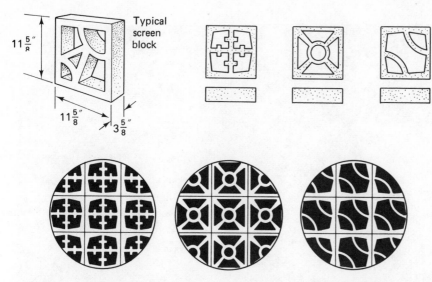

Figure 6-26: These drawings show the dimension of a standard concrete block and some of the many types of decorative screen block available (*courtesy of National Concrete Masonry Association and Portland Cement Association*).

7:

Bricklaying &
Projects in Brick

Brick is one of the oldest building materials known to man. Simple baked clay bricks were in use at least fifty centuries ago and perhaps longer. Some of the bricks found in ancient excavations are still brightly glazed in a variety of attractive colors whose process was only rediscovered by modern man in the last century.

Simple brick structures are among the easiest to build. Conversely, advanced bricklaying is done by highly skilled craftsmen. Garden walls, barbecues, terraces—all these and more can be competently made by the novice. But it takes years of practice to attempt some of the complicated archways and corbeling done by the masters.

Bricklaying Techniques

In this book, the essentials of bricklaying are described. With these instructions, you should be able to erect a number of elementary structures. But save the wall-to-wall fireplaces for the experts. Or, at the very least, try a barbecue first.

KINDS OF BRICK

Brick comes in a great many shapes and sizes, but 2¼"×3¾"×8" is the one most used by the do-it-yourselfer. This is the "common" or "standard" American brick. The larger kinds sometimes used include Norman brick (2¾"×3¾"×12") and Roman brick (1½"×3¾"×12"). Dimensions may vary slightly, so check with your local brickyard or

Figure 7-1: While this is an easy beginner's project, it is also a splendid classic use of good brick (*courtesy of Sakrete, Inc.*).

Figure 7-2: A handsome brick wall creates privacy inside without seeming unfriendly, particularly if it is as well conceived and landscaped as this one (*courtesy of National Association of Nurserymen*).

building supply dealer early in the planning stages of your project. Brick may be solid or cored (with two rows of holes down the length of the brick) as long as the coring does not exceed 25 percent of the volume of the brick.

Most brick colors range from earth reds through buffs to creams, varying according to the type of clay used and the production process. With the addition of chemicals, brickmakers can now produce an endless variety of colors and textures. Again, check your local source of supply to see what is available.

A tribute to the material's durability is the popularity of old brick—brick that has already seen one lifetime of service and is ready for another go-round. Its patina of warmth and mellowness is hard to match, so good used brick often costs more than new brick.

BRICKLAYING TOOLS

As a beginning bricklayer, your tool investment can be minimal: a pointed 10" trowel, a broad-bladed brick chisel, a hammer, a pointing tool (you can use a short length of ½" pipe for the job), a level, and some cord. In addition, you will need a shovel and a container for mixing mortar. An ordinary wheelbarrow is fine; you can move it along as your job progresses. Or you can just do your mixing on a piece of plywood or any other clean surface.

BRICKWORK FOUNDATIONS

The foundation for brickwork depends, of course, on the project. A brick patio may simply be laid in a leveling bed of sand or mortar. For most projects, however, a concrete footing of foundation is required. The size and depth of the footing are determined partly by where you live (it must be deep enough so that it will not be disturbed by frost heaving) and partly by the size of the project. For a larger project, you may want to have the foundation put in by a contractor, then take over the job from there.

MORTAR FOR BRICKWORK

Whatever it is, your brick structure can be only as strong as the mortar that holds it together. Proper proportions for your mix are one part Portland cement, one-half part hydrated lime, and four parts clean sand. You can buy mortar mix with cement and lime already blended. Order the sand from your building supply dealer since the free kind from the beach is too rough and dirty.

Thoroughly blend together the dry ingredients, turning them over and over with the shovel. Scoop out a hollow in the middle of the mixture and gradually add water, mixing it in with the shovel. The mortar should have the consistency of soft "mud" (as the pros say); that is, it should slide easily from the trowel. Make sure it is completely mixed, with no dry spots. Make only as much as you can use in about a half hour, adding a little water occasionally to keep the mortar workable. If it becomes too stiff, discard it and whip up a new batch.

Brick should be damp when laid. Otherwise, it will quickly absorb the moisture from the mortar, not allowing enough time to set up properly. But if the brick is too wet, it will dilute the mortar, causing the brick to slip. Your best bet is to spray the bricks lightly with a garden hose an hour or so before they are used. Just before you go to work, slightly dampen the foundation or other area where the brick is to be laid.

Figure 7-3: Always wet brick before laying it. Hose it lightly about an hour before you begin working with it (*courtesy of Louisville Cement Company*).

BRICKWORK PATTERNS

The pattern or "bond" of your brickwork depends on the project as well as your personal preference. It should be laid out so that the smallest unit with which you will build is a half brick. Whether the structure is one or two bricks wide also depends on the project; single-brick width will be more than adequate for a low planter box; a high wall should be of double width (or two "wythes"). But regardless of width or bond, basic bricklaying techniques are the same.

Start laying brick at the corners of your project, building them up three or four courses (rows) high, dovetailed at right angles. Use the level and square frequently to keep things in true. When you have built up one corner, go on to the next one, lining it up with the first by means of a straightedge or line level. With the two corners in place, push nails into the soft mortar between the first two courses and run a string between them, or use a wood tension holder. This line will serve as a guide for placement of the intermediate bricks; lining them up with the string will keep the course level and the wall plumb, without bulges or curves. When the first course is laid, move the string up and repeat the procedure for each course.

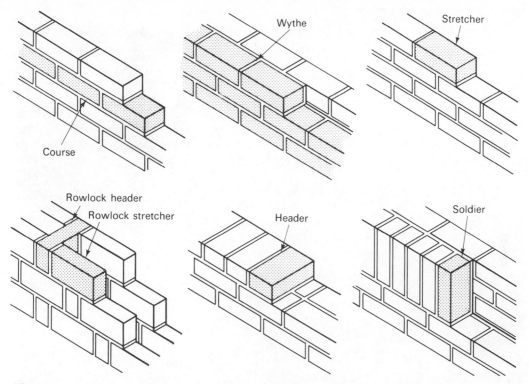

Wythe

Stretcher

Course

Rowlock header

Rowlock stretcher

Header

Soldier

Figure 7-4: A visual "glossary" of common bricklaying terms (*courtesy of Brick Institute of America*).

Figure 7-5: Constant attention is necessary to lay brick level, plumb, and straight. A string line helps keep bricks level, and the regular use of a carpenter's or mason's level to check all dimensions ensures that everything is in alignment (*courtesy of Sakrete, Inc.*).

To lay the brick, take a slice of mortar on the trowel and place it on the foundation (or the brick course below), laying it on about ½-inch thick and long enough for two bricks. Remember, you're a beginner; as your technique improves, you will be able to lay three or four bricks at a time. Furrow the mortar with the point of the trowel, making sure it is the full width of the brick, then "butter" the end of the brick, completely

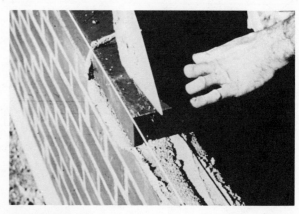

Figure 7-6: Set brick in place and push it down gently with the edge of the trowel. Note the furrowed mortar bed and the excess mortar oozing out where brick was buttered. Both are signs of good bricklaying technique.

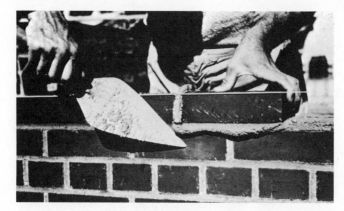

Figure 7-7: After brick is set in correct alignment, it is held there with one hand while the excess mortar is struck off with the edge of the trowel (*courtesy of Louisville Cement Co.*).

covering the end surface, and set firmly in place. Trim off excess mortar, butter the next brick, and set it in place against the first, allowing a ½" joint between.

IMPORTANT CHECKS & DOUBLE CHECKS

Don't forget to keep checking with that level. If you find your wall is running out of line, don't attempt to tap bricks back into place once they have been set. Take up the brick, scrape off the mortar, and reset it. Otherwise, you will almost surely have a hollow spot, and thus a weakened area, in the mortar joint.

When you have to cut a brick to fit, first place it on a solid base. With the brick chisel and hammer, tap all around it at the cutting line, beveling the cut slightly inward. When it is grooved on all sides, hold the chisel against the brick's wide face and give it a sharp blow; the brick will break apart. (Once you get a little practice you can try one sharp blow with a brick chisel or the back of your hammer.)

As each course is completed and before the mortar has hardened,

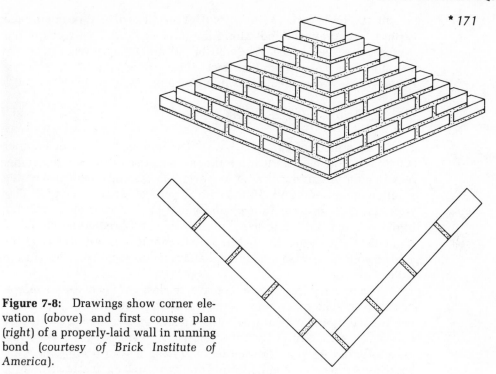

Figure 7-8: Drawings show corner elevation (*above*) and first course plan (*right*) of a properly-laid wall in running bond (*courtesy of Brick Institute of America*).

Figure 7-9: Proper method and correct tools for cutting brick are shown here. Don't make the common mistake of using a brick hammer to strike the brick chisel. Use a heavy "mash" hammer like this one and protect your eyes (*courtesy of Hand Tools Institute*).

smooth the joints with a pointing tool (or the piece of ½" pipe mentioned earlier). Just draw the tool along the joint to produce a smooth and uniform concave surface. While flush, "V" and other types of joints are sometimes used for decorative effects, the concave joint is by far the best for making a water-repellent seal between bricks.

CLEANING UP THE WORK

Keep a piece of damp burlap at hand and use it to remove mortar stains. Wipe the face of the brick after each course or so. Any stains that remain after the mortar has set for several days can be removed with a solution of muriatic acid diluted with 10 parts of water. Be careful! This stuff can hurt, so wear rubber gloves and protect your eyes. Wet the brickwork and scrub on the solution with a stiff-bristled brush. Rinse immediately with plenty of clear water. Should you splash any of the acid on your skin, wash it off immediately and thoroughly with soap and water.

And now the last brick is in place, the last vestige of excess mortar has been scraped away, and no trace of a stain remains on your brick-work. But the job is not quite finished. For best results, treat it gently for a couple of weeks. Mortar should set slowly, and an occasional watering, especially during hot, dry weather, will help. If your brick project is a barbecue, hold off your appetite and don't fire up for at least two or three weeks.

Brick Patios

Brick is excellent material for patio surfaces. It is durable, easily laid, and imparts a very handsome, mellow look to most houses. A brick patio is particularly simple to do if you try it without mortar in a bed of sand.

If you have naturally sandy soil, the brick can be laid directly in the original earth, after it is scooped out and leveled. For other soils, the job is almost as easy except that you have to excavate the topsoil and add enough sand to fill. Either way you'll also need sand for filling the cracks between bricks.

A brick patio surrounded by railroad ties can give a nice rustic touch to a patio. They are particularly useful when the ground slopes and one end of a patio must be raised to provide a level surface. If your slope is very bad, forget brick entirely and go to a wood deck (Chapter 9).

Instead of ties for edging, you can use brick set on end or redwood 2×4s, or some other lumber that pleases you. The technique is basically the same regardless of material. Make sure, though, that the material is weather-resistant. Redwood and red cedar may be used without preservatives. Other types of wood can be used too, but they must receive a

Figure 7-10: Brick and railroad ties combine to make an attractive terrace, particularly where there is a slope.

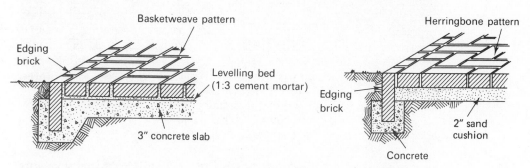

Figure 7-11: You can also use brick for edging. Drawings show cross section of brick-in-mortar and brick-in-sand terrace.

heavy coat of penta ("Wood-Life," etc.) or creosote. The best railroad ties are pressure-treated with creosote and should last as long as the brick.

Ties are heavy enough in themselves and need no bracing. If you use 2×4s, you should drive a 12" stake into the ground behind them every four feet. Brick set on end (a "sailor" course) should be placed into a small bed of concrete.

To lay the field brick, excavate to about four and a quarter inches deep. Lay down a 2" level bed of sand and simply set the bricks in the sand, leveling each one as it is laid. Fine sand is then swept over the surface, filling the joints and locking each brick in place. The whole surface is then watered down, resanded, and watered again. The watering forces the fine particles of sand downward, filling gaps in the bed and between the bricks.

If you are using a running bond, plain common brick will do as well

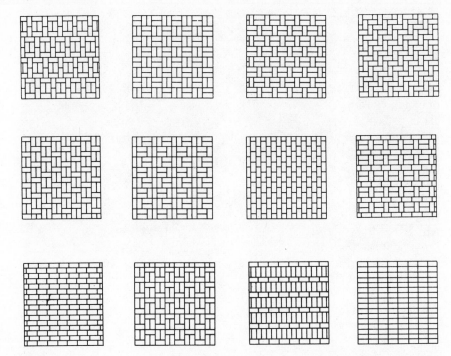

Figure 7-12: Interesting patterns may be obtained with these centuries-old brickwork layouts. Reminder: paving brick may be necessary for some of the patterns you choose. Either ask your masonry dealer or try the layout with a few bricks. (*As a general guide, paving brick is required for any pattern that uses a brick exactly twice as long as it is wide.*)

as anything. Any modular pattern, however, is difficult to achieve with common brick because there will be uneven gaps between the bricks. For other patterns, use special paving brick, which measures exactly 4"×8" and fits easily into any type of bond.

In areas of severe winters, the mortarless method may result in heaved bricks and uneven pavement. Actually, this is not a serious problem, because a little waviness is not unacceptable in a rustic setting. Furthermore, the heaved brick can be returned to position by digging out the sand beneath and replacing it. (If the fit is too tight, chip off an edge, or replace some surrounding brick.)

You may prefer, however, to eliminate frost problems by digging six inches below the frost line and filling in with gravel approximately six and three-quarter inches below the intended surface of your patio. Then lay a concrete slab about four inches thick over the gravel (see Chapter 5). Next spread a ½" mortar bed on top of the cured concrete and lay common brick in the mortar with ½" mortar joints between. This is, of course, a lot more work, but you can be sure that a patio of this construction isn't going to shift or heave.

Large Brick Walls

Large brick walls and load-bearing walls are built with the same basic techniques as the smaller wall previously described, but they must be stronger and more durable. Sometimes a double brick wall is built. Or one made with concrete block, wood, structural clay tile or other materials is used for a back-up wall; then the brick is "veneered" in front.

When a double brick wall is built, "headers," or brick laid lengthwise across both walls, are provided in regular sequence no less than every seven courses. Various patterns can be worked out by alternating the bond. English bond, for example, has one course of stretchers followed by one of headers. Flemish bond alternates headers and stretchers in each course. Occasionally, "rowlock" headers are used, which means that the crossing brick is laid on its narrow side.

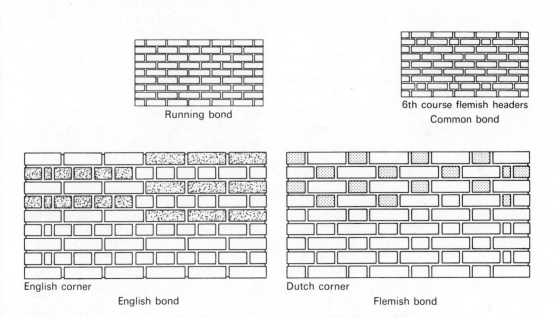

Running bond

6th course flemish headers
Common bond

English corner
English bond

Dutch corner
Flemish bond

Figure 7-13: The most popular patterns for double brick walls are diagrammed above. Shaded areas represent ties between the two withes. In the case of running bond, metal straps are used for ties.

Brick Barbecues

Before you build a brick barbecue, you'll want to locate it properly since it is not a movable item. Probably the best way to find the best place for it—particularly if you don't have a patio yet—is to observe where the family naturally congregates in the backyard. Where is the picnic table set up? Where is the portable barbecue? What seems to be a comfortable site for outdoor cooking?

Other likely places for a barbecue are near a swimming pool, garden house, "Florida room," or gazebo. A clump of trees or shrubbery will provide shade, privacy, and natural windbreak—but beware of low-lying branches which can catch on fire. And use a high chimney when among trees or next to the house, garage, etc.

Another consideration is whether or not utilities are available. If you're installing a gas-fired barbecue, you'll obviously need a gas line. Check to see that there are no serious obstacles in the way such as a favorite flower bed or swimming pool. Of course, there's always "bottled" gas such as propane which is made with LPG (liquified petroleum gas), if running a gas line is too difficult.

Electricity is not a must for a simple barbecue, but you'll need some source of power for a spit or other appliance. It's always nice to have light close by, too, for evening use. Also, you may need a water source. Check with local building codes. Is a permit required? Are there setback regulations?

LAYING THE FOUNDATION

Whether your barbecue is made of brick or something else, you'll need a strong foundation to support all that weight. The thickness of the concrete will depend on the type of soil on which you're building, the local climate, and whether you use reinforcing wire. Poor weight-bearing soils such as loose sand or loam will necessitate a thicker slab. So will severe freezing conditions.

In most of Canada and the northern U.S. "prolonged freezing areas" means that you should go below the frost line or down 16 inches at least, to prevent winter damage to your barbecue. In the southern U.S. or other frost-free areas, you may not need a concrete base at all if your soil is firm. A few inches of gravel or cinders may do the trick. But if there is any possibility at all of below-freezing temperatures, don't take a chance. Install a concrete base of at least four inches.

When planning, determine the dimensions of the bottom row of brick or other material, then add at least two inches all around. If the ground is level and the surrounding soil compact, you may be able to lay the concrete without forms. When forms are used, add another two inches in each direction.

Lay out the area as described, then mark with a string. If you set the string a little above the soil line and use a line level, you can use the same string to determine the correct depth of your excavation. Just add the height above the soil line to the depth of the excavation and measure down. If you want a 12" deep foundation, for example, set the string two inches above the soil line and dig a 14" deep hole.

When the forms are built, it helps to coat the inside with some old, heavy oil. This will facilitate removal of the wood after the foundation has cured. Check each side of the form with a level, then use a long straightedge with the level on top to check opposite walls and diagonal corners for level.

There's another step here that is too often skipped by the inexperienced do-it-yourselfer. Before you pour the concrete, soak the excavation thoroughly with the garden hose and let the water stand in it for a while. Start to pour when it's almost drained. If the mix is put into a dry hole, the water in the concrete will be sucked out; that in turn will cause too rapid drying and a crumbly foundation.

For smaller areas, dry ready-mixed products like Sakrete simplify the job greatly. (The same holds true for mortar and other cement mixes.) If you prefer to mix your own, however, the proportions are one part Portland cement to three parts sand and four parts gravel (see page 125 on concrete ordering, mixing and placing).

SETTING THE BRICK

Use chalk to draw the outline of the barbecue two inches in from the edges of the foundation. Set dry bricks in place to check your measurements, allowing approximately a half inch between each one to represent a mortar joint. If everything seems to fit, you can start laying brick.

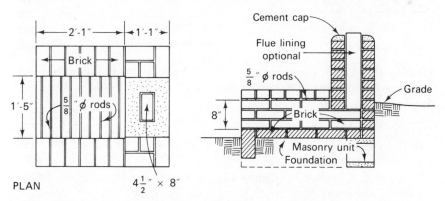

Figure 7-14: This simple barbecue unit can be made with brick and ⅝" or ½" steel rods.

If you are using grates set into the mortar, be sure to put them in place while the mortar is still wet. When laying the firebed, pitch it slightly toward the front to allow for drainage (from ¼ to ⅜ inch).

When mortaring the top course of the brick, try to achieve a smooth surface without concave or beveled joints. This type of top is much easier to work on. You may want to cover the top course with a layer of concrete, ceramic tile, stone, or other material, but a smooth brick finish

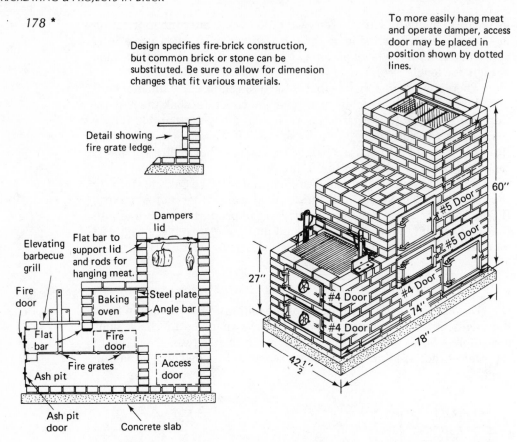

Design specifies fire-brick construction, but common brick or stone can be substituted. Be sure to allow for dimension changes that fit various materials.

To more easily hang meat and operate damper, access door may be placed in position shown by dotted lines.

Detail showing fire grate ledge.

Elevating barbecue grill

Flat bar to support lid and rods for hanging meat.

Dampers lid

Fire door

Baking oven

Steel plate

Angle bar

Flat bar

Fire door

Access door

Fire grates

Ash pit

Ash pit door

Concrete slab

#5 Door
#5 Door
#4 Door
#4 Door
#4 Door
60"
27"
74"
78"
42½"

Figure 7-15: This combination baking oven, barbecue, and Chinese oven features metal accessories from Miller Materials Co., 797 Marina Blvd., San Leandro, California 94577.

will do just as well. Pitch the top row slightly away from the fire so that water will drain away.

Firebrick, which is always used for indoor fireplaces, is not as necessary outdoors because there is usually plenty of air circulation, which keeps the temperature of the brick from becoming as hot as it would in an enclosed area. Furthermore, firebrick is brittle and can be damaged by cold winter weather.

If you do use firebrick, lay it so that the large surface faces the fire. Use special fireclay-cement mortar, or substitute fireclay for lime in your own mix. And butter firebrick lightly, allowing only ¹/₁₆ to ¼ inch between bricks for better insulation.

Cut firebrick more carefully, too, making shallow guide cuts on all four sides before giving the sharp final blow. And don't dampen firebrick. It should be as dry as possible when it is laid.

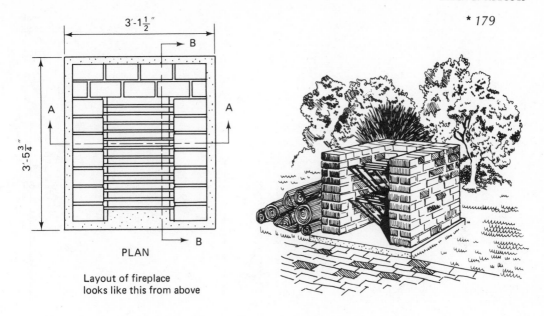

PLAN

Layout of fireplace
looks like this from above

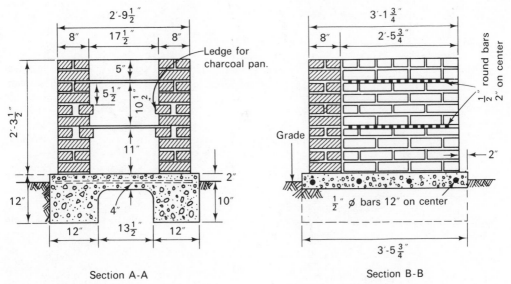

Section A-A

Front cross section shows the footings and slab.
Note ledge for charcoal pan.

Section B-B

Sideview cross-section — Note the reinforcing
bars and spacing of grill.

Figure 7-16: Standard ½″ steel bars are used for this firepit and grille (*courtesy of Glen-Gary Corporation*).

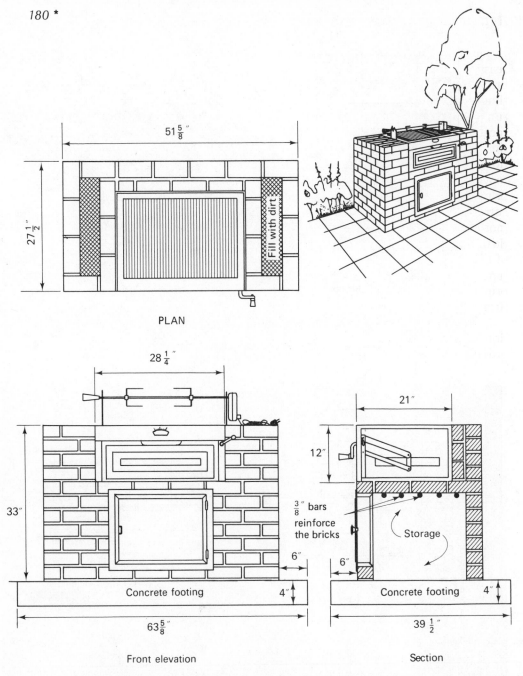

PLAN

Front elevation

Section

Figure 7-17: This fireplace-barbecue uses reinforcing bars to support the brick top, with metal doors, adjustable grate and an electric spit. Parts are available from Superior Fireplace Company, 4325 Artesia Avenue, Fullerton, California 92633.

Repointing Old Brickwork

Virtually no maintenance is necessary for brick—one of the main reasons for its enduring popularity. Occasionally, however, the overall brickwork may need "repointing." Frost upheavals or the like sometimes make mortar crumble, or you may have to break through a wall to run a pipe. The repointing procedure starts when you chip out all the loose mortar. Professional bricklayers use special abrasive wheels for this, but a cold chisel and mash hammer will do the job for the average do-it-yourselfer. When the old loose, crumbling mortar has been removed (no need to remove the solid stuff), clean out the joints with a stiff brush or an air blast if you have a compressor. Be sure to wet the surrounding surfaces just before you apply the new mortar. Push the mortar back into the cleaned joint in one continuous operation. You can do this with a trowel, but a special S-shaped pointing tool is best. A piece of half-inch pipe will be needed with the trowel to tool the joint. The repointing technique is not much different from that used in regular bricklaying, except that the mortar is pushed into the joint much more firmly than when laying brick originally.

You may also find that mortar crumbles or pulls away from junctions of brick and materials such as wood. In that case, a silicone calk provide a more flexible bond between the materials.

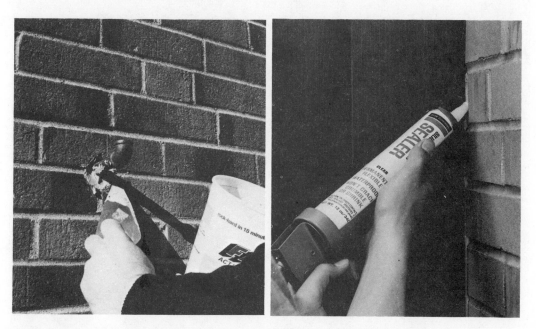

Figure 7-18: Where mortar has eroded or been chipped away, special pointing mortar like this Set product is used (*left*); while a silicone sealer is in order between brick and wood (*right*).

8:

Working with Building Stone

In pre-historic times man lived in caves in the earth and rock. Later he learned to make shelters by piling up stones—probably one of the oldest building materials still in use. Later still, man erected monumental edifices, such as the Pyramids of Egypt. They give ample evidence that he had learned how to hew and transport very large stones to use in structures and they still endure as marvels of construction and engineering.

Building stone is still widely available, the type, color, and shape depending on the geology of the area. But, despite the wide variety of appearance, there are really only two categories functionally—rubble and stratified building stone. Rubble refers to the naturally rounded, very hard boulders that are piled rather than laid up. (Often builders use mortar to hold them together.) Basalt, granite and similar round stones are used in rubble masonry, while stratified or ashler stonework is done with sandstone, shale, and other flat, layered rocks, referred to generally as flagstone.

Since rubble stonework is so tough and flinty-hard, it holds up extremely well to weather and temperature extremes. There is very little that can harm a structure made of such naturally erosion-proof material, but rubble stones are extremely difficult to work with. Sometimes they can be cracked with a sledge hammer, but it is virtually impossible to cut, chisel or otherwise alter their shape. Ordinarily you either use them as is or you don't use them at all.

Because of their wide availability, boulders are often used for rough boundary walls, fireplaces, and the like. It is easy to use this material as long as a structure is low and not too massive. As the work

Figure 8-1: Building stone is defined as either rubble or stratified. Rubble is rounded, very hard rock and is generally used with mortar (*left*); while stratified rock is layered and most often put up without mortar (*the "dry-wall" technique*).

goes higher, it is more difficult to lift the building stones, and as a structure gets bigger, it is harder to work out a pleasing pattern. Rubble is good for fireplaces, though, because the stone is impervious to flame and heat and will not "pop" or crack. And rubble stone walls are often built while clearing boulders off the land—a cheap and easy project.

Most building stone is of the stratified, flagstone variety. The stone is long, layered, and comparatively easy to cut with a cold chisel and heavy hammer. It is possible to construct an attractive design, as long as the stone is laid in its natural direction and you don't try to get too fancy with it. For a fireplace or barbecue, however, hard-burned brick should be used in the firepit, because heat will chip, crack or even "explode" ashlar stones.

Wet and Dry Wall Methods

Unlike brick, concrete block or other masonry, stone does not require mortar to bind building units. The builder has the option, in most cases, of building his wall "wet" or "dry." The do-it-yourselfers choose "dry" because it so much easier.

But ease of construction is not the only reason for using dry construction. A retaining wall, for example, holds back a lot of earth, and the extra pressure exerted by rainwater is often enough to crack the mortar and break down the wall. When the wall is built without mortar, water seeps through every chink and relieves the pressure that would build behind a solid, mortared surface.

Granite, limestone, marble, sandstone, slate, or quartzite are suggested for most ashlar stonework. Some of the potential uses for attractive stonework are patios, barbecues, walkways, steps, planters, and walls of all sorts. Don't neglect stone for indoors, either, as it is most striking in a fireplace or planter.

Figure 8-2: Building stone is beautiful both outdoors *and* in as this ashlar construction shows.

If stone is easy to lay, it is very hard to cut. For this reason, many people buy stone precut into squares, rectangles and circles. The cost is considerably more, however, than buying stone by the ton and doing the cutting yourself. Actually, if you use random or rustic patterns, you can take advantage of the fact that stone *breaks* quite easily and keep cutting to a minimum.

How to Order Building Stone

Garden supply houses are usually the best sources for cut stone in regular sizes. Uncut stone can be found at stone or masonry dealers. Look in the yellow pages under "Stone, Natural" for a local supplier.

You will find that stone is very heavy and that you may need a ton for even small projects. The retaining wall shown on page 187 required over three tons of rough stone plus another half ton of square materials for steps and coping.

Since stone is relatively expensive, don't pile it any thicker than you have to. A high retaining wall may need to be 12 to 18 inches thick, but small ones do not, especially if laid dry. Your stone dealer will be the best judge, but it shouldn't be necessary to lay stone any more than six inches thick for a moderate-sized wall. In some cases, four or five inches

186 *   will be enough. Actually, you should resign yourself to wide tolerances, because of the difficulty of cutting the stone to exact measurements.

Where a wide wall is desired, it may be best to use stone as a veneer. A stone veneer wall is built in much the same way as brick veneer, with concrete footings and block back-up. The stone is attached by metal ties or clips. Lay the stone with the flat side out and use mortar between pieces. Tell the stone dealer that you will be using the material as veneer so that he can sell you stone of the same thickness. You will probably find that the only kind available is four inches thick even though two inches is really all you need.

Building a Stone Wall

One nice thing about working with stone is that you can afford to be somewhat casual in your layout. With drywall construction, you will be putting up the stone piece by piece (all varying sizes), with no permanent ties, and you can pull it all down and start over if you wish. Even with mortar, the pieces are so irregular that planning is impossible.

If you plan on steps, save some large pieces for treads. When the stone arrives, however, don't be distressed if the truck driver dumps the load and smashes up most of it. He is saving you a lot of future work.

Figure 8-3:   A load of typical building stone delivered and ready for sorting and use. Note that the dumping simply helped with the preliminary breaking and sizing.

In some cases, a concrete footing will be necessary. Like all footings, it should be placed six inches below the frost line and at least two feet below the surface. You should not need a footing, though, with a mortarless wall unless the soil is very mushy or unstable.

When you build with mortar, the technique is much like bricklaying. Lay down a bed of mortar on the footing, butter one end of a stone piece, place it, and strike off the excess. Butter another piece, press it firmly against the first one, and so on.

You will run into trouble with stone if you try to make even courses and neat mortar joints. There is no way (or need) to achieve the kind of exactness necessary with brick. Just put up a piece of stone with the straightest edge out, fill all joints with mortar and go on to the next. The only "bond" you should be concerned with is not laying one joint on top of the other. Try to use stone of the same thickness for each course and keep the tops generally level, but you can adjust unevenness as you go along. Use varying size mortar joints to take up the slack.

For dry construction, start one or two courses below the surface, making the joints extra tight and the tops level. Use extra-large, thick pieces of stone for this since it is in essence your foundation. The soil should be dug out with a square-end garden spade to a depth of about four inches and a bed of sand laid first (unless the soil is itself sandy of course).

Figure 8-4: Before and after views of a new, raw backyard. Part of the hill at the right was eventually cut away and piled next to the foundation in order to furnish a level play area for children; then a stone retaining wall was built to hold up the new earth. Note the attractive set of stone steps.

Figure 8-5: Here a "Payloader" cuts the earth away from the hill and levels it on the area in front.

As long as you aren't using mortar, you can be even less fussy about fitting the pieces. Stone is very heavy and its surfaces are all essentially abrasive. When stone is laid on stone, the little projections lock against each other and are very difficult to dislodge. For that reason, try to get as much bearing surface between each surface as possible. But don't worry about gaps or uneven courses unless the stones tip and lose contact with the ones above and below. It doesn't matter what the sides and back of each piece look like, since no one sees them. Actually, the back should be as jagged as possible to provide a better tie with the soil.

Figure 8-6: The first stones of the retaining wall are laid down about six inches below grade level. Succeeding layers are positioned so that no joint rests directly over another.

Sooner or later you'll use up the pieces of stone that were broken when the load was dumped. Then you'll have to start breaking or cutting some new ones. For a truly rustic look, just drop the stones on a hard surface so they'll break into irregular pieces. You should be able to get a relatively straight surface on one of the edges and, if you don't, you can always cut the piece in half, thereby getting straight edges on two pieces. But try using the uneven pieces without cutting. You'll be surprised how straight the wall will look overall, even though individual pieces are rather jagged.

Figure 8-7: Although this ashlar wall was laid so the straightest edges are in front, many of the individual stones are far from straight. The overall look is pretty even-looking, nevertheless. Note that large, heavy pieces are used to build the outside corners.

If you prefer straight edges for your wall, tap a line on the surface with your hammer and cold chisel. If you're looking for a high degree of accuracy, tap all around the stone, but this is very time-consuming. Most of the time, you can get a pretty straight cut by scoring just the top. Once the top is scored, give the chisel some heavy whacks up and down the lines. Eventually the whole line will crack and fall into two or more pieces.

For greater wall strength, taper your wall backward one inch for every six inches in height. Also tie the wall into the soil behind it by inserting a long piece sideways about every 2 feet. The best pieces for this are shaped like an isosceles triangle.

Backfill when the wall is 6″ high. If the soil contains a high percentage of decayed organic matter, use a layer of sand or gravel directly behind the wall about six inches thick. Tamp down firmly and soak with water; when dry, tamp again and fill with more water. This packs the dirt tightly, bonding the jagged edges of the stones.

Figure 8-8: Stone-breaking technique: first score the piece with a mash hammer and cold chisel (*left*); then strike a few hard blows up and down the scored line (*right*) to make a good break.

Figure 8-9: Because the back end of this stone wall is quite jagged, small pieces are used as fill where large stones are too narrow. A long piece is inserted lengthwise every two feet or so in order to anchor or tie the wall into the earth.

As you work through your stone pile, you should set aside thicker pieces with squared ends. They will be useful for the topping course—or stairwell, if you build one. Some stone masons advise mortaring this course even if the others are dry, but chances are that the mortar will crack with the frost anyway. You're better off simply butting the ends together and packing in the soil behind. Kids and dogs may knock these pieces off, but you can just set them in place again.

Figure 8-10: Everytime you add six inches in height to the wall, backfill, tamp and water. Repeat tamping and watering, adding more backfill as necessary. In this way, the wall becomes bonded to the hill as the work progresses.

Figure 8-11: It is almost impossible to het a straight line across the top of a stone wall; but try to keep the stones reasonably level. Use a long 2 x 4 and a spirit level to check your work.

192 * Outdoor Steps

An easy and economical way to make good-looking stone steps is to lay a veneer over existing concrete. If you like the rustic steps in the photos, however, they must be built from the ground up. They can be built as part of the retaining wall or separately.

Stone stairs should be built into the grade rather than project from it. Thus, the sides of the stairwell and risers are miniature retaining walls and should be constructed as such. The stairwell should be dug out in its entirety before starting and, if combined with a retaining wall, built along with the wall. Outside corners should be constructed of large, heavy square or rectangular pieces, and the inside corners should be dovetailed as with brick.

Figure 8-12: Sides of a stone stairwell are, in effect, small retaining walls and should be built accordingly. Large, squarish stones work best as treads.

When your wall gets to the height of the first tread (seven to eight inches), build a small wall on either side and another foundation wall underneath the front of the tread. The side walls should go back far enough so that you have a solid foundation for the tread on both sides. If you don't have enough large, squarish pieces for treads, you can buy them extra from the stone dealer. When the wall is finished, dress the soil and plant it with some sort of groundcover. This prevents erosion of the soil.

Walks, Patios, Etc.

Stone has long been a favorite for handsome patios, sidewalks, and other horizontal applications. "Flagstone" here means any stratified stone that splits into flat pieces suitable for paving. Most ashlar stones will do just that.

Again, it is easier and less expensive to lay this type of stone dry, in the same manner as you would mortarless brick (Chapter 7). Here, of course, "bond" is meaningless, even with cut stone. If you prefer to use mortar, use it for the bed instead of sand, and fill up all chinks.

Figure 8-13: Square-cut flagstone is available from most large nurseries as well as stone dealers, and makes an excellent patio floor, with or without mortar.

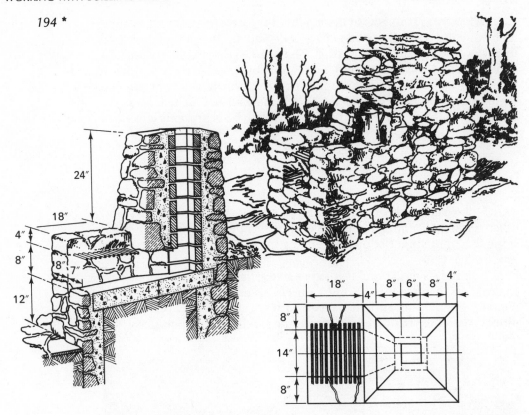

Figure 8-14: Plans for building a rustic rubble barbecue. Note concrete firepit and clay flue lining.

A common and worthwhile variation is laying stone over poured concrete. It is usually unfruitful to put down a slab underneath the stone, but if the slab is already there, you can lay stone on top.

Maintenance

When it comes to maintenance, stone is like brick—none, or almost none—is needed. Some people do apply a clear masonry sealer, but it isn't necessary and just means extra work. But like brick, stone may need occasional repointing if laid with mortar. Read the section (page 181) about brick repointing, since the same technique applies to stone. The only difference may be in tooling of the joint. Flat applications such as this for a flagstone terrace should be tooled level with the stone. Any other joints are repaired to match the original ones.

Figure 8-15: The mortar between stones, like that used in brick, sometimes deteriorates with weather and usage. When this happens, the joints are re-pointed to prevent further erosion of the mortar. Special pointing tool makes job easier (*courtesy of Western Wood Products Association*).

9:

Decks for Every House

When you look at a handsome deck and note how it seems to add horizontal dimension to a house, you are struck mainly by its good looks. (It's hard to build an ugly deck.) Actually, decks have another quality that is matched by few other structures. They are extremely flexible in design. A deck can be built off a first or second floor, with entrances from the family room, living room, dining room, kitchen, bedroom, or bath —any room, in fact. A deck can be one-level, two-level, multilevel and attached or not—as you prefer. But, best of all, a deck can be erected on any size or shape lot. If your home is on a slope, a deck can be built where a patio would be impossible. Even if you're on the edge of a ravine, you can cantilever a small deck over it and take advantage of that spectacular view.

A Patio-Deck

Although most decks are raised above the ground on piers or some other type of foundation, it is possible to build a wood deck on the ground. In that case it is probably more of a patio than a deck. To build a wood deck on the ground, it is necessary first to prepare the earth beneath it. If the area is not already paved with concrete or similar material, remove all vegetation, then level and tamp the soil. If the drainage is poor, remove soil to a depth of three inches and fill with gravel.

A typical layout for a deck might measure 10 × 10 feet in 30″ squares. The dimensions can be altered, of course, to suit your own

Figure 9-1: A deck can serve many purposes. This one provides a pleasant place to sun and relax, lengthens the house line and serves as a roof for the carport below (*courtesy Western Wood Products Association*).

Figure 9-2: Decks come in many shapes and sizes.

situation. Simply add or deduct squares to fit. Construction grade or better redwood can be used for the wood framing, and clear all-heart redwood is recommended for the decking. If you use other woods, make sure that a good preservative is applied before use.

Make and check the framing layout carefully before you cut the lumber. Note that the wood squares are 30 inches square (actually, you

Figure 9-3: The high smaller deck (*left*) takes complete advantage of the view, and is set off nicely by the rustic Ruf-X siding. The high deck (*right*) is made of western Canadian woods.

Figure 9-4: Western cedar in tiers makes this large deck an attractive one also.

Figure 9-5: The levels of this high deck are staggered so it won't seem too large.

Figure 9-6: Again western cedar enhances the good lines and functional excellence of this tiered deck.

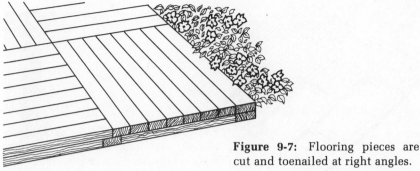

Figure 9-7: Flooring pieces are cut and toenailed at right angles.

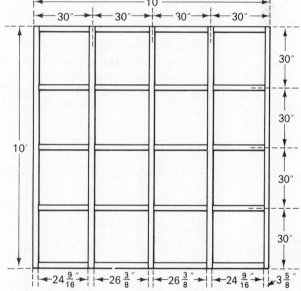

Figure 9-8: Deck framing is 30″ o.c.

can vary that size if you wish), so the framing will be 30″ o.c. This means, as in wall construction, that the edge framing members must be brought in 1-13/16″ or half the width of the framing material. In other words, the spaces between each framing member will be 26-5/8″ except around the perimeter, where the distance will be 24-9/16″ to the edge boards.

For such a 10-foot square deck, cut five 10-foot rails from 2×4s and lay them parallel on the ground. Then cut 10 pieces of 2×4 26-5/8″ long and toenail these cross pieces between the center three rails. Cut ten more pieces 24-9/16″ long and use them for end rails. Nails should be 8d stainless steel, aluminum, or hot-dipped galvanized to prevent rust and staining. Check for level and square as you proceed.

Decking is made from 128 2×4s, each 30″ long. Each of the 16 squares of the grid should be covered by eight parallel 2×4s spaced

Figure 9-9: Boards for the decking are nailed to the frame so that each square faces the opposite way. Fasten them with hot-dipped galvanized 8d nails.

approximately 3/16-inch apart. Form a parquet pattern by laying each square opposite to the last one. Use two 16d non-corroding nails at each end to nail decking to the frame. (Incidentally, these nails are 3/16″ in diameter and make a fine measuring device between decking boards.) To avoid cracking or splitting the ends of the decking material, it is best to predrill nail holes at the ends of each piece.

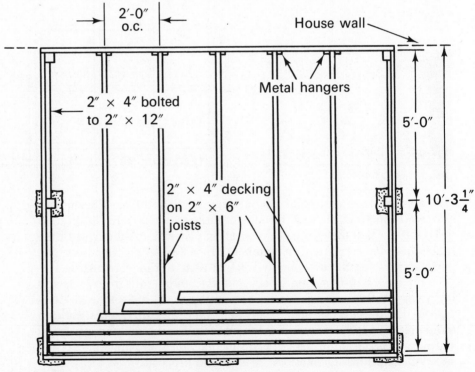

Figure 9-10: Construction plans show how to make a ground-level deck. Foundations and flooring details are diagrammed at the top of the next page.

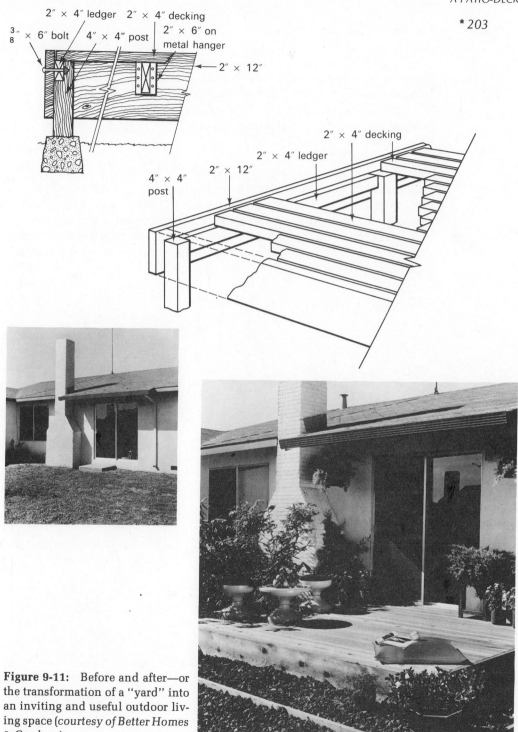

Figure 9-11: Before and after—or the transformation of a "yard" into an inviting and useful outdoor living space (*courtesy of Better Homes & Gardens*).

204 * Above-Ground Decks

Although some specific above-ground deck plans are illustrated here, they are not suitable for every home. Individual home styles, sizes and siting will usually demand an individually styled deck.

The ideal thing to do when planning a deck is to hire an architect to design one for you. This, however, costs money—and a lot of it—even assuming you can find an architect who wants a comparatively small job like this.

You can design your own deck, and usually without trouble as long as the deck is relatively small, doesn't span too great a distance, rests on sturdy posts, and is attached securely to the house. The more complex the deck is, of course, the more likely you are to meet difficulties.

A thorough study of the following design and construction principles, however, should enable you to adapt any type of plan, or design your own from scratch.

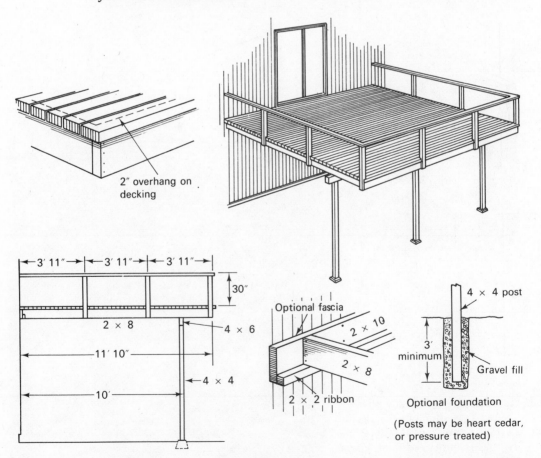

Figure 9-12: Construction plans for a second-story deck with partial cantilever.

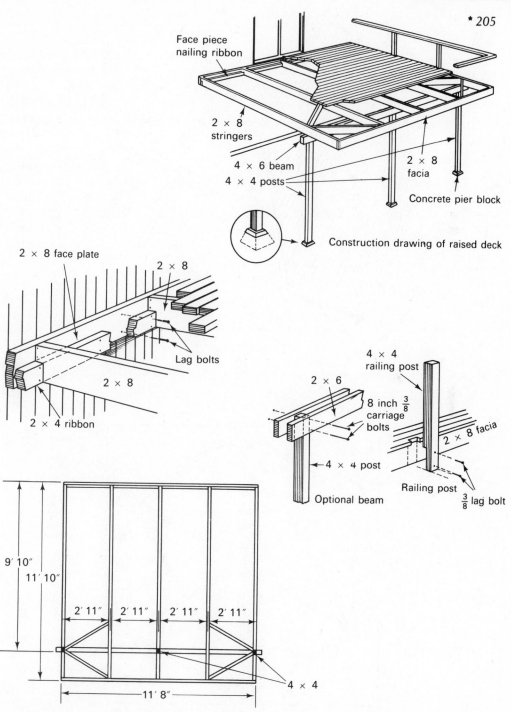

Face piece
nailing ribbon

2 × 8
stringers

4 × 6 beam

4 × 4 posts

2 × 8
facia

Concrete pier block

Construction drawing of raised deck

2 × 8 face plate

2 × 8

Lag bolts

2 × 8

2 × 4 ribbon

4 × 4
railing post

2 × 6

8 inch $\frac{3}{8}$
carriage
bolts

2 × 8 facia

4 × 4 post

Railing post

$\frac{3}{8}$ lag bolt

Optional beam

9′ 10″

11′ 10″

2′ 11″   2′ 11″   2′ 11″   2′ 11″

4 × 4

11′ 8″

Figure 9-12 continued: Details show how the deck is fastened and reinforced.

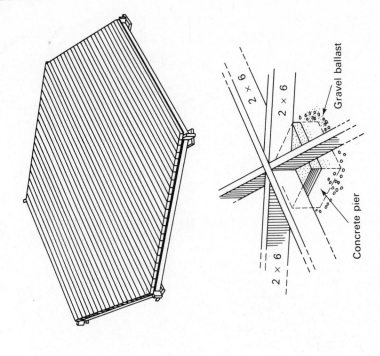

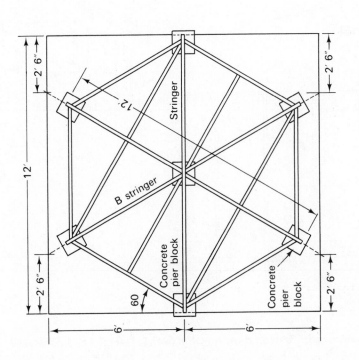

Figure 9-13: Construction plan for a hexagonal detached deck

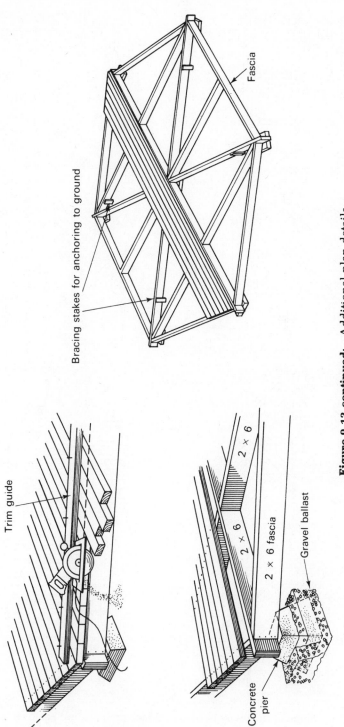

Figure 9-13 continued: Additional plan details

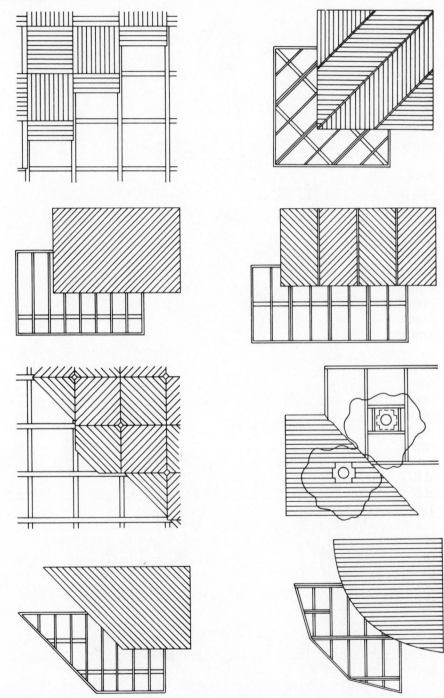

Figure 9-14: Some of the many varieties of deck patterns and basic structural layouts (*courtesy of California Redwood Association*).

FRAMING SPANS AND SIZES

The allowable spans for decking, joists, and beams and the size of posts depend not only on the size, grade, and spacing of the members but also on the species. Species such as Douglas fir, Southern pine, and Western larch allow greater spans than some of the less dense pines, cedars, and redwood, for example. Normally, deck members are designed to carry about the same load as the floors of a dwelling.

The arrangement of the structural members can vary somewhat because of orientation of the deck, position of the house, slope of the lot, etc. However, basically, the beams are supported by the posts (anchored to footings), which in turn support the floor joists. The deck boards are then fastened to the joists. When beams are spaced more closely together, the joists can be eliminated if the deck boards are thick enough to span between the beams. Railings are located around the perimeter of the deck if required for safety (low-level decks are often constructed without edge railings). When the deck is fastened to the house in some manner, the deck is normally rigid enough to eliminate the need for post bracing. In high free-standing decks, the use of post bracing is good practice.

Post sizes: Common sizes for wood posts used in supporting beams and floor framing for wood decks are 4×4, 4×6, and 6×6 inches. The size of the post required is based on the span and spacing of beams, the load, and the height of the post. Most decks are designed for a live load of 40 pounds per square foot with an additional allowance of 10 pounds per square foot for the weight of the material. The suggested sizes of posts required for various heights under several beam spans and spacings are listed in Table 9-1. Under normal conditions, the minimum dimension of the post should be the same as the beam width to simplify the method of fastening the two together. Thus, a 4×8 beam (on edge) might use a 4×4 or a 4×6 post, depending on the height, and so forth.

Beam spans: The nominal sizes of beams for various spacings and spans are listed in Table 9-2. These sizes are based on such species as Douglas fir, southern pine, and western larch for one group, western hemlock and white fir for a second group, and the soft pines, cedars, spruces, and redwood for a third group. Recommended lumber grade is No. 2 or better.

Joist spans: The approximate allowable spans for joists used in outdoor decks are listed in Table 9-3—both for the denser species of Group 1 and the less dense species of Groups 2 and 3. These spans are based on the loads as for posts (above).

Deck board spans: Deck boards are mainly used in nominal two-inch thickness and in widths of three and four inches. Decking can also be made of 2×3s or 2×4s placed on edge, or of 1×4 boards. Deck spans are listed in Table 9-4.

Table 9-1: Minimum Post Sizes (wood beam supports) [a]

Species group [b]	Post sizes	Load area based on beam spacing x post spacing									
		36	48	60	72	84	96	108	120	132	144
1:	4"x4"	up to 12-ft. heights_____				up to 10-ft heights___		up to 8-ft. heights ___			
	4"x6"					up to 12-ft. heights_____			up to 10-ft. ___		
	6"x6"								up to 12-ft. ___		
2:	4"x4"	up to 12-ft. ___	up to 10-ft. hts. _____			up to 8-ft. heights_____					
	4"x6"			up to 12-ft. hts. _____		up to 10-ft. heights_____					
	6"x6"					up to 12-ft. heights _____					
3:	4"x4"	up to 12'	up to 10-ft. ___	up to 8-ft. hts._____		up to 6-ft. heights_____					
	4"x6"		up to 12-ft. ___	up to 10-ft. hts._____		up to 8-ft. heights_____					
	6"x6"				up to 12-ft. heights_____						

[a] Based on 40 p.s.f. deck live load plus 10 p.s.f. dead load. Grade is Standard & Better for 4"x4" posts and No. 1 & Better for larger sizes.
[b] Group 1: Douglas-fir-larch and southern pine; Group 2: Hemlock-fir and Douglas-fir south; **Group 3:** Western pines and cedars, redwood, and spruces.

Example: *If the beam supports are spaced 8'6" o.c. and the posts are 11'6" o.c., then the load area is 98; use next larger area 108.*

FASTENERS

The strength of any wood structure or component is in great measure dependent upon the fastenings that hold its parts together. The most common wood fasteners are nails and spikes, followed by screws, lag screws, bolts, and metal connectors and straps of various shapes. An important factor for the outdoor use of fasteners is their finish. Metal fasteners should be rust-proofed in some manner or made of rust-resistant metals. Galvanized and cadmium-plated finishes are most common. Aluminum, stainless steel, copper, brass, and other rust-proof fasteners are also satisfactory. Hot-dip galvanized, aluminum, or stainless steel fasteners are the most successful for such species as redwood. They prevent staining of the wood under exposed conditions. Remember, a rusted nail, washer, or bolt head is not only unsightly but difficult to remove and replace. Often it is also a factor in weakening a connection.

Grooved nails are the most satisfactory sort to use in the construction of outdoor units if screws or bolts are not used. Smooth shank nails often lose their holding power when exposed to wetting and drying cycles. Annular grooved nails (ring shank) and spiral grooved nails are the best for nailing decks. Such a nail or spike is valuable because its withdrawal resistance endures even after repeated wetting and drying cycles. Such nails should be used for the construction of exposed units if screws, lag screws, or bolts are not used.

Table 9-2: Minimum Beam Sizes and Spans [a]

Species group	Beam sizes	Spacing between beams in feet								
		4	5	6	7	8	9	10	11	12
1:	4"x6"	up to 6-ft. spans								
	3"x8"	up to 8-ft.		up to 7'	up to 6-ft. spans					
	4"x8"	up to 10'	up to 9'	up to 8'	up to 7-ft.		up to 6-ft. spans			
	3"x10"	up to 11'	up to 10'	up to 9'	up to 8-ft.		up to 7-ft.		up to 6-ft.	
	4"x10"	up to 12'	up to 11'	up to 10'	up to 9-ft.		up to 8-ft.		up to 7-ft.	
	3"x12"			up to 12'	up to 11'	up to 10'	up to 9-ft.		up to 8-ft. spans	
	4"x12"			up to 12-ft.		up to 11'	up to 10-ft.		up to 9-ft.	
	6"x10"					up to 12'	up to 11'	up to 10-ft. spans		
	6"x12"						up to 12-ft. spans			
2:	4"x6"	up to 6-ft.								
	3"x8"	up to 7-ft.		up to 6-ft.						
	4"x8"	up to 9'	up to 8'	up to 7-ft.		up to 6-ft.				
	3"x10"	up to 10'	up to 9'	up to 8'	up to 7-ft.		up to 6-ft. spans			
	4"x10"	up to 11'	up to 10'	up to 9'	up to 8-ft.		up to 7-ft. spans			up to 6'
	3"x12"	up to 12'	up to 11'	up to 10'	up to 9'	up to 8-ft.		up to 7-ft. spans		
	4"x12"			up to 12'	up to 11'	up to 10-ft.		up to 9-ft.		up to 8-ft.
	6"x10"			up to 12'	up to 11'	up to 10-ft.		up to 9-ft. spans		
	6"x12"				up to 12-ft. spans			up to 11-ft.		up to 10'
3:	4"x6"	up to 6'								
	3"x8"	up to 7'	up to 6'							
	4"x8"	up to 8'	up to 7'	up to 6-ft.						
	3"x10"	up to 9'	up to 8'	up to 7'	up to 6-ft. spans					
	4"x10"	up to 10'	up to 9'	up to 8-ft.		up to 7-ft.		up to 6-ft. spans		
	3"x12"	up to 11'	up to 10'	up to 9'	up to 8'	up to 7-ft. spans			up to 6-ft.	
	4"x12"	up to 12'	up to 11'	up to 10'	up to 9-ft.		up to 8-ft.		up to 7-ft.	
	6"x10"			up to 12'	up to 11'	up to 10'	up to 9-ft.		up to 8-ft. spans	
	6"x12"			up to 12-ft.		up to 11-ft.		up to 10-ft.		up to 8'

[a] Beams are on edge. Spans are center to center distances between posts or supports. (Based on 40 p.s.f. deck live load plus 10 p.s.f. dead load. Grade is No. 2 or Better; No. 2, medium grain southern pine.)

[b] **Group 1:** Douglas fir-larch and southern pine; **Group 2:** Hemlock-fir and Douglas-fir south; **Group 3:** Western pines and cedars, redwood, and spruces.

Example: If the beams are 9'8" apart and the species in Group 2, read the 10-ft. column—3x10 up to 6-ft. spans, 4x10 or 3x12 up to 7-ft. spans, 4x12 or 6x10 up to 9-ft. spans, 6x12 up to 11-ft. spans

Wood screws may be used in areas where nails are normally specified if cost is not a factor. The flathead screw is best for exposed surfaces because it does not extend beyond the surface. The new variable speed drills (with a screwdriver bit) are excellent for applying screws, since screws will take a lot more time to hand-apply than nails.

Lag screws are commonly used to fasten a relatively thick piece

Table 9-3: Maximum Allowable Spans for Deck Joists [a]

Species group [b]	Joist sizes	Joist spacing (in inches)		
		16" o.c.	**24" o.c.**	**32" o.c.**
1:	2"x6"	9'-9"	7'-11"	6'-2"
	2"x8"	12'-10"	10'-6"	8'-1"
	2"x10"	16'-5"	13'-4"	10'-4"
2:	2"x6"	8'-7"	7'-0"	5'-8"
	2"x8"	11'-4"	9'-3"	7'-6"
	2"x10"	14'-6"	11'-10"	9'-6"
3:	2"x6"	7'-9"	6'-2"	5'-0"
	2"x8"	10'-2"	8'-1"	6'-8"
	2"x10"	13'-0"	10'-4"	8'-6"

[a] Joists are on edge. Spans are center to center distances between beams or supports. Based on 40 p.s.f. deck live loads plus 10 p.s.f. dead load. Grade is No. 2 or Better; No. 2 medium grain southern pine.

[b] **Group 1:** Douglas-fir-larch and southern pine; **Group 2:** Hemlock-fir and Douglas-fir south; **Group 3:** Western pines and cedars, redwood, and spruces.

Table 9-4: Maximum Allowable Spans for Spaced Deck Boards [a]

Species group [b]	Maximum allowable span in inches [c]					
	Boards laid flat				Boards laid on edge	
	1 x 4	**2 x 2**	**2 x 3**	**2 x 4**	**2 x 3**	**2 x 4**
1:	16"	60"	60"	60"	90"	144"
2:	14"	48"	48"	48"	78"	120"
3:	12"	42"	42"	42"	66"	108"

[a] These spans are based on the assumption that more than one floor board carries normal loads. If concentrated loads are a rule, spans should be reduced accordingly.

[b] **Group 1:** Douglas-fir-larch and southern pine; **Group 2:** Hemlock-fir and Douglas-fir south; **Group 3:** Western pines and cedars, redwood, and spruces.

[c] Based on Construction grade or better (Select Structural, Appearance, No. 1 or No. 2).

such as 2×6 to a thicker member where a through bolt cannot be used. Lead holes must be used and the lag screw turned in its entire length. Use a large washer under the head. Lead holes for the threaded portion should be about two-thirds the diameter of the lag screw for the softer woods such as redwood or cedar and three-fourths the diameter for the dense hardwoods and such species as Douglas fir.

Machine bolts and **carriage bolts** are simple fasteners and especially good where rigidity is important. They are used for small connections such as railings-to-posts and for large members when combined with timber connectors. Both types are commonly used in light frame construction.

The carriage bolt is normally used without a washer under the head. A squared section at the bolt head resists turning as it is tightened. Washers should always be used under the head of the machine bolt and under the nut of both types. Bolt holes should be the exact diameter of the bolt.

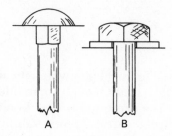

Figure 9-15: The squared section under the head of a carriage bolt (**A**) resists turning; use washers under the heads of machine bolts (**B**) to prevent their digging into the wood while turning.

A   B

SITE PREPARATION

Site preparation for construction of a wood deck is usually less costly than that for a concrete terrace. When the site is steep, it is difficult to grade and to treat the backslopes in preparing a base for the concrete slab. In grading the site for a wood deck, one must normally consider only proper drainage, disturbing the natural terrain as little as possible. Grading should be enough to insure water runoff, with usually just a minor leveling of too uneven ground.

There may also be some need for control of weed growth beneath the deck. Without some control or deterrent, such growth can lead to high moisture content of wood members and subsequent decay hazards where decks are near the grade. Common methods for such control are the application of a weed killer to the plants or the use of a membrane such as 4- or 6-mil polyethylene or 30-pound asphalt saturated felt. Such coverings should be placed just before the deck boards are laid. Stones, bricks or other permanent means of anchoring the membranes in place should be used around the perimeter and in any interior surface variations which may be present. A few holes should be punched in the covering so that not all of the rain will run off and cause erosion.

FOOTINGS FOR DECK POSTS

Concrete footings below the surface are normally used for treated posts or poles. Two such types may be used. The first consists of a

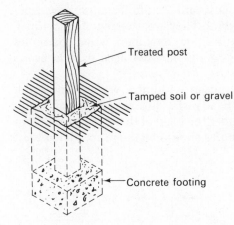

Treated post

Tamped soil or gravel

Concrete footing

Figure 9-16: This type of footing is poured first underground, then the post rests upon and is backfilled with tamped soil or gravel.

poured footing upon which the wood members rest. Embedment depth should be only enough to provide lateral resistance, usually two to three feet. The exception is in cold climates where frost may penetrate to a depth of four feet or more. Minimum size for concrete footings in normal soils should be 12×12×8 inches. Where spacing of the poles is over six feet, 20×20×10 inches or larger sizes are preferred.

Another type of below-grade footing is the poured-in-place type. In such construction, the poles are pre-aligned, plumbed, and supported temporarily by wood cleats above the bottom of the excavated hole. Concrete is then poured below and around the butt end of the pole. A

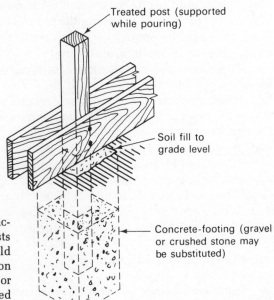

Treated post (supported while pouring)

Soil fill to grade level

Figure 9-17: Another acceptable way to anchor posts is to nail wood cleats to hold the post in proper position while concrete (or gravel or crushed stone) is poured around the bottom.

Concrete-footing (gravel or crushed stone may be substituted)

minimum thickness of eight inches of concrete below the bottom of the pole is advisable. Soil may be added above the concrete when necessary for protection in cold weather. Such footings do not require tamped soil around the pole to provide lateral resistance. All poles or posts embedded in the soil should always be pressure treated for long life.

You can buy or make pre-cast footings with pedestals for attaching the posts. These exposed footings should extend at least six inches above grade.

POST-TO-FOOTING ANCHORAGE

The anchorage of supporting posts to footings with top surfaces above grade is important as they should not only resist lateral movement but also uplift stresses which can occur during periods of high winds. These anchorages should be designed for good drainage and so that the bottoms of the posts do not come in direct contact with wet concrete. It is also important that the post ends be given a dip treatment of water-repellent preservative. They are then anchored in concrete in various ways.

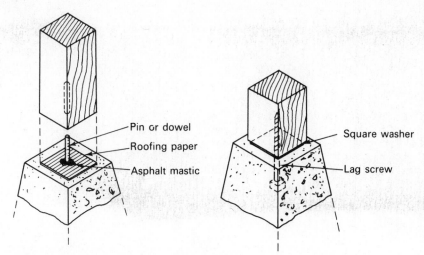

Figure 9-18: Two good ways to attach posts to concrete anchors.

BEAM-TO-POST CONNECTION

Beams are members to which the floor boards are directly fastened or which support a system of joists. Beams may be single large or small members or consist of two smaller members fastened to each side of the posts. When a solid deck is to be constructed, the beams should be sloped away from the house at least one inch every 8 to 10 feet.

Single beams, when four inches or wider, usually bear on a post.

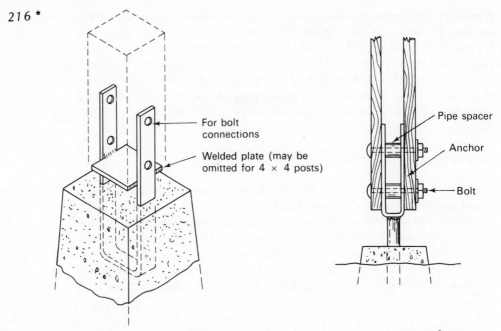

For bolt
connections

Welded plate (may be
omitted for 4 × 4 posts)

Pipe spacer

Anchor

Bolt

Figure 9-19: Two other good ways to attach posts to concrete anchors.

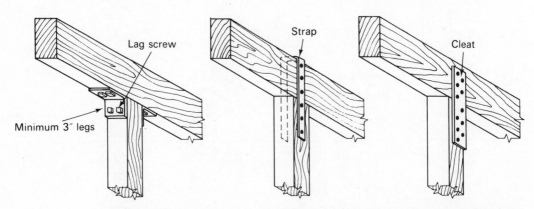

Lag screw

Minimum 3″ legs

Strap

Cleat

Figure 9-20: Three common methods are shown for attaching single beams to single posts—all good construction techniques. (Toe-nailing is not recommended.)

When this system is used, the posts must be trimmed evenly at the top so that the beam bears equally on all posts. Use a line level or other method to establish this alignment.

To attach these beams, use 1×4 lumber or a plywood (exterior grade) cleat located on two sides of the post. Nail the cleats to the beam and post with 8d annular (ring groove) nails. Another good fastening method is to use angle irons on both sides. A 3×3-inch angle iron (or larger) should be used so that fasteners can be turned in easily. Use lag screws. A metal strap fastened to the beam and the post can also be used for single beams. A ⅛×3″ or larger strap, pre-formed to ensure a good fit, will provide an adequate connection. Use 10d ring-groove nails for the smaller members and ¼″ lag screws for larger members.

When a double post made of two 3×6 members is used, a single beam is usually placed between them. Double or split beams are normally bolted to the top of the posts, one on each side. Notching the top of the beam as shown provides greater load capacity. A piece of asphalt felt or a metal flashing over the joint will provide some protection for the post end-grain.

It is sometimes advantageous to use the post which supports the beam as a railing post too. In such a design, the beam is bolted to the post, which extends above the deck to support the railing members.

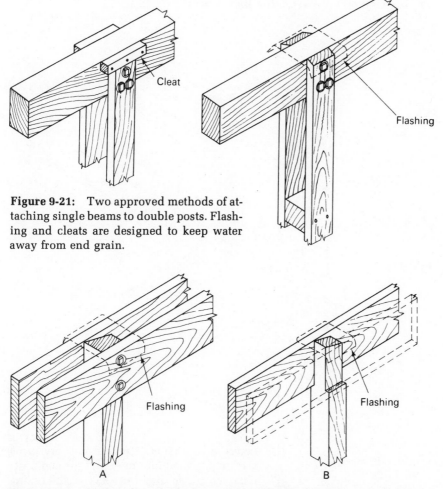

Figure 9-21: Two approved methods of attaching single beams to double posts. Flashing and cleats are designed to keep water away from end grain.

Figure 9-22: Preferred methods for attaching double beams to single posts. Notching the tops of the posts (right) increases the load capacity.

When the deck is adjacent to the house, some method of connecting beams or joists to the house is normally required. This may consist of supporting such members through metal hangers, wood ledgers or angle irons, or utilizing the top of the masonry foundation or basement wall. It is usually good practice to design the deck so that the top of the deck boards are just under the sill of the door leading to the deck. This provides protection from rains as well as easy access to the deck.

Beams: One method of connecting the beam to the house is the use of metal beam hangers. These may be fastened directly to a floor framing member such as a joist header or to a 2×8 or 2×10 which has been bolted or lag-screwed to the house framing. Use 6d or longer nails or the short, large-diameter nails often furnished with commercial hangers for fastening. Hangers are available for all beams up to 6×14.

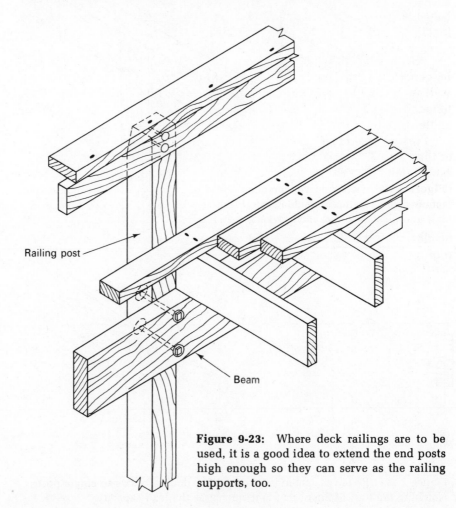

Railing post

Beam

Figure 9-23: Where deck railings are to be used, it is a good idea to extend the end posts high enough so they can serve as the railing supports, too.

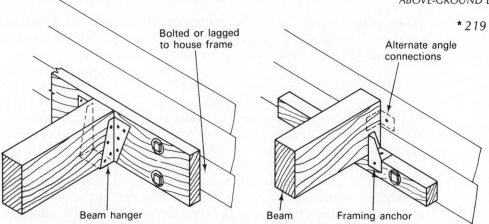

Figure 9-24: Where deck beams are perpendicular to the house, they can be attached by means of beam hangers attached to a header (*left*) or by resting on a bolted ledger with additional support from a framing anchor or metal angle (*right*).

Beams can also be secured to the house proper by bearing on ledgers which have been anchored to the floor framing or to the masonry wall with expansion shields and lag screws. The beam should be fastened to the ledger or to the house with a framing anchor or a small metal angle.

Joists. When joists of the deck are perpendicular to the side or end of the house, they are connected in much the same manner as beams, except that fasteners are smaller. Often a lag screw is used to fasten the ledger to the house. Joists are then toe nailed to ledger and house or fastened with small metal clips.

Joists can also be fastened with joist hangers to a 2×8 or 2×10 header (lag screwed to the house). Six-penny nails or 1¼″ galvanized roofing nails are used to secure the hangers to the joist and to the header.

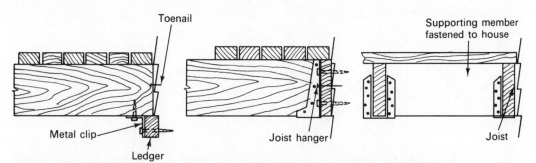

Figure 9-25: Where deck joists are perpendicular to the house, they are supported in the same way as beams, except that the hardware is smaller (*left & center*); where joists are parallel to the house, no fastening is necessary as long as beams are attached (*right*).

220 *

When joists are parallel to the house, no ledger or other fastening member is normally required. If they are supported by beams, the beams, of course, are then connected to the house.

BRACING

On uneven sites or sloping lots, posts are often five or more feet in height. When the deck is free (not attached to the house), it is good practice to use bracing between posts to provide lateral resistance. Treated poles or posts embedded in the soil or in concrete footings usually have sufficient resistance to lateral forces, and such construction normally requires no additional bracing. However, when posts rest directly on concrete footings or pedestals and unsupported heights are more than five feet, some system of bracing should be used. Braces between adjacent posts serve the same purpose as bracing in the walls of a house. Some methods of bracing are illustrated on page 000.

JOIST-TO-BEAM CONNECTIONS

When beams are spaced two to five feet apart and 2×4 Douglas fir or similar deck boards are used, there is no need to use joists to support the decking. The beams thus serve as both fastening and support members for the two-inch deck boards. However, if the spans between beams are more than the recommended spans in Table 9-2 (page 000), it is necessary to use joists between the beams or set the 2×4 on edge for decking. To provide rigidity to the structure, the joists must be fastened to the beam in one of several ways.

Joists bearing directly on the beams may be toenailed to the beam with one or two nails on each side. Use 10d nails and avoid splitting. When uplift stresses are inclined to be great in high wind areas, supplementary metal strapping might be used in addition to the toenailing.

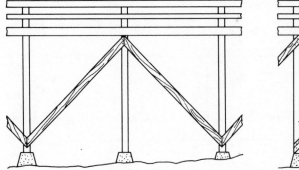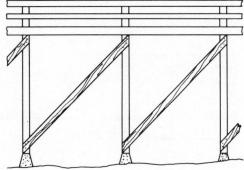

Figure 9-26: Two of the more effective ways of providing extra stability to a deck by means of braces and gussets.

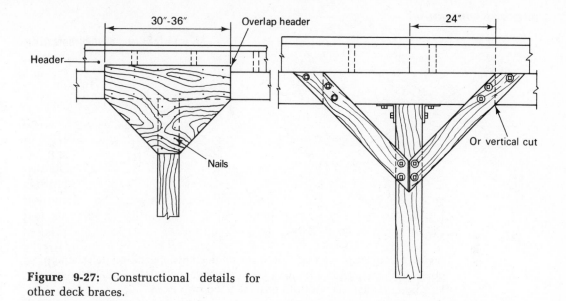

Figure 9-27: Constructional details for other deck braces.

Use 24- to 26-gage galvanized strapping and nail with one-inch galvanized roofing nails. When a header is used at the joist ends, nail the header into the end of each joist. Have the header overhang the beam by one-half inch to provide a good drip edge.

Joists located between beams and flush with their tops may be connected in two ways. One utilizes a 2×3 or 2×4 ledger which is spiked to the beam. Joists are cut between beams and toenailed to the beams at each end. The joint can be improved by the use of small metal clips.

Another method utilizes a metal joist hanger. The hanger is first nailed to the end of the joist with 1″ to 1¼″ galvanized roofing nails and then to the beam. Several types of joist hangers are available.

FASTENING DECK BOARDS

Use two 12d nails for 2×3 and 2×4 decking laid flat. For 2×3s or 2 × 4s on edge, use one fastener per joist. Always use 5″ nails for 2 × 3s on edge and 5″ flathead screws for 2 × 4s set on edge.

Space all deck boards (flat or vertical) one-eighth to one-fourth inch apart (use 8d or 10d nails for ⅛″ spacing and 16d nails for ¼″ spacing). End joints of flat deck boards should be made over the center of the joist or beam. Flat grain boards are always placed "bark" side up; that is, with the outside of the wood uppermost (as it is cut from the tree). When this upper face gets wet, it crowns slightly. Consequently water drains off that side of the lumber more easily. End joints of any deck boards on edge should be made over a spaced double joint, a nominal four-inch or wider single beam, or a two-inch joint with nailing cleats on each side. Always, of course, dip ends of deckboards in water-repellent preservative before installing.

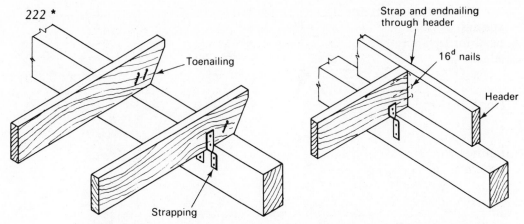

Figure 9-28: Approved joist-to-beam connections: toenailing (*left*); strapping (*lower left*); strap and endnailing through header (*right*). Note that header overlaps beam by half its width to provide good drip edge.

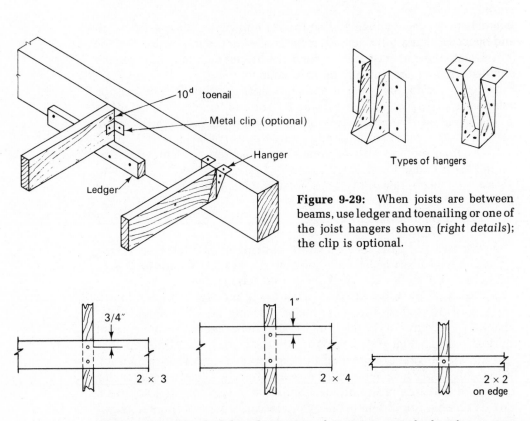

Figure 9-29: When joists are between beams, use ledger and toenailing or one of the joist hangers shown (*right details*); the clip is optional.

Figure 9-30: Flat deck boards (2x3's and 2x4's) are attached with two non-corroding nails while one 5″ flathead screw is used with 2 x 2 boards laid on edge.

Always pre-drill ends of 2×3 or 2×4 (flat) deck boards of the denser species, or when there is a tendency to split. Pre-drill when screws are used for fastening and all fastening points of deck boards placed on edge.

Deck Railings

Low-level decks located just above the grade normally require no railings. However, if the site is sloped, some type of protective railing or system of balusters might be needed because of the height of the deck.

RAILING POSTS

The key members of a railing are the posts. Posts must be large enough and well fastened to give strength to the railing. Some types of vertical members such as the post can also serve as a part of a bench or similar edge structure of the deck. Railings should be designed for a lateral load of at least 20 pounds per lineal foot. Thus, posts must be rigid and spaced properly to resist such loads.

One method of providing posts for the deck railing, as previously mentioned, is by the extension of the posts which support the beams. When single or double beams are fastened in this manner, the posts can extend above the deck floor and serve for fastening the railing and other

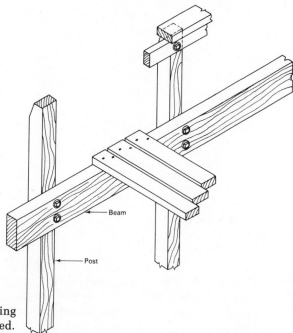

Beam

Post

Figure 9-31: Details of railing posts with framing posts extended.

224 * horizontal members. Railing heights may vary between 30 and 40 inches, or higher when a bench or wind screen is involved. Posts should be spaced no more than six feet apart for a 2×4 horizontal top rail and eight feet apart when a 2×6 or larger rail is used.

When supporting posts cannot be extended above the deck, a joist or beam may be available to which the posts can be secured. Posts can then be attached at the edge. Such posts can be made from 2×6s for spans less than four feet, from 4×4s or 2×8s for four to six-foot spans, and from 4 × 6s or 3 × 8s for six- to eight-foot spans. Each post should be bolted to the edge beam with two ⅜" bolts—or larger if the post is very large. This system can also be used when the railing consists of a number of small baluster-like posts. When such posts are made of 2×2s or 2×3s and spaced 12 to 16 inches apart, the top fastener into the beam should be either a ¼" or ⅜" bolt or lag screw. The bottom fastener can then be a 12d or larger nail. Pre-drill when necessary to prevent splitting. Wider spacings or larger size posts require two bolts. A ⅛" to ¼" space should be allowed between the ends of floor boards and posts.

The ends of beams or joists along the edge of the deck can also be used to fasten the railing posts. Single posts or double posts (one on each side) are bolted to the ends of the joists or beams. Space the bolts as far apart as practical for better lateral resistance.

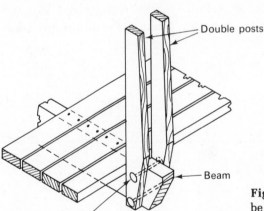

Figure 9-32: Double posts can be used at the beam ends of the deck to support deck railings.

Deck Benches

High-deck benches: At times there is an advantage in using a bench along the edge of a high deck, combining utility with protection. The vertical back supporting members (bench posts), spaced no more than six feet apart, are bolted to the beams. They can also be fastened to extensions of the floor joists. When beams are more than six feet apart, the bench post can be fastened to an edge joist in much the same manner

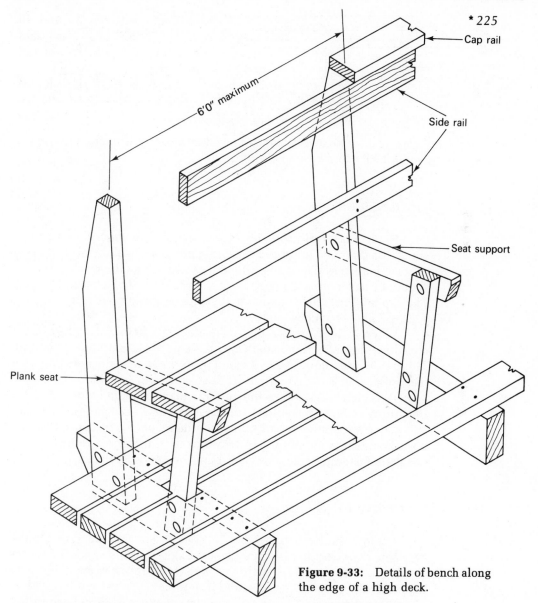

Figure 9-33: Details of bench along the edge of a high deck.

as railing posts. The backs and seat supports should be spaced no more than six feet apart when nominal two-inch plank seats are used.

Low-deck benches: Benches can also be used along the edge of low decks. These can be simple plank seats which serve as a back drop for the deck. Such bench seats require vertical members fastened to the joists or beams with cross cleats. For 2×4 seats, vertical supports should be bolted to a joist or beam and spaced no more than six feet apart. A single wide support (2×10) or double (two 2×4s) supports can be used.

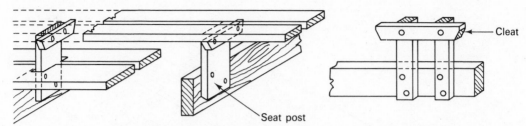

Figure 9-34: Two ways to support low-deck benches: with one wide support (*left*) or with two thin supports (*right*).

RAILINGS

Horizontal railings: The top horizontal members of a railing should be arranged to protect the end grain of vertical members such as posts or balusters. The upper side rail, which is usually a 2×4 or wider, should be fastened to the posts with a lag screw or bolt at each crossing. The cap rail then can be nailed to the edge of the top rail with 12d nails spaced 12 to 16 inches apart.

When railing posts are spaced more than about two feet apart, additional horizontal members may be required as a protective barrier. These side rails should be 2×4 when posts are spaced no more than four feet apart. Use 2×6s when posts are spaced over four feet apart.

Rail fastenings: When the upper side rail is bolted to the post, the remaining rails can be nailed to the posts. Use two 12d nails at each post and splice side rails and all horizontal members at the centerline of a post. Posts must be more than two inches in thickness to provide an adequate fastening area at each side of the center splice.

Stairways for Decks

Often a stairway is needed to give access to a deck or for use between decks with different levels. Exterior stairs are constructed much the same as stairs within a house, except that members with exposed end grain or surfaces that trap moisture must not be used.

Stair stringers: A basic stair consists of stair stringers (also called the stair carriage) and treads. Additional parts include balusters and side cap rails and, on occasion, risers. The supporting members of a stair are the stringers. Stringers are used in pairs spaced no more than three feet apart. They are usually made of 2×10s or 2×12s. Stringers must be well secured to the framing of the deck. They are normally supported by a ledger or by the extension of a joist or beam. For example, a 2×3 of 2×4 ledger nailed to the bottom of an edge framing member with 12d nails supports the notched stringer and toe-nailing or small metal clips

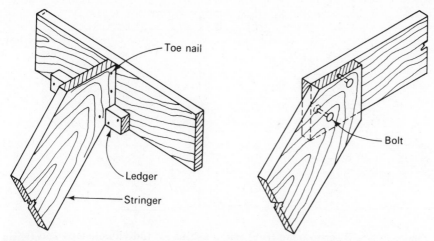

Figure 9-35: Stair stringers are supported at the side of the framing member with ledger and notches and at the end with bolts.

are used to secure the carriage in place. Stair stringers can also be bolted to the ends of joists or beams when they are spaced no more than about three feet apart. Use at least two ½" galvanized bolts to fasten the stringer to the beam or joist.

The bottom of the stair stringers should be anchored to a solid base and be isolated from any source of moisture. Metal angles are most frequently used. They should be thick enough to raise the stringer off the concrete which is sloped for drainage. The angles may also be fastened to a treated wood member anchored in the concrete or in the ground.

Tread and riser size: The relation of the tread width to the riser height is important in determining the number of steps required and thus the total length or "run" of the stair. For ease of ascent, the rise of each step times the tread width should equal 72 to 75 inches. Thus, for an 8" riser (considered maximum for stairs), a 9" tread is necessary, or with a 7½" riser, a 10" tread. The number of risers and treads can be found when the total height of the stair is known. Divide total rise in inches by 7½ (each riser) and select the nearest whole number. Thus, if the total rise is 100 inches, the number of risers would be 13 and the total run about 120 inches.

Tread support: A good method of tread support consists of 2×4 ledgers or cleats bolted to the stair stringers and extended to form supports for the plank treads. The ledgers can be sloped back slightly so that rain will drain off the treads. Nail 2×10 or 2×12-inch treads to the ledgers with three 12d nails at each stringer. Rust-proof wood screws three inches in length can also be used. Always place plank treads with bark side up to prevent cupping and retention of rain water. Treads can also be made of two 2×6 planks, but the span must be limited to 42 inches for less dense woods.

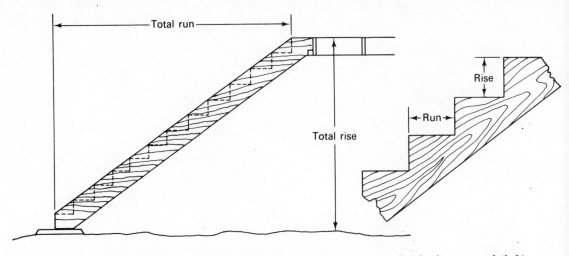

Figure 9-36: Riser-to-tread (run) relationships for individual steps and (*left*) total rise and run of a staircase.

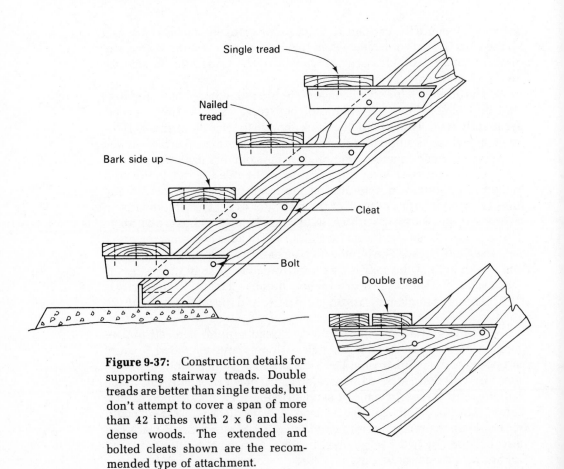

Figure 9-37: Construction details for supporting stairway treads. Double treads are better than single treads, but don't attempt to cover a span of more than 42 inches with 2 x 6 and less-dense woods. The extended and bolted cleats shown are the recommended type of attachment.

Stair railings: On moderate- to full-eight stairs with one or both sides unprotected, some type of railing is advisable. Railings for stairs are constructed much the same as railings for the deck. In fact, from the standpoint of appearance, they should have the same design. Railings normally consist of posts fastened to stair stringers and supplementary members such as top and intermediate rails.

Many variations of post and rail combinations can be used, but all designs should obviously consider safety and utility as well as pleasing appearance.

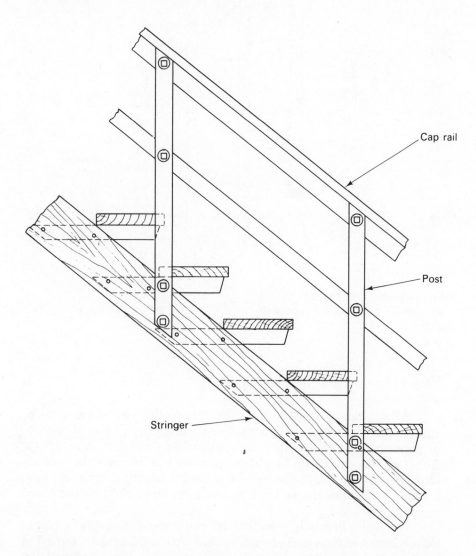

Cap rail

Post

Stringer

Figure 9-38: Details for constructing a staircase railing with widely-spaced stair posts.

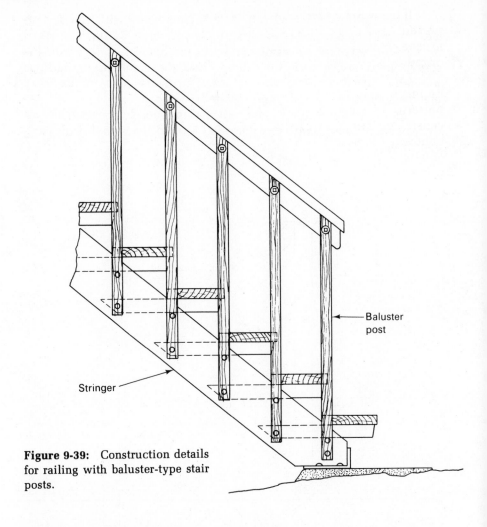

Baluster post

Stringer

Figure 9-39: Construction details for railing with baluster-type stair posts.

Preservatives & Finishes for Decks

All outdoor woodwork should be treated with a wood preservative of some sort. For wood not in contact with the ground, a coat of "penta" or pentachlorophenol with a water repellent is usually satisfactory. Although this can be applied when your deck is finished, the penta is more effective when the lumber is soaked in solution before nailing. Soaking penetrates the end grain, saw cuts, etc. and gives the wood much longer life.

For wood that is in contact with the ground, creosote or pentachlorophenol in heavy oil should be used. All wood actually buried in the ground should be pressure-treated with creosote. (You can buy it that way.)

If the wood is visible and to be finished, creosote or heavy oil will
prevent good adhesion. Penta is the only possibility here. It is also wise
to use a naturally decay-resistant type of wood such as all-heart redwood
or red cedar.

For easy maintenance and a rustic look, decks can be completely
unfinished. Another coat of penta applied after construction will help
preserve the wood, but you don't even need this with redwood or red
cedar. You can, if you want, use a penetrating sealer or sealer-stain,
although a natural finish looks best. Paint is not recommended, but if
you insist, be sure to use at least two coats of porch and deck paint over a
primer.

Figure 10-1: Simple and easy to build, this wooden shed is made with exterior quality plywood and stock lumber.

10:

Garden Sheds, Storage Units & Carports

If you've ever read all the way through your homeowner's insurance policy, you may have run across the term "appurtenant structures." "Structures" we all understand, but what is this mysterious "appurtenant"? A quick review of the dictionary reminds us that an appurtenant structure is an outdoor building which is incidental to the main structure (your house). In other words, an appurtenant structure is a garage, gazebo, storage shed, garden shelter, or any building other than the house itself. And this is what this chapter is all about.

Garden Sheds

A simple wooden shed is roomy, practical, and easy to build. In any contest with metal sheds, it's a winner both in good looks and cost. Outdoor storage structures that will hold lawnmower and garden tools, plus the peat moss, the fertilizer, the trowels and pots are bound to be useful the year round as well as during the growing season. Complete plans and a list of materials may be obtained from The American Plywood Association, 1118 A Street, Tacoma, Washington 98401. Ask for Handy Plan A C 206-BR 2-2283 if you like the looks of the one illustrated on the facing page.

A Versatile Storage Center

This handsome storage facility is large, complex, and different-looking. Its abundant nooks and crannies provide niches for every-

Figure 10-2: Here a complex storage center combines functional design and versatility.

thing—gardening equipment, lawn party supplies, swimming pool accessories, and many other items. It's a four-unit, demountable outdoor storage center, and attractive any way you look at it. It's versatile, too, with a counter-height potting bench, deep storage cabinets, shelves, and two storage closets so large you can also use them for poolside dressing rooms.

The unit with the wide, fold-down potting bench is ideal for storing garden tools and supplies. You can keep pots, gloves, labels, and pencils close at hand on the two shelves in front of the bench. Use the cabinets above and below to store seeds, bulbs, transplanting solutions, and root hormones. For barbecues, convert the unit to serve as a storage/work center. (The shelf space, cabinets, and counter really come in handy for food and beverage service.)

A lawn mower and sweeper can be set in the unit with the spacious open area at ground level. Doors on the upper part conceal a roomy two-shelf cabinet for wrenches, screwdrivers, and other small tools.

In the two units with full-height double doors, you can store rakes, hoes, and shovels, along with a wheelbarrow, bags of peat moss, fertilizer, and bark mulch. Depending on individual needs, add shelves or wall hooks for sprayers, chain saw, hedge and grass trimmers, hose, sprinklers, and lopping shears. For security, lock hardware may be installed on all doors.

Basic plywood connections are designed to interlock and fasten with pegs for easy assembly. Only roofs, minimum lumber parts, and hardware require any screws, so the center can be demounted and moved anytime.

Your local building material dealer can supply most of the materials you'll need. Before starting, study the plans carefully so all details are clearly in mind.

Cutting and Framing: Saw off all shiplap edges from Texture 1-11 plywood panels. (Finished panel should be 47¼" wide.) Then lay out plywood panels as shown in the sutting diagrams (Texture 1-11 panels with grooved side up). Use a straightedge and carpenter's square for accuracy. As always, allow for saw kerfs when plotting dimensions. Lightly mark all pieces for identification later, then cut out pieces. For easier fitting, cut slots 1/16 inch longer and wider than shown on cutting diagrams, if desired.

On panels B-1 and D-1, the hole location for pegs is critical. To assure a more precise alignment of holes in these panels, place the panels flat with the tabs facing each other. Place 1¼" spacer blocks at each end of the panels, lap panel D-1 tabs over panel B-1 tabs and clamp panels together for drilling. (Check the diagram for alignment before drilling.) Drill through both panels as marked. When all plywood cutting and drilling is complete, fill plywood edges with surfacing putty, allow to dry, and sand smooth.

Cut lumber to required lengths for shelf supports as you go. Note that front and back 1 × 2s of roof frame must be beveled on top as shown in detail drawing.

Refer to roof framing drawings for locations of lumber framing members on roofs. Position each piece on bottom of roofs, pre-drill, and screw lumber framing to roofs.

Wipe all plywood parts clean, determine color(s) you want for all four units, then apply undercoat to MDO plywood surfaces. Edges should receive several undercoats before applying finish coat. When undercoat is thoroughly dry, apply finish coat.

Stain exterior of Texture 1-11 plywood and interior of panels wherever desired in color(s) of your choice. Allow all painted and stained parts to dry thoroughly. Label parts with masking tape.

Basic Assembly: Assemble the center where you plan to use it. In choosing the site, keep in mind that the area should allow for good drainage. It may be necessary to provide some type of foundation. Ask your building material dealer for his recommendation on the foundation material and building method best suited to your needs (probably a concrete slab).

During assembly, adhesive may be used at all panel joints to assure a tight fit. Begin by butting panel C-1 to panel A-1 (in a vertical position) so that the largest slots of both panels are closest together. Then, overlap panel C-1 on panel A-1 so that the largest slots of both panels are aligned. Now insert tabs of panel D-1 through aligned slots of panels C-1 and A-1. (Tabs of panel D-1 must be inserted through slots of panel C-1 first, then on through panel A-1 slots.) Panel D-1 will now be perpendicular to both panels. Do not insert pegs at this time.

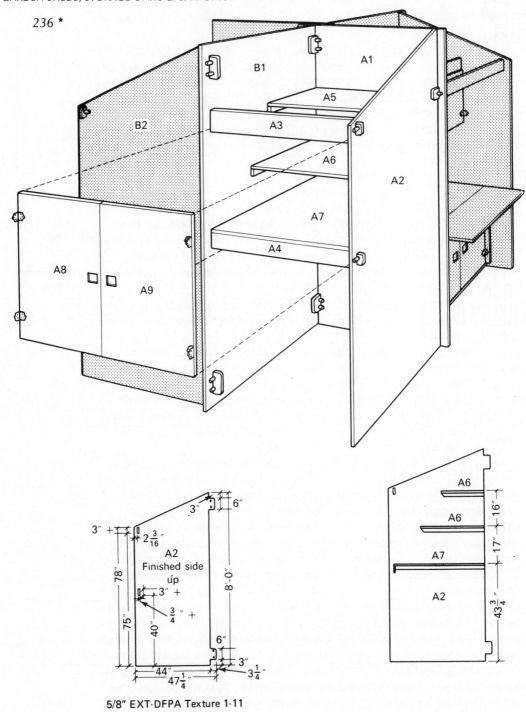

5/8" EXT-DFPA Texture 1-11

Figure 10-3: Construction details for the storage center's Unit A side.

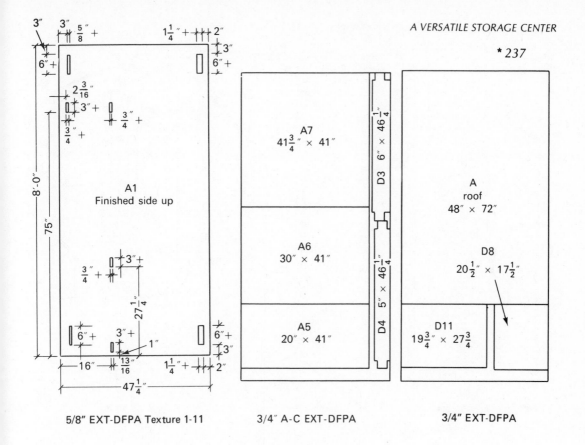

Figure 10-4: Cutting diagrams for the Unit A details on page 236.

To form the fourth partition (opposite panel D-1), insert tabs of panel B-1 through aligned slots of panels A-1 and C-1, so that panel B-1 will be perpendicular to both. (Be sure tabs of panel B-1 are nearest to outside edge of panel A-1 where B-1 tabs insert into A-1 slots.) Now fasten all panels at center with 3½" pegs.

Next, assemble sides of all units into outer slots of partition panels. As you connect sides to partitions, arrange textured surface of side panels to face out. Insert tabs of panel A-2 into slots of panel A-1, tabs of panel B-2 into slots of panel B-1, tabs of panel C-2 into slots of panel C-1, and tabs of panel D-2 into slots of panel D-1. (Do not insert pegs unless required for temporary fastening.)

Refer to drawings of Units A, B, C, and D for locations of cross beams with tabs. Note that cross beams are generally lettered and numbered in sequence of assembly. Beginning with Unit A and working through Unit D, assemble cross beams in all units. After all are in place, fasten the cross beams and panels with three-inch pegs.

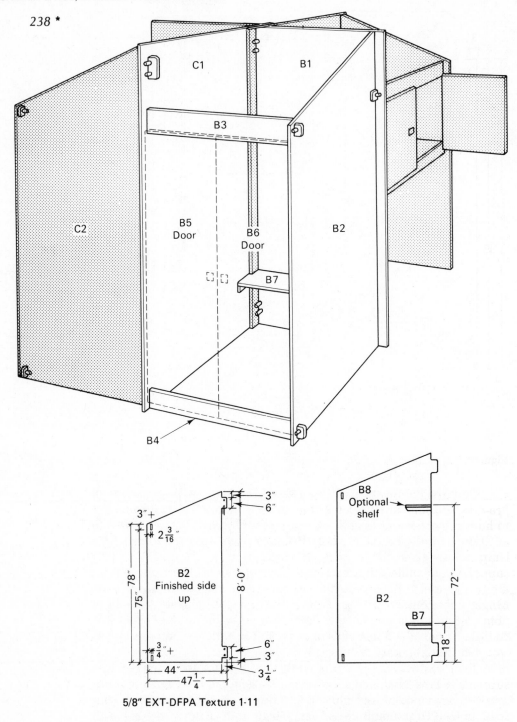

5/8" EXT-DFPA Texture 1-11

Figure 10-5:   Construction details for the storage center's Unit B side.

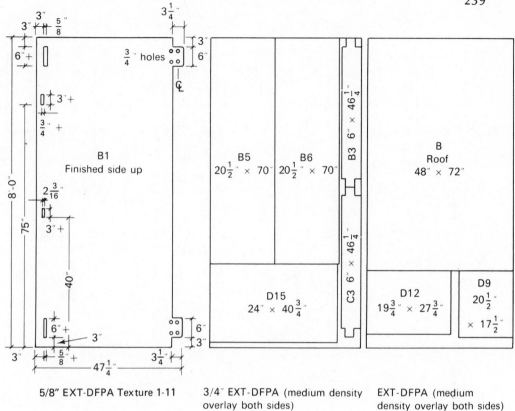

3/4" EXT-DFPA (medium density overlay both sides)

EXT-DFPA (medium density overlay both sides)

5/8" EXT-DFPA Texture 1-11

Figure 10-6: Cutting diagrams for the Unit B details on the opposite page.

Complete basic assembly by placing framed roofs over each unit. Pre-drill and screw through framing and into plywood on all four sides to hold each roof in place.

Door Shelf and Bench Assembly: Refer to side view drawings of Units A, B, and C for locations of shelf supports. Pre-drill and screw shelf supports in position shown for Units A, B, and C. Now, hinge doors on Units A, B, and C. (Doors on all units must be slightly rounded at inside hinged edge to fit tightly.) Place shelves on supports. You will have to notch left rear of panel B shelf to fit. Attach door pulls and catches to complete these three units.

On Unit D, install lower shelf supports so that top of supports are flush in height with top of cross-beam D-4. Also install fold-down bench supports at the same height, so that outside support edges are flush with outside edges of panels A-1 and D-2. (See Unit D drawing.) Place shelf D-10 on shelf supports and screw into position. (The left rear corner of all shelves in this unit must be notched to fit.)

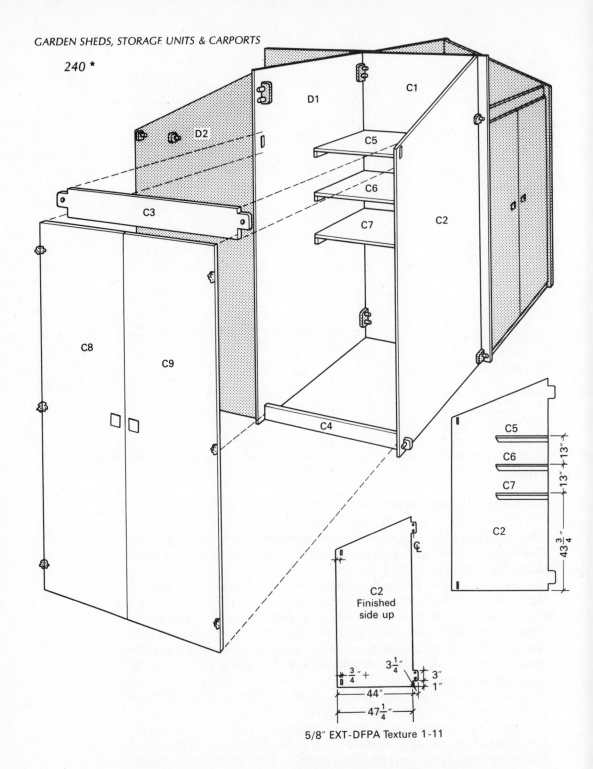

Figure 10-7: Construction details for the storage center's Unit C side.

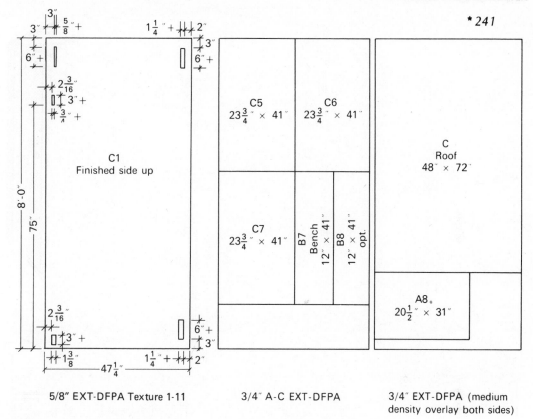

5/8″ EXT-DFPA Texture 1-11   3/4″ A-C EXT-DFPA   3/4″ EXT-DFPA (medium
                                                               density overlay both sides)

Figure 10-8:   Cutting diagrams for the Unit C details opposite.

Next, install 1×3 cabinet-door hinge supports for lower cabinets.
The top edge of these supports should be flush with top of cross-beam
D-4, and tight against the cross beam vertically. Then hinge the cabinet
doors onto the supports so that the top edges of the doors are flush with
the top of the door supports and cross beam D-4. The doors should close
tight against top and bottom cross beams.

Now hinge D-15 fold-down bench to top edge of shelf D-10. Fold
bench into closed (vertical) position and mark top edge height on panels
A-1 and D-2. This is the maximum height to install D-7 shelf supports.
Place shelf D-7 in position over supports.

Hinge top cabinet doors to panels A-1 and D-2 so that bottom edges
of doors are 1/16″ above bottom edge of shelf D-7. Doors should close
tight against this shelf and cross beam D-3.

Install shelf supports for shelves D-13 and D-14 at desired heights
between shelves D-7 and D-10. Place shelves in position, install door
pulls and friction latches to complete assembly of unit. All panel tabs
and wood pegs can be touched up with paint or stain as required.

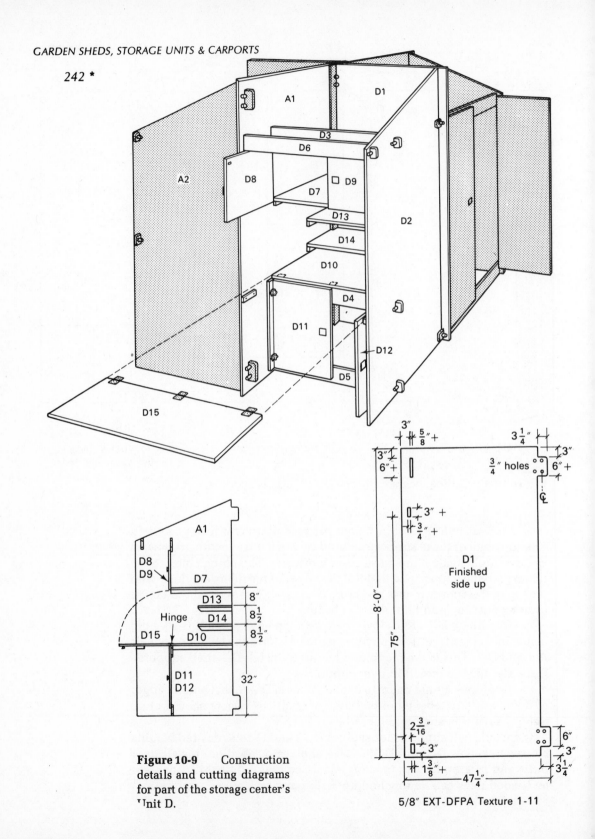

Figure 10-9 Construction details and cutting diagrams for part of the storage center's Unit D.

5/8″ EXT-DFPA Texture 1-11

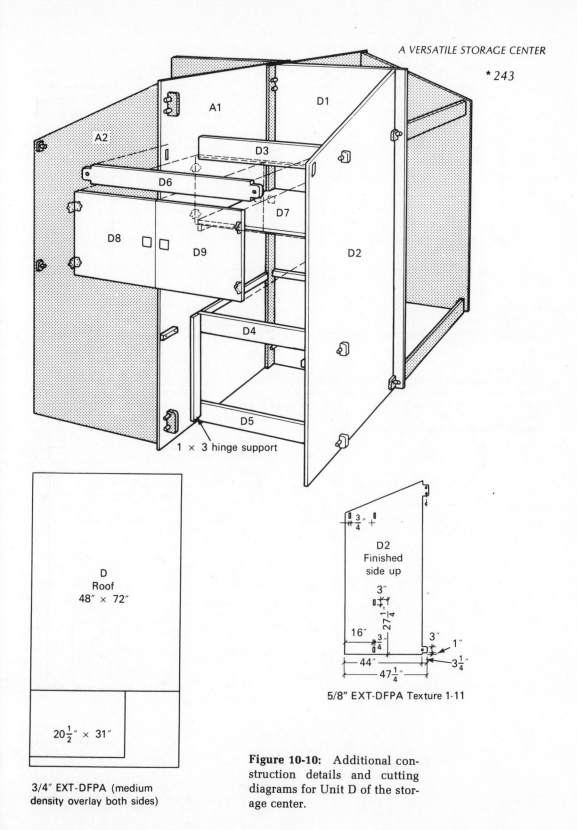

A1

D1

A2

D3

D6

D7

D8

D9

D2

D4

D5

1 × 3 hinge support

D
Roof
48″ × 72″

$20\frac{1}{2}″ \times 31″$

3/4″ EXT-DFPA (medium
density overlay both sides)

$\frac{3}{4}″$

D2
Finished
side up

3″

$27\frac{1}{4}″$

16″

$\frac{3}{4}″$

3″

1″

44″

$47\frac{1}{4}″$

$3\frac{1}{4}″$

5/8″ EXT-DFPA Texture 1-11

Figure 10-10: Additional construction details and cutting diagrams for Unit D of the storage center.

PLAN VIEW

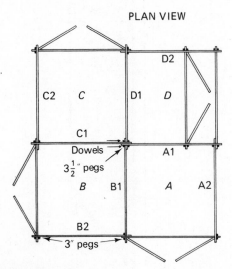

Overlap slots of panel C-1 on largest slots of panel A-1 so slots align. Insert tabs on panel D-1 into slots of panel C-1 and through slots of panel A-1.

Insert tabs of panel B-1 into aligned slots of panel A-1 and C-1, so panel B-1 tabs are to the left of panel D-1 tabs.

Figure 10-11: Plan view of the storage center's layout and details for the spacing and for drilling members of the storage center sections.

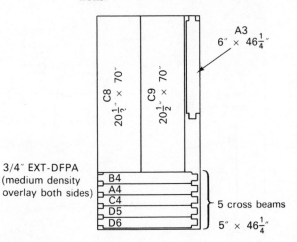

3/4″ EXT-DFPA (medium density overlay both sides)

Cross beam details

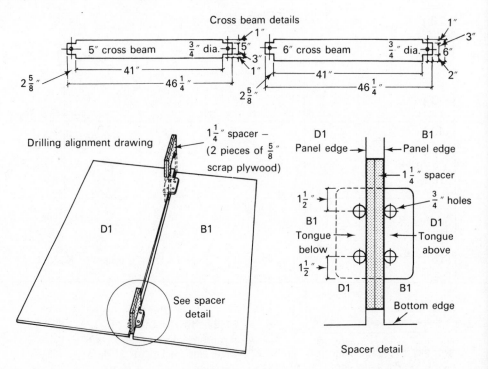

Spacer detail

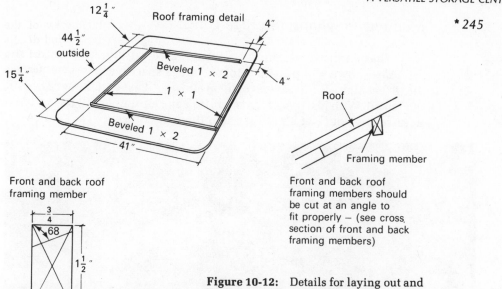

Roof framing detail

12¼″

44½″ outside

15¼″

Beveled 1 × 2

1 × 1

Beveled 1 × 2

41″

4″

4″

Roof

Framing member

Front and back roof framing member

¾

68

1½″

Cross section

Front and back roof framing members should be cut at an angle to fit properly — (see cross section of front and back framing members)

Figure 10-12: Details for laying out and building the frame for the storage center's roof.

Materials List for Storage Center

Quantity	Wood	Usage
8 panels	⅝″×4′×8′ EXT-DFPA Texture 1-11 plywood	basic unit structure
6 panels	¾″×4′×8′ EXT-DFPA MDO plywood (Medium Density Overlay) both sides	roof, doors, crossbeams
3 panels	¾″×4′×8′ EXT-DFPA A-C plywood	shelves, crossbeams
140 lin. ft.	1×2 lumber	roof frame, shelf supports
30 lin. ft.	1×1 lumber	roof frame
5 lin. ft.	1×3 lumber	cabinet door hinge supports
16 lin. ft.	¾″ diameter dowel stock	pegs for connecting basic parts

Quantity	Hardware	Usage
13 pair	hinges	doors, fold-down bench
14	friction catches	doors, fold-down bench
188	1-¼″ No. 10 flathead wood screws	framing, roof connection
11	door pulls	doors, fold-down bench
	lock hardware for doors (optional)	

246 *   Modular Playhouse/Storage Units

These units represent the ultimate in versatility. Even one of the modules shown will provide a lot of storage space (each is 4 feet square and 8 feet high). Build several of them and you'll have all the space you'll ever need. With just two of the modules you can support all the optional accessories—but not all at the same time, of course.

Figure 10-13:   The lean-to greenhouse (*above*) fits well with these handsome modules built for a dedicated gardner. **Figure 10-14:**   The same sort of modules (*below*) also suit the needs of people whose garden and lawn are often the scene of gracious outdoor entertainment for family and friends.

Accessories include a picnic table and bench (or work table) stretched between storage units, plus a monkey bar/ladder and two types of crawl-through roofs to fit between units. A standard lean-to greenhouse may be fitted in nicely with these modules, as shown in the larger photo. (The latter may be purchased from Lord & Burnham Co., Irvington, N.Y. 10533).

PLANS FOR THE BASIC MODULE

Lay out the plywood sheets for the modules you are building and cut out the pieces. Four panels are needed for each module, plus one or two for each accessory. True the edges and fill any defects. Allow the surfacing putty to dry, then sand smooth.

Attach the 2×2 frame assembly on both side panels, back and front panels of the module, using glue and 6d galvanized finishing nails. Glue and nail the 4×4 foundation as well. The optional shelf or peg supports may also be installed and drilled for pegs at this point.

Round any sharp corners slightly with a sanding block, and clean MDO plywood surfaces with a tack cloth to prepare for painting. Select a good quality paint and stain, and finish all exterior surfaces. Use different colors on different sections for a bright, cheerful effect.

When paint is thoroughly dry, begin assembly of the unit. (During assembly, use exterior adhesive at all basic joints.) Set both side panels on edge with a back facing up and lightly clamp the plywood base and roof to the side panels. Drill ¼-inch bolt holes through the base and roof panels and framing members. Fasten the roof to the sides with wing nuts and bolts. Then lay the back panel in place, drill bolt holes through the back panel, and insert bolts. At this point, drill bolt holes into roof and base, through framing members of the back panel, and insert bolts through the roof holes. Then turn the unit on its back, lay the front panel in place, and drill through the roof and framing members of the front panel. Insert bolts through new holes in the roof panel and secure with wing nuts. Also drill holes through front panel and side framing members; insert bolts and secure with wing nuts, but remove the base entirely. Nail and glue the plywood base to the 4 × 4 foundation. Using the pilot holes in the plywood base, drill through the foundation. If a concrete foundation is desired, consult the optional plans; otherwise, proceed as follows.

Countersink bolt holes in the bottom of the foundation, insert 6" carriage bolts, and set the side panels with roof onto the foundation assembly. Fasten all parts of module with wing nuts. (Casters may also be fastened to the 4×4 foundation.)

Apply the piano hinge, door catch, lock (optional), and handle to the door. While a plywood door handle adds an interesting visual touch, standard door hardware will work as well and may be easier to install. Finally, hang the door in place. Add shelves and pegs as desired. Recommended minimum peg length is four inches.

248 *

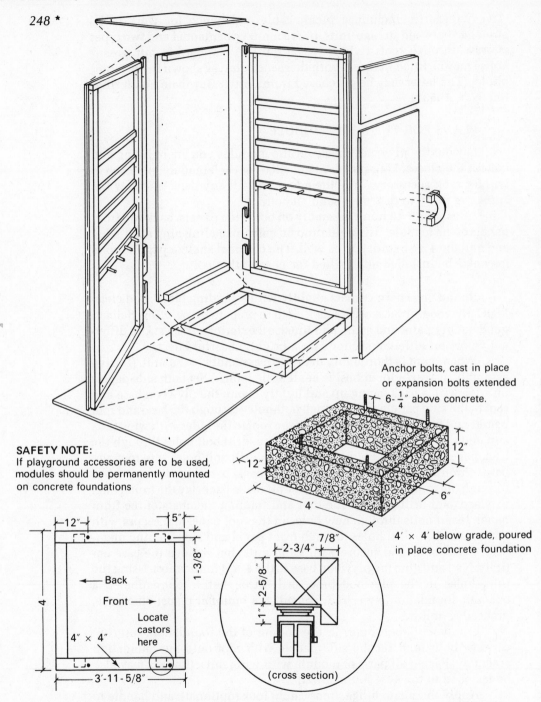

Anchor bolts, cast in place or expansion bolts extended 6-$\frac{1}{4}$" above concrete.

12"

12"

6"

4'

4' × 4' below grade, poured in place concrete foundation

SAFETY NOTE:
If playground accessories are to be used, modules should be permanently mounted on concrete foundations

12"

5"

1-3/8"

Back

Front →

4

Locate castors here

4" × 4"

3'-11-5/8"

7/8"

2-3/4"

2-5/8"

1"

(cross section)

Figure 10-15: Construction details for the foundation, framework, and sheathing of the basic module used for the Playhouse/storage units.

Materials List for Modular Playhouse/Storage Units *249

Quantity	Wood (for each module)	Usage
1 panel	¾"×4'×8' EXT-DFPA A-C plywood	roof, base
2 panels	¾"×4'×8' EXT-DFPA MDO or A-C plywood	front, back
2 panels	¾"×4'×8' EXT-DFPA rough-sawn or other plywood	sides
16 lin. ft.	4×4 lumber	foundation
60 lin. ft.	2×2 lumber	framing
40 lin. ft.	1×2 lumber	shelf rests
1 piece	½" dowel (4-ft. length, or as needed)	shelf pegs
scrap	2×3 lumber	optional wood handle

Quantity	Hardware (for each module)	Usage
1 lb.	6d galvanized finishing nails	
1 lb.	16d galvanized common nails	
20	¼"×2-¾" galvanized carriage bolts & wing nuts	
6	¼"×6" galvanized carriage bolts & wing nuts	
1	72" piano hinge	
1 box	¾" No. 4 brass flathead screws	
1	door catch	
1 set	casters or concrete base (optional)	
2	3/16"×4" galvanized carriage bolts, washers & wing nuts	optional wood handle
8	1-½" No. 10 galvanized flathead screws	optional wood handle

Quantity	Wood (for all accessories)	Usage
5 panels	¾"×4'×8' EXT-DFPA MDO or A-C plywood	optional accessories

If you plan to build more than one module and use accessories, drill holes for connectors. Connector installation can be made any time with bolts. You may also want to add a greenhouse. That requires the adjustment of the greenhouse base to equalize the height between the storage unit and roof of the lean-to. If the greenhouse is offset as shown, a back wall of plywood must be provided, the length depending on the area exposed by the offset. The width of the door that would open inside the greenhouse should also be reduced by about half to prevent the top of the door from striking the greenhouse roof.

ACCESSORIES FOR THE MODULES

Decide on the accessories you want to make. For all accessories, cut dowels to length. If 2⅝" dowels are unavailable, use 3×3s shaped as shown in the "Flat Roof" diagram. Next, lay out plywood panels and cut

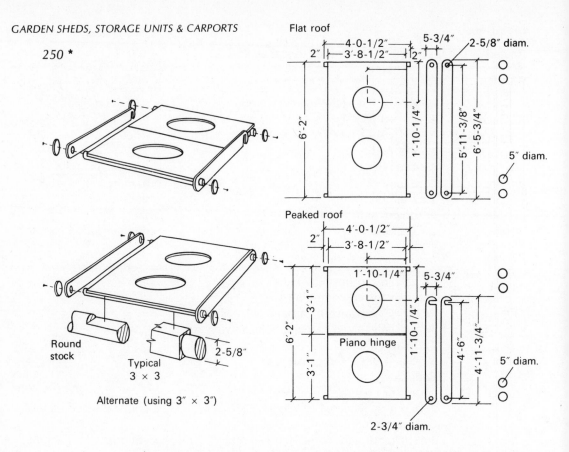

Figure 10-16: Construction details for both flat and peaked roof members used with the modular units.

out pieces. Then sand edges, slightly rounding corners, and fill exposed edge defects. Sand smooth when dry.

For all dowels except those in monkey-bar/ladder accessory, measure in from ends as shown in "Flat Roof" and crosscut ¾" deep at marks. Saw lengthwise between crosscuts as shown for the particular accessory you are making to form a flat surface. Also, pre-drill all round plywood end caps for screw holes.

Flat Roof: Glue and nail ends of the plywood roof on the dowels. Then glue each long edge of plywood roof, and slip holes of plywood end beams over dowels. Nail end beams onto roof edges. Screw the plywood caps onto glued dowel ends as shown.

Peaked Roof: Hinge the plywood roof ends together. Pre-drill screw holes at each end of hinged roof, pre-drilling flattened dowel at the same time. Then glue ends of plywood roof and fasten roof panel ends to dowels with screws. Nails may be substituted for screws in plywood-dowel connection if children will not be climbing on roof.

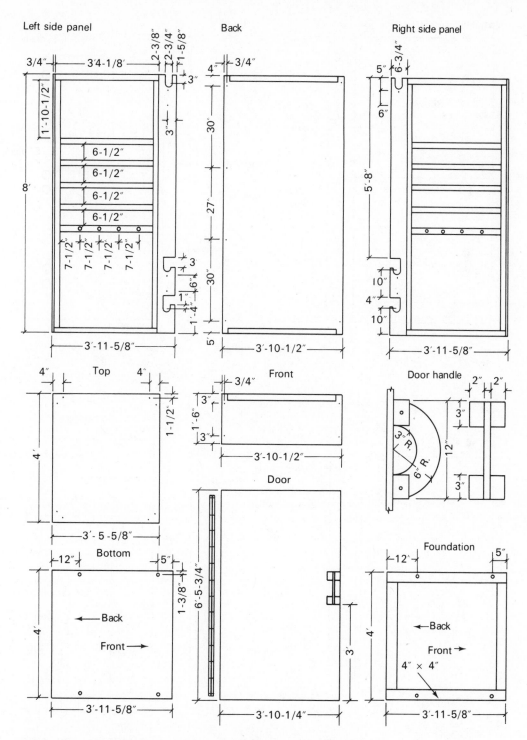

Figure 10-17: Additional construction details for the modules.

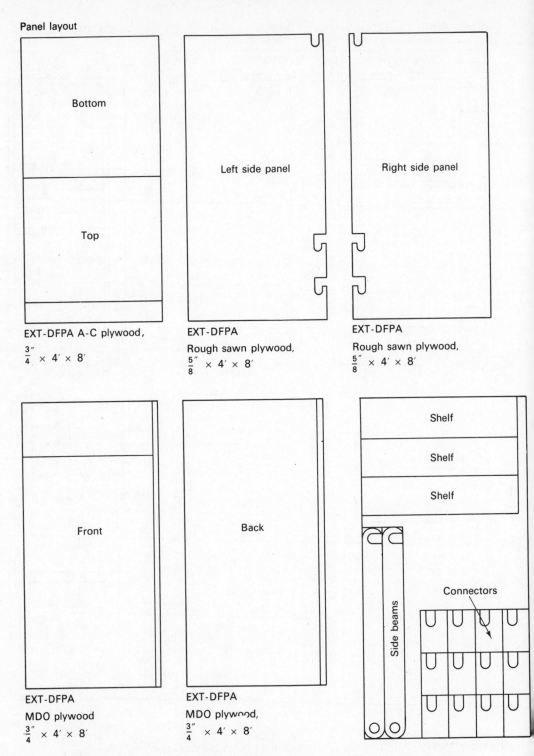

Figure 10-18: Other cutting diagrams and shelf details for the modules.

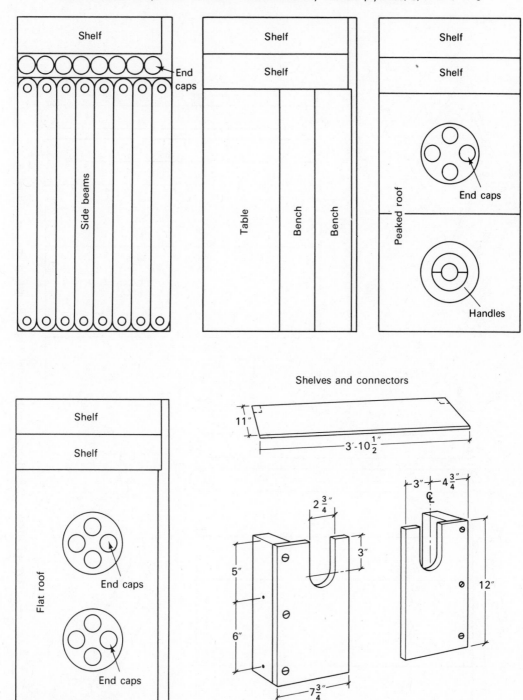

PANEL LAYOUT (5 panels) EXT-DFPA medium density overlaid plywood, 3/4″ × 4′ × 8′

Shelf

End caps

Side beams

Shelf

Shelf

Table

Bench

Bench

Shelf

Shelf

Peaked roof

End caps

Handles

Flat roof

Shelf

Shelf

End caps

End caps

Shelves and connectors

11″

3′-10½″

2¾″

3″

5″

6″

7¾″

3″ 4¾″

12″

Figure 10-19: Shelf and panel layouts for the modular.

254 *

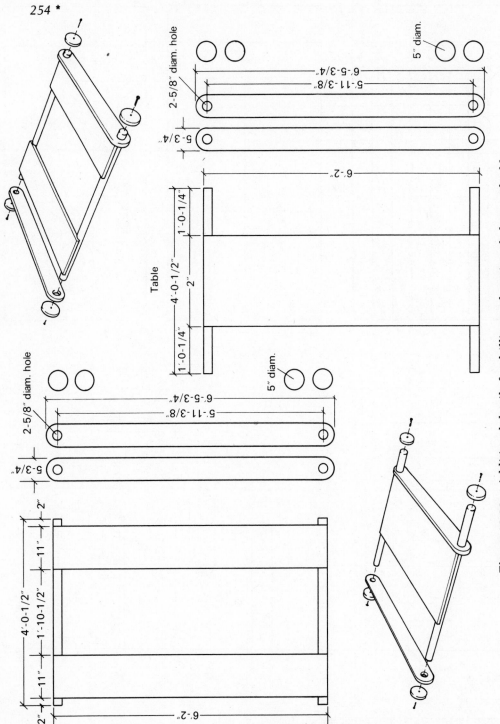

Figure 10-20: Additional details for drilling and cutting shelves and table.

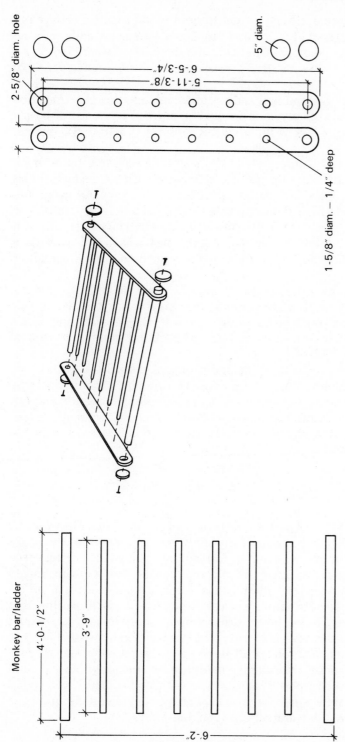

Figure 10-21: Construction details for the modular's monkey bar-ladder accessory.

256 *   (Optional: secure eye bolts in roof to hold nylon rope for children to climb.) Slip holes of plywood end-beam connectors over ends of dowel as shown. Screw the plywood caps onto the glued dowel ends.

Table: See drawing. Basic instructions are the same as for "Flat Roof" assembly.

Benches: Glue and nail ends of plywood onto dowels. Then glue outside edges of each plywood bench. Slip holes of plywood end beams onto bench edges. Screw the plywood caps onto glued dowel ends as shown.

Monkey Bar/Ladder: Along the center of each end beam, mark evenly spaced locations for each 1⅝" dowel and drill 1⅝" diameter holes (¼" deep) into one side of each beam. Glue 1⅝" dowel ends, insert into end beams, and pre-drill the opposite side of end beams for screws. The dowel is also less apt to rotate in use if you pre-drill off center into each dowel. Then slip the 2⅝" dowels through holes in each end beam. Glue these dowel ends, and screw the plywood caps onto the dowel ends as shown.

Shelves and Connectors: Five shelves per module are recommended; however, they are optional. You may want more than or less than five, or none at all—depending on your storage requirements. **Note:** Be sure to notch corners of shelves to fit around framing at back of module.

Connectors are required if modules are not placed back-to-back and you wish to attach accessories. Determine the number of connectors you need by considering the number of modules you plan to build and the module arrangements you may use. For instance, if two modules are placed side-to-side with accessories between, you may need as many as twelve connectors.

Carport-Patio Shelter

Who needs a carport when there is a garage? Quite a few people, oddly enough. In recent years many families who were pressed for space and reluctant to move have transformed their garage into living space —and that leaves cars out in the cold and the rain. And for many houses garages can be awkward or impractical—or just too expensive to build.

So a good way to help shield a car from the worst of the weather is to build a carport. An even better idea is to build a back-to-back carport and patio. But the best idea is to put some storage area between.

This plan incorporates all three—a sheltered patio and carport, plus three large separate storage modules, two opening into the patio and one into the carport. (You can reverse this, of course, if you wish.) Thus, you provide cover for your vehicle, your garden tools, and your family all in one integrated, good-looking unit.

Figure 10-22: Here a carport-patio is attached to one side of a house.

Figure 10-23: Two versions of a free-standing patio-carport shelter—one with a center storage unit (*left*).

This carport-patio shelter can be attached to any side of the house or be built as a separate, free-standing structure. The plan and drawings show the carport enclosed on three sides, but you can leave it open in warmer climates if desired.

THE FOUNDATION

When you have all the materials on hand (see page 261), begin by laying out the post and wall footings. First, stake out the corners and intersections of post footings with rear wall and edge of slab in front.

258 *

Scale: 1/32″ = 1′-0″

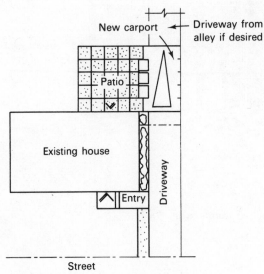

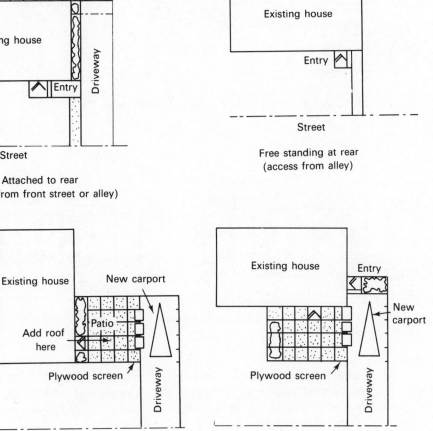

Figure 10-24: Four plans showing convenient ways to lay out attractive and useful carport-patios.

Scale: $\frac{3}{16}'' = 1' -0''$

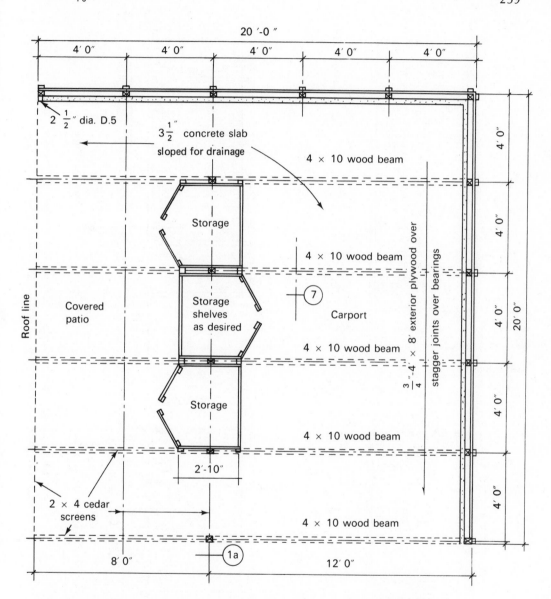

Figure 10-25: Plan view of the carport-patio shown at the top of page 257.

Then check for square by measuring diagonally across from corner to corner. When dimensions are the same on each diagonal, the building is in square. Now dig a 2-ft. wide trench to a depth below local frost line for the foundation wall along the rear and right side. Dig 2-ft. sq. holes at each post foot location.

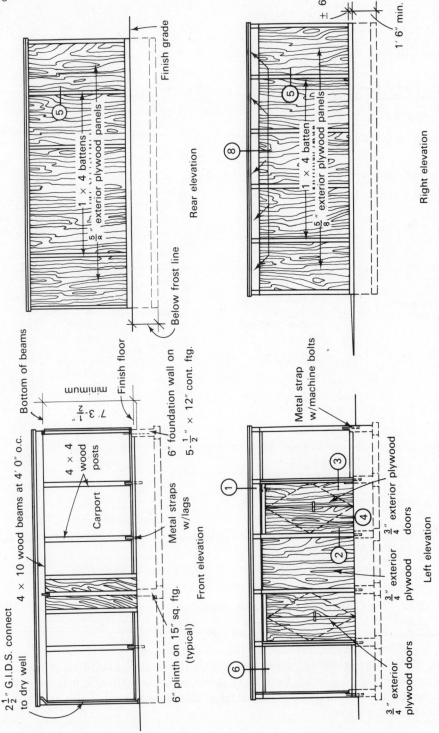

Figure 10-26: Construction details for the central storage unit shown in the plan view of the carport-patio overleaf.

Materials List for Carport-Patio Shelter

Quantity	Wood	Usage
12½ panels	¾"×4'×8' EXT-DFPA A-C plywood	roof
10 panels	⅝"×4'×8' EXT-DFPA A-A plywood	walls
6 panels	¾"×4'×8' EXT-DFPA A-C plywood	storage cabinet doors & back
6 panels	½"×4'×8' EXT-DFPA A-C plywood	storage cabinet top, ends, partitions
6 pieces	20' of 4×10 lumber	beams
16 pieces	8' of 4×4 lumber	posts
4 pieces	12' of 2×4 lumber	plates
20 pieces	8' of 2×4 lumber	plates, cabinet door headers, framing
11 pieces	8' of 2×4 cedar	patio screeds
5 pieces	8' of 2×2 lumber	roof blocking
8 pieces	10' of 1×3 lumber	roof fascia
15 pieces	8' of 1×3 lumber	cabinet door stiffeners
12 pieces	8' of 1×4 lumber	battens
1 piece	12' of 1×2 lumber	cabinet door stops
4 pieces	8' of ½"×3 lumber	post casting

Quantity	Hardware & Miscellany	
21	⅛"×2"×16" metal anchor straps	
15	24 gage 2"×10" sheet metal straps	
10	standard joist anchors	
22	½"×3" lag screws	
10	½"×4-½" machine bolts, washers, and nuts	
6 pairs	3-½"×3-½" fast-pin zinc-coated butt hinges	
3	2-½" safety hasps	
40	aluminum plyclips for ¾" plywood	

Nails and other fastenings as required.

7-½ lin. ft. (approx.) of 2-½" downspout with base plate and nipple.

80 lin. ft. of 24 gage galvanized gravel stop.

4" drain tile and gravel for drywell.

Concrete reinforcing bars, paint, stain, and miscellaneous finishing materials, as required.

Now set batter boards approximately two feet out from corners and the intersection of the post line with rear wall and front edge of slab. Stretch strings to locate outside face of foundation wall and post line. Check for square again by taping the diagonals to corners where strings intersect.

Stake 2×6s on edge for footings along the rear and right side. Build wall forms for foundation to the required height with 2×4s and plywood or boards. Set outside form panels on top edge of 2×6 footing forms and

262 *

Scale 1-1/2″ = 1-0″

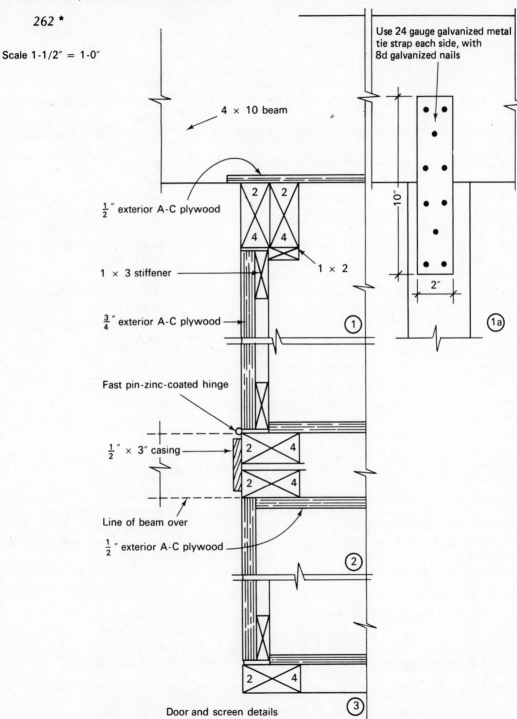

Use 24 gauge galvanized metal tie strap each side, with 8d galvanized nails

4 × 10 beam

½″ exterior A-C plywood

1 × 3 stiffener

1 × 2

¾″ exterior A-C plywood

①

⑩

10″

2″

Fast pin-zinc-coated hinge

½″ × 3″ casing

Line of beam over

½″ exterior A-C plywood

②

Door and screen details

③

Figure 10-27: Additional construction details for the central storage unit.

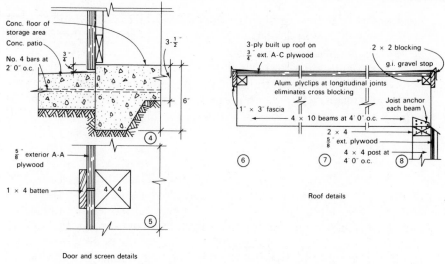

Door and screen details

Figure 10-27 continued: The diagram of the unit is on page 261.

nail into position with inside face lined up with batter board strings. Set inside form panels so that forms are six inches apart. Install one row of form ties about half way up from top of footing and nail wood bracing on 2×4s across the top where required. Install wood spreaders between forms as needed. Build bottomless boxes for post footings from 2×6 scrap lumber. Assemble 6"×6" plinth forms from scrap wood and nail to 2×4s fastened across post footing forms. (You may be able to buy or adapt precast footings that will work. Show plan to your masonry dealer.) Pour concrete into forms and then insert ⅛"×2"×16" metal straps into the concrete foundation at each post location. Insert double straps into plinths at each post footing. Treat 2×4 plates with toxic water repellent. Using a carpenter's level, set plates on top of freshly poured wall with 20d nails driven into bottom side to act as plate anchors. (See Chapters 5 & 6 for more on concrete.)

FRAMING

Remove formwork after concrete has sufficiently hardened. Cut 4×4 posts to length, fasten with ½" lags to metal straps, holding them upright with temporary diagonal braces to the 2×4 plate on foundation walls. Also, position and fasten posts to straps from footing plinths. Now nail a 2×4 continuous plate across the posts on the far carport wall.

Cut 4×10 beams to length and fasten to top plate with metal joist anchors on both sides of each beam. Use galvanized tie straps and nails in other locations where beams are connected directly to posts. Keep

264 *　beams aligned with temporary bracing across the tops. It would be well at this stage of construction to apply two coats of stain or other finish to all the beams, posts, and plates.

Prime both sides and the edges of exterior plywood wall panels before installation. When the prime coat is dry, fasten panels to posts, plates, and beams with 8d non-corrosive common nails, 6" o.c. along all edges.

THE ROOF

After applying a coat of primer to the "A" face and edges of the ¾" exterior plywood roof panels, fasten them to the tops of the beams with end edges staggered. Use aluminum "plyclips" at 16" centers and fasten panels with 8d common nails 6" o.c. along edges at bearings. Install 2×2 blocking between beams at outside edges to provide nailing for the 1×3 fascia which should be back-primed before installation. Set galvanized nipple and base plate for 2½" diameter downspout.

Application of the built-up roof is the next step. Call in a professional roof applicator for this job. He can recommend the best and most economical roof to meet the requirements in your locality. Have the roofer or a sheet metal shop make up and install the shop-primed galvanized gravel stop to insure a neat installation.

THE SLAB

Prepare for the pouring and finishing of the patio and carport slab by setting 2×4 cedar screeds in a 4'×4' pattern as shown. Set the screeds to effect a slope of approximately ⅛-inch per foot from the rear to front of the carport and from the front of the storage cabinets to the edge of the patio slab. Note that the edge of the slab at the storage cabinet fronts is deepened and reinforcing steel is installed at 24" centers to keep the slab from cracking at this point. Use a broomed finish for the carport and patio slab. (See Chapter 5.)

CABINETS

Construction of the storage cabinets is one of the last steps. Use ½" exterior plywood for the walls, partitions and roof with 2×4s at outside corners for additional strength. Double 2×4s over door openings act as headers between double 2×4 spacers at post locations. Doors are made of ¾" exterior plywood with 1×3 stiffeners along all edges, nailed and glued. Edges of ½" plywood partitions act as stops along jambs. Nail a 1×2 to header at top to form a stop. Hang doors with a pair of zinc-coated fast-pin butts and install suitable catches and hasps. Install shelving to suit.

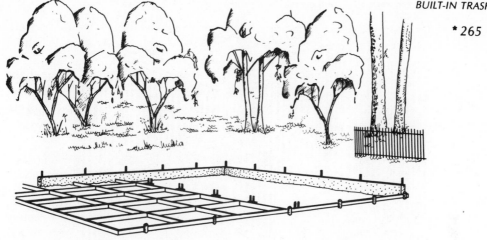

Figure 10-28: Layout for pouring and finishing the concrete for the patio and carport slabs detailed on pages 256–64.

Use a good quality exterior house paint and stain on your new structure. Over the prime undercoat apply two coats of exterior house paint on all plywood surfaces, fascia board, and metal gravel stop. A colorful motif may be achieved by painting the wall panels and storage cabinet doors in alternate harmonizing colors. After paint has thoroughly dried, apply 1×4 wood battens (prestained with two coats) over plywood joints at each post location on rear and right side walls. Fasten with 8d galvanized nails and set slightly below the surface.

Built-in Trash Bin

This project will foil marauding dogs, keep cans neat and clean, and eliminate garbage-can eyesore. The bin can be built right into the fence so that you don't have to walk out of your yard, or you can make it as a separate unit. A hinged lid covers the bin, and as a built-in, the open can permits sanitation crews to slide the can in and out without entering your property.

The plan shows standard plywood for the bin itself and Texture 1-11 for the fence, but you can reverse them or use the same type for both (or other materials, if you prefer). The bin is cut out of one sheet of plywood. You can double or even triple the width for more cans. The fence, of course, depends on both your needs and tastes (see Chapter 4). The only other materials are a 4-foot length of 2×4 for the base, a pair of hinges, some glue, and a couple pounds of galvanized, stainless or aluminum nails.

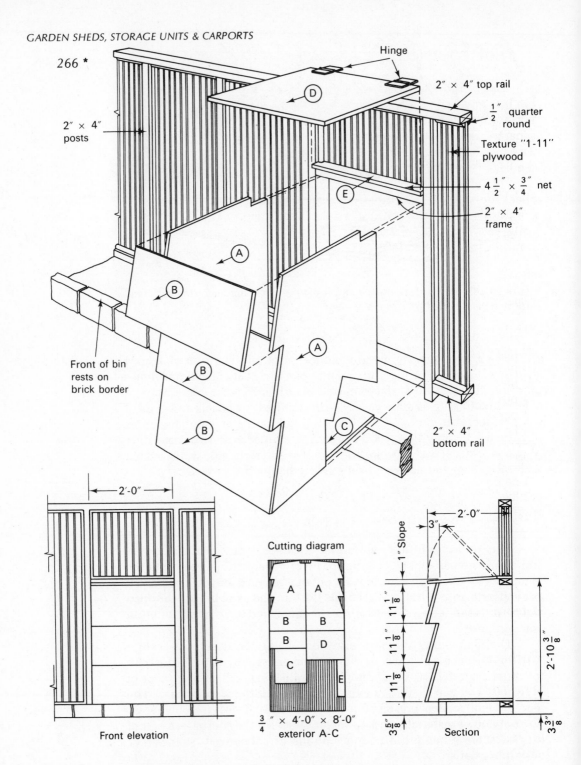

Hinge

2″ × 4″ top rail

$\frac{1}{2}$″ quarter round

Texture "1-11" plywood

$4\frac{1}{2}$″ × $\frac{3}{4}$″ net

2″ × 4″ frame

2″ × 4″ posts

2″ × 4″ bottom rail

Front of bin rests on brick border

2′-0″

Front elevation

Cutting diagram

$\frac{3}{4}$″ × 4′-0″ × 8′-0″ exterior A-C

1″ Slope

2′-0″

3″

$11\frac{1}{8}$″

$11\frac{1}{8}$″

$11\frac{1}{8}$″

$11\frac{1}{8}$″

$3\frac{5}{8}$″

$3\frac{3}{8}$″

2′-10$\frac{3}{8}$″

Section

Figure 10-29: Plan view and construction details for the built-in trash bin.

Examine the plan carefully before you do anything. If you build the bin into an existing fence, check dimensions to see if everything fits. If not, alter them to suit your purposes. When you build this trash bin as a separate unit, omit the notches at the top of the side pieces and nail to 2×4 framing. You'll also need another piece of plywood 24″ × 36⅝″ for the back if you do not build it "in."

Lay out and cut the parts after you study the cutting diagram. Then check the cut pieces and true all edges with a sandpaper block. Assemble the side panels square and flush with the back edge of the bottom panel, using glue and 6d finishing nails. Nail and glue the three louvers to the front, leaving the bottoms open to allow air circulation.

Materials List for Built-In Trash Bin

Quantity	Wood Dimensions	Usage	Key*
2 pieces	24″×33-⅝″	sides	A
3 pieces	11″×24″	louvers	B
1 piece	21″×22½″	bottom	C
1 piece	19″×24″	lid	D
1 piece	4½″×24″	hinge support	E
14 lin. ft.	2×4 lumber	framing	

Quantity	Hardware
1 pair	brass hinges
2 lbs.	6d aluminum finishing nails

* "Keyed" parts cut from one 4×8 panel of ¾″ plywood EXT-DFPAA-C plywood.

Fit and nail the hinge support strip. Attach the hinges, fill all holes and defects with surfacing putty, then finish as recommended for all exterior wood.

Barbecue Buffet

Tired of fumbling for the necessary equipment when you have a backyard barbecue? This compact, handsome buffet holds barbecue tools, charcoal, lighter, and condiments and serves as a convenient storage unit for the grill. It can be attached to the house or used free-standing. Use it not only for storage, but as a work and serving table —just as you would an indoor buffet.

Figure 10-30: The barbecue buffet, here attached to the house, has excellent working spaces.

Figure 10-31: Closed, the barbecue buffet presents a tidy, pleasant facade.

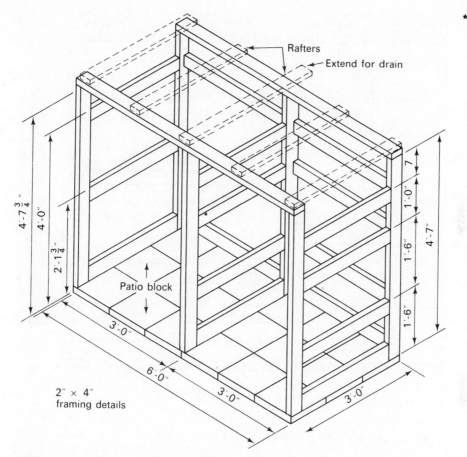

Figure 10-32: Framing details for the barbecue buffet.

The first step in building the Barbecue Buffet is careful selection of a well-drained site on which to place the flooring of foot-square concrete patio blocks. They should be leveled carefully, since the frame will rest directly on the perimeter. Or the unit also can be attached directly to a wood deck, with the deck for its floor. Or, a 3×6-ft. concrete slab can be poured (as described in Chapter 5).

Framing starts with one middle and two end sections. Check drawings and Materials List for sizes. The middle and outside end section are identical, so the first can be a pattern for the second. Horizontal members tie the sections together into a boxlike frame which is toenailed and set in place on the foundation. Basic framing is 2×4 fir, pine, or other locally available lumber (see the framing diagram). Install plywood partition. Attached units are nailed to the house; free-standing units are secured by helical concrete nails or other fasteners appropriate to the foundation.

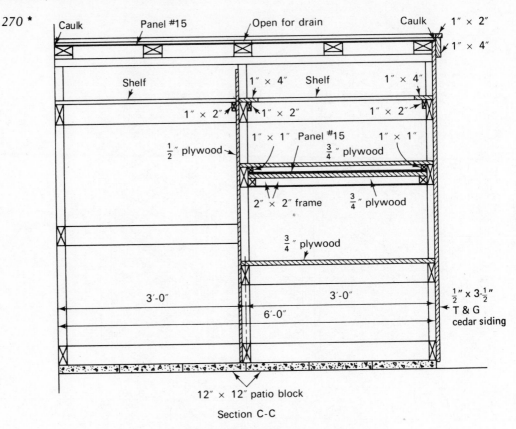

Section C-C

Figure 10-33: Siding details for the barbecue buffet.

Cut ¾″ plywood panels for shelving as follows:

* One piece 36¾″ × 35¼″
* One piece 36¾″ × 32½″
* One piece 36¾″ × 12″
* One piece 34¾″ × 18″
* One piece 33¾″ × 33¾″

Then cut a sheet of ½″ plywood to 54″ × 34″ inches for the partition. Also cut a plastic- or metal-clad (15) plywood panel to make one 41″×73″ piece for the roof and another 23″ × 33¾″ for the sliding shelf. Make two 10″ long runners from 1″ × 1″ or 1″ × 2″ stock.

The metal- or plastic-clad ¼″ plywood panel is used for both the roof and slide-out shelf. The roof, sloping to the back at a quarter-inch to the foot, is attached with neoprene washer roofing nails, 12 inches apart, over the five rafters. Kitchen-counter laminated plastic will also provide a shelf surface that is easily cleaned and won't be scarred by hot pans or utensils. A 1×4 fascia surrounds the unit at the top and is cut out at the

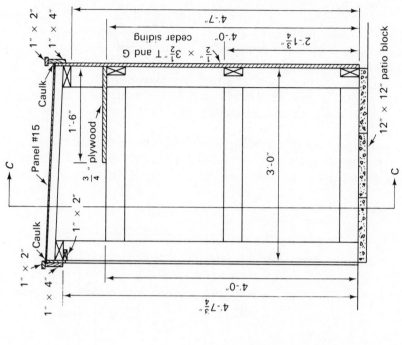

Section B-B

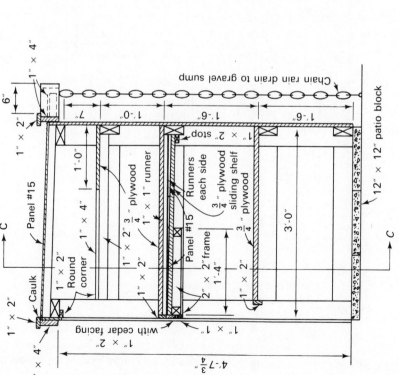

Section A-A

Figure 10-34:   Additional construction details for the barbecue buffet.

272 *

back for drainage along an extended center rafter and down an Oriental-style chain drain (see Section A-A).

The wide storage shelf above the pull-out shelf fits in easier if it is sawn in half, then set together in place. Install other shelves per Sections A-A and C-C. Where shelves have no "resting spot" on the frame, use 1×1 or 1×2 cleats as shown. Sliding shelf rests on 2×2 frame, with a piece of 1×2 at bottom rear for a stop (see above). Runners come next. Bottom doors are opened to hold the shelf up when pulled out, but you can make it self-supporting with the appropriate drawer hardware, if you prefer.

Doors are made from Z-frames of 1×4 lumber and built-up ½"×3½" cedar siding. The same siding is nailed to the side(s) and to the back. Strips of 1×2 or 1×4 cedar are used as fascia for the front framing pieces.

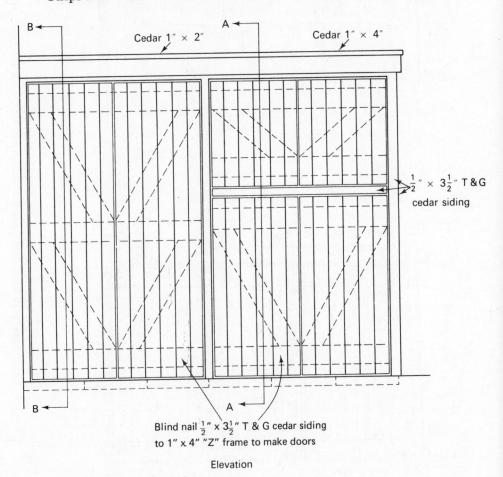

Elevation

Figure 10-35: Plan showing framing and construction details for barbecue-buffet doors.

Note that the unit in the photos has a notched 1×4 next to the house siding. The configuration of that piece depends on the particular house. Free-standing units take a piece of standard 1×2.

All doors are hung with Colonial-style "wrought-iron" hinges (or other varieties to suit). Pulls should be the same style. The cedar can be allowed to weather naturally, or it can be stained or painted. Saw-textured siding is suggested if it is to be stained.

Materials List for Barbecue Buffet

Quantity	Wood	Usage
2 panels	¾"×4'×8' EXT-DFPA A-C plywood	shelving
1 panel	¼"×4'×8' EXT-DFPA C-C plywood (or piece already metal—or plastic-clad)	roof, sliding shelf
1 panel	½"×3'×5' EXT-DFPA C-C plywood	partition
12 pieces	2×4 lumber 8 ft. long	framing
1 piece	2×2 lumber 8 ft. long	cleats
5 pieces	1×4 lumber 8 ft. long	shelving, supports
4 pieces	1×2 lumber 8 ft. long	cleats
3 pieces	1×1 lumber 9 ft. long	cleats
3 pieces	1×4 cedar 8 ft. long	fascia
3 pieces	1×2 cedar 8 ft. long	fascia
66 pieces	½"×3-½" tongue & groove cedar 5 ft. long	siding
12 pieces	½"×3-½" tongue & groove cedar 5 ft. long	siding (free-standing unit only)
1 piece	1×4 exterior cedar 4 ft. long	fascia (free-standing unit only)
18	12×12 patio blocks (or other foundation material)	
1 piece	4'×8' laminated plastic (if metal—or plastic-clad plywood unavailable)	
	calk, stain, etc.	as required

Quantity	Hardware
2 lbs.	10d galvanized common nails
2 lbs.	8d galvanized common nails
3 lbs.	6d galvanized finishing nails
3 lbs.	roofing nails with neoprene washers
7	drawer pulls
6 pairs	hinges
6	friction catches
1	5' chain

Figure 11-1: A family pool, even the built-in kind, is not beyond the means of most middle-income Americans (*courtesy of Hallmark Pools*).

11:

Pools & Potpourri

Residential Pools

Time was when a private pool was the showcase of the wealthy, the ultimate luxury that showed that, indeed, its owner had "arrived." But now the backyard pool is within the grasp of almost everyone. The new metal-walled vinyl-liner pools in the ground are surprisingly less expensive—compared to what it used to cost to make that kind of splash (pun intended). And even the poorest among us can afford a tiny kiddy pool.

There are over a million pools in use in the U.S. and Canada, and at least another 80,000 are installed every year—not including the round, above-ground types that are so common. Of course, there are some people who are sorry they went to all the expense, and there are some who wouldn't buy a house with a built-in pool if you paid them (mostly families with very small children). Still, a private "swimming hole" can be your vacation-at-home on many a hot, sweltering day—and even on cooler ones if you have a heater. There is no highway traffic to fight while burning expensive gas and there are no wall-to-wall people at the beach—nothing but you, your family, the sun, the birds and bees. For many people, this is the ultimate in outdoor living.

Those who are interested in a pool should familiarize themselves with the three chief types. Remember, you can save a thousand dollars or so on a built-in pool by doing it yourself, but in that case forget about concrete, Gunite, fiberglass, or anything except the vinyl-liner sort. Basically, pools fall into three categories or types according to their location.

Figure 11-2: An in-ground pool can have a rectangle, oval, dogleg, or a special shape such as this large 42 x 44 foot award-winning beauty which includes a hydrotherapy unit (*courtesy of National Swimming Pool Institute*).

Basic Types of Pools

* **In-Ground Models:** The Cadillacs of the industry, they are often made of concrete—either poured or applied pneumatically (Gunite)—or they have a vinyl liner laid over reinforced metal walls of aluminum or steel. Fiberglass in-ground pools are also popular in the Midwest and some other areas.
* **Above-Ground Models:** They are usually made with a vinyl liner over aluminum or steel—or sometimes over wood—and with a wood decking. Only the rectangular or oval types, at least 12 ft. wide by 24 ft. long are considered in this category. (Smaller, round pools are thought to be more for cooling off than for swimming.)
* **On-Ground Models:** Basically they are the same as above-ground models except that a diving "hopper" is dug into the ground at one end. A deck is usually an integral part of the package. (This type seems to be disappearing.)

Of the residential pools built in recent years, almost 47 percent were constructed with pneumatically applied concrete, over 42 percent with plastic liners, and 6 percent of poured concrete. The rest, or less than 5 percent, were made with fiberglass or other materials.

Figure 11-3: Above-ground models have many advantages, including lower cost and no increase in taxes—usually (*courtesy of National Swimming Pool Institute*).

Sizes and Shapes

Most in-ground pools are custom built, so the variety of sizes and shapes is considerable. Above-ground pools and most in-ground pools with vinyl liners come in multiples of four feet. In other words, you can get a 20' × 32' but not a 13' × 38' pool ordinarily. Some companies also offer variations of the dogleg and the reverse dogleg, for example. Poured, Gunite, and similar types can be as long or short as you desire —and virtually any shape. Free-form fiberglass pools are also available.

A 12×24 ft. pool is usually considered the minimum size, but the vast majority (about 85 percent) range from 16' × 30' to 20' × 40'. The size is largely determined by use, location, and—most important— budget. The larger the pool, obviously, the more it costs, but price-per-square-foot does diminish.

Shape has some bearing on costs, too. If you're hooked on an unusual shape, be prepared to pay more than the person who chooses the traditional rectangle.

Allow 36 square feet per swimmer and 100 square feet per diver. With a diving board, 7½ feet of depth is the minimum. Consult the National Swimming Pool Institute, 2000 K St., N.W., Washington, D.C. 20006, for standard specifications.

Recommended Pool Depths by Style

Dimensions in	Styles				
Linear Feet*	A	B	C	D	E
12'×24'	8'-0	7'-0	6'-0	5'-6	3'-0
16'×32'	9'-0	13'-6	6'-0	8'-0	3'-6
16'×36'	13'-0	13'-6	6'-0	8'-0	3'-6
18'×36'	9'-0	15'-0	7'-0	8'-6	5'-0
20'×48'	11'-6	16'-6	7'-4	9'-0	4'-8
24'×48'	17'-0	18'-0	8'-8	9'-6	4'-4

*Width and length for five styles available from Buster Crabbe Pools, Cascade Industries, Inc.

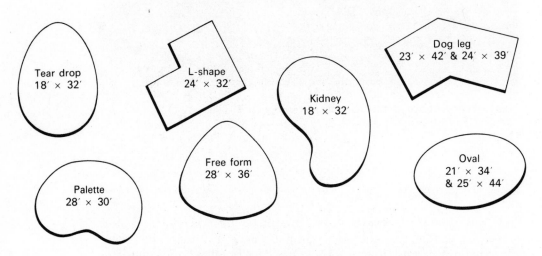

Figure 11-4: Most pool manufacturers offer a wide variety of shapes and sizes—even in the prefabricated types. These drawings illustrate the wide selection in Buster Crabbe pool designs (*courtesy of Cascade Industries, Inc.*).

WHERE TO PUT THE POOL

Too often people assume that a pool has to be in a certain spot, next to the house, for example. It is true that, all else being equal, a pool should be placed next to the house. But there are other considerations, many of them more important than proximity.

One of the most important factors in siting a pool is the optimal amount of sunlight afforded at the proposed site. Sun is important for sunbathing, for warm water, and for general pleasure. Even if the water is warm and you have no intention of getting a suntan, there is just something about sitting in the sun next to the pool that is undeniably

Figure 11-5:   Be sure for the sake of swimming fun to locate your pool where the sunlight prevails. When shade or a place for a cooling drink is needed, a covered shadescreen and bench will provide both. Here they are made of Douglas fir.

nice—for want of a better word. So ask yourself an important question. Do you want to swim in the shade while the sun is shining just beyond the pool?

Choose sun if you can, and stay away from trees. Not only do they block off the sunlight, they drop leaves and seeds into the pool. Their roots can make problems too, so build as far away from large trees as possible. And, locate your pool where drainage will not be a problem.

A swimming pool dealer can help you choose a good location. Other things he might help with are economical ways to relocate pipes and utilities and what to do about underground water or any excavation necessitated by hard rock.

How Much Do Pools Cost?

You don't have to spend any more than five dollars to get something for the kids to splash around in. If you have something more exotic in mind, you may still be in for a mildly pleasant surprise. While the price of contractor-built pools has risen along with every other custom service, the development of in-ground pools with steel sidewalls and

Figure 11-6: You may find pools a better buy than you expect. The beautifully landscaped concrete pool above (*left*) was built for less than $8,500 in 1974, and the fiberglass pool (*right*) sold for just under $7,000 during that same year (*courtesy of National Swimming Pool Institute*).

vinyl liners for in-ground pools did help lower prices somewhat. (Recent shortages have caused an upward revision, however.)

The price range of pools is wide—with small concrete or Gunite pools beginning at $5000. Pools 20×40 and larger will cost at least 50 percent more. Vinyl-lined in-ground pools, however, will run about half these prices.

Above-ground pools are considerably cheaper. Prices for all pools in California, Florida, and other areas where competition is keen will be slightly lower than in less competitive areas. Concrete walls must be thicker in colder areas, running up the cost of this type of pool. Availability of materials and skilled labor is another factor affecting regional costs.

There are often seasonal differences as well as regional ones, with many end-of-year discounts. If demand rises, prices will probably rise. It follows, then, that off-season is a good time to buy.

DIFFERENT TYPES OF POOLS

How do we compare one pool type to another or one contractor's design to the others? The merits to be considered include:

* Interior finish
* Shapes and sizes available
* Structural strength
* Contractor versus owner installation
* Initial cost—complete
* Cost of maintenance
* Depreciation rate
* Inherent dangers—if any

Figure 11-7: This concrete beauty looks so much like a natural part of the landscape that it almost seems a shame to swim in it.

Concrete Pools

Besides the three basic kinds of concrete pools (poured, Gunite and dry-pack), there are two less-used types, pre-cast and block.

Poured: Interior finish varies with the quality of workmanship. Structurally, this is an excellent choice, particularly when steel reinforcing rods are used, but is not preferred for free forms (use Gunite). Depreciation is low if correctly installed. This is not a job for the do-it-yourselfer. Initial as well as maintenance costs are relatively high, but it should last many years with no extraordinary maintenance or repair costs such as new liners. The only inherent danger is the possibility of serious cracks, which are difficult to mend.

Pneumatically Applied (Gunite): This type is quite strong if properly installed with steel reinforcing rods. Interior finish is very good, but it must be applied by skilled workmen. Almost any shape is possible, which is Gunite's principal advantage. Strictly a contractor's job, the costs run about the same as poured concrete, although maintenance is slightly lower. Depreciation is fairly low. Inherent dangers are minimal, except that Gunite is subject to lime deposits and algae accumulation. Serious cases of such fouling require sand blasting and etching with acid.

Dry Pack: This pool is somewhat of a hybrid in construction, a cross between poured concrete and Gunite. Dry pack means that stiff, heavy concrete is poured and molded over reinforcing wire. No forms

Figure 11-8: Here the above-ground pool shown was blended with the house plan so that it seems built into the ground. This type of installation is particularly effective where the land slopes away from the dwelling (*courtesy of National Swimming Pool Institute*).

are used, so that an infinite variety of shapes is possible. It is quite strong, but not as strong structurally as poured concrete or Gunite. The walls slope and the finish is rough and somewhat porous; consequently, swimmers are more subject to bruises and abrasions. Cost is considerably less than the previous two methods, but maintenance is slightly higher. Depreciation depends on quality of installation but is generally somewhat higher than poured or Gunite, especially in northern climates. Check very carefully into contractors' credentials.

Pre-Cast: Walls for these pools are cast at the factory and are lowered into place at the site. Corners, floor and structural strengthening are cast at the site. Installation is rapid and economical. Interior finish and maintenance costs are similar to poured, but structural strength and depreciation are not as good as poured or Gunite. Again, this is not a job for the handyman.

Block: The chief advantage of block construction is the ease of installation. A reasonably skilled do-it-yourselfer can put in a block pool himself, with occasional help. All shapes are possible, but walls must be vertical. The cost is quite low, even if the pool is installed by a contractor. Maintenance is also low, but block walls are not particularly strong and frequently crack and leak. Depreciation is therefore rather high. Interior paint or plaster finish is unsatisfactory, but improved by vinyl liner or cement coat.

Vinyl Pools

These pools come in many varieties. They can go into the ground, above the ground, or on the ground. Structural members can be wood, metal or even concrete; the common denominator is the vinyl liner inside the frame.

Figure 11-9: Vinyl-lined pools in the ground are not much more expensive than a similar pool above ground. Chief difference is the excavation cost (*courtesy of Buster Crabbe Pools*).

Figure 11-10: Another above-ground pool that looks as if it always belonged here. This very attractive pool was made entirely of western red cedar-supports, wall panels, decking, etc. It has a vinyl liner inside (*courtesy of Council of Forest Industries*).

284 *   Steel-above-Ground Pools

This very popular type has replaced the old wooden above-ground pools by and large. There are many manufacturers and contractors. Structural strength is generally good, but investigate the particular brand thoroughly. Buy the heaviest, strongest steel available. Both original and maintenance costs are relatively low—lower than in-ground varieties but higher than wood.

Depreciation is moderate. Interior finish is very good. The structure should hold up for a long time, but most have wooden decks which may deteriorate quickly from all the water sloshing around. The liner itself is the biggest casualty, although newer ones are much tougher than the older ones. Figure on replacing the liner after about ten years, at a cost of several hundred dollars. Vandalism and other damage to the liner is a constant danger, but repairs can now be made under water with relative ease and little expense. It can be installed by the owner (with a few helpers).

Steel-in-Ground Pools

The same general comments apply here as to steel above the ground. The big differences are higher original cost and depreciation. Excavation is the big cost factor; it can run at least $1000 and perhaps a lot more, especially if bedrock is encountered. On the other hand, expensive decks are eliminated and depreciation is much better. The price compared to that of concrete has made this type quite popular. Structurally, in-ground steel is better than above-ground steel if the pool is properly installed. Deflection of the walls could be a problem with poor installation. Except for the excavation, it can be installed by owner.

Aluminum Pools

They are similar in most respects to the steel models discussed above. Aluminum costs a little more, but it is lighter in weight and does not rust. It can be weak if too light, so be sure to specify the heaviest gauge.

Wood Pools

The granddaddy of the above-ground swimming pool is still relatively inexpensive. Although not so popular any more with the manufacturers, it is a good do-it-yourself project with proper plans and patience. Wood should be carefully chosen for decay-resistance and/or impregnated with preservative. Wood should be inspected yearly and kept in good condition. Depreciation is relatively rapid for wood pools with rather high maintenance costs. It is similar in other respects to other vinyl pools.

Fiberglass Pools

While comparatively new for pools, fiberglass is an excellent material. It is rather expensive, but the finish is usually excellent and maintenance is quite low. Occasionally the gel finish has been known to wear off after a few years, and repainting may be necessary.

Installation is strictly a job for a good contractor. Use great care in selecting one. Qualified contractors are scarce, except in the Midwest where fiberglass pools are second only to vinyl in-ground types in sales. Structural strength is good with adequate reinforcement. Depreciation is very low, but this is still a rather unknown quantity.

IN-GROUND VS. ABOVE-GROUND POOLS

One of the big selling points of above-ground pools used to be that they could be taken down and moved. Rarely does anyone do that, however. In reality, the pool becomes part of the property.

Above-ground types do have advantages, though. Probably the biggest advantage is cost. There is no excavation, no drilling or blasting and—perhaps best of all—usually no tax. There are some localities which have considered above-ground pools a permanent addition, but most municipalities do not tax above or even on-ground pools.

Better looking than they used to be, most above-ground pools have effective masking devices for the rather unsightly understructure and filtering machinery. On a large lot, they may add to the richness of the home, but they are a problem on smaller lots. Decking adds at least four feet in width and eight feet in length, which means you'll probably settle for a smaller pool than you wanted—and hardly any backyard at all.

Another problem is the view. If the view beyond your yard is at all interesting, an above-ground pool will block it. And there'll be little garden space. On the other hand, an above-ground pool deck fits very nicely where the land slopes away from the house. It might be better not to put any pool on a small lot; but if you do, it probably should be below ground unless you have an unusual lot that adapts better to the above-ground type.

Everything about an above-ground pool pertains as well to the on-ground varieties, with the exception of the hopper for the diving areas. For all practical purposes, an on-ground pool is impossible to move when you move—unless you think the new owner will like four-foot holes in the ground. Installing a hopper is also more work, although

286 * it is done by hand, as opposed to the mechanical excavation necessary for below-ground pools.

The Best Pool To Choose

There is really no question about the best choice if you can afford it. An in-ground pool, either concrete or vinyl-lined, fits nicely into any landscape. It looks better, takes up less space, and is more satisfying to use and maintain.

On the debit side, there is no getting away from the fact that this type of pool will cost money. It's not only more expensive to install, it adds to your property tax. A rough rule of thumb is to add 25 percent to your assessed valuation when you put in a below-ground pool. The extra tax will probably be $100 and up for most homes. Check your local assessor before you build to make sure, and to avoid future shock.

Another thing to check is the local fencing statute. Authorities in practically every built-up area require a fence around a built-in pool. Sometimes fencing is not mandated for an above-ground or on-ground pool because many already have a built-in fence around the deck, usually with retractable steps to prevent little feet from straying into danger.

Figure 11-11: Most municipal statutes require childproof fencing around a built-in pool. There's no reason for the fence to be ugly, though. This good-looking design features Douglas fir framing, with resawn red cedar 1 x 4's for the main sections.

Figure 11-12: One of the items that run up pool costs is a retaining wall. But the wall itself can be made extremely handsome and look distinctive, as this one does. Note the unusual, rustic "diving board" in the foreground (*courtesy of National Swimming Pool Institute*).

Quite a few jurisdictions do, however, require a fence no matter what the style of pool; and this attitude seems to be growing. If you have to fence in an above-ground pool, the extra cost detracts seriously from the advantage of that type. You should really have a pool below ground if you can. Vinyl in-ground pools are really not that much more costly than those above-ground so long as the excavation doesn't require blasting, retaining walls, or other extras. See Chapter 4 for a discussion of fences and how to build them.

FILLING THE POOL WITH WATER

When you fill your new pool for the first time, the water may appear cloudy or "turbid." Don't be alarmed. Your pool is filled with the same drinking water you use in your home—water that you assume is sparkling clear. By the glassful most tap water does *appear* clear. By the poolful, the same water may not.

To clear the pool, turn on the filter and let the pool stand unused for a day. Minute solids—particles of calcium, iron, and other minerals—will be filtered out or will settle to the bottom. Pool water will turn sparkling clear.

288 *   MAINTAINING CORRECT POOL "RESIDUAL"

From the very first day you fill your pool, its purity must be guarded (and maintained) by a chemical disinfectant. Some purifying chemical, whether chlorine, bromine, or iodine, must be maintained in your pool water. And enough of it must "reside" there to kill disease-carrying bacteria brought into the water by bathers.

The amount of chemical residual which must be present in pool water is expressed as so many parts of disinfectant per million parts of water, abbreviated "ppm." The same quantitative measure is used to express the amount of any other chemical added or present in pool water.

Chlorine is the most widely used of the accepted disinfectants for swimming pools. Used as a disinfectant, at least 0.6 and preferably 1.0 ppm of free residual chlorine must at all times be present in pool water to kill bacteria and maintain water purity. Less free residual than one part in one million parts of water may fail to kill bacteria. (These recommended concentrations apply to chlorine only and do not reflect the concentrations required when using other types of disinfectants.)

Critical though this residual is for pool purity, it represents a very small amount of chemical. Less than one drop of chlorine in every 1,000,000 drops of pool water is enough, providing the chemical is 100 percent active.

Factors Affecting Longevity of Disinfectant Residuals. There are six factors that commonly affect the in-pool longevity of chlorine and other disinfectants.

* **Bathing load:** The greater the number of swimmers, the more disinfectant is used up.
* **Sunlight:** The greater the sun's intensity, the faster the dissipation of disinfectant residual.
* **Water temperature:** The warmer the pool's water, the shorter the life of most chemicals used as disinfectants.
* **Winds and rain:** They carry dust, bacteria, algae spores, and other debris into the pool, overworking chemical disinfectants and reducing their power to sanitize.
* **pH "balance":** The higher the pH of pool water, the slower-acting most pool disinfectants are; so more disinfectant must usually be added to maintain the proper bacteria-killing residual. The ideal pH range for pool water is 7.2–7.6.
* **Total alkalinity:** If the amount of alkaline salts present in pool water is below 80 to 100 ppm, the total alkalinity is low. Then the pH will fluctuate widely and pool plaster may etch. If the total alkalinity is too high, pH will tend to be maintained at a higher than desired level and cause scale and cloudy water.

Testing the Water for Disinfectant Residual: A simple test kit (available at your pool supplier) lets you test pool water quickly and

easily to make sure that it contains the proper chlorine or other disinfectant residual. If the test kit indicates that pool water contains too little
residual, you must add enough disinfectant to restore the proper (and
recommended) residual level. Test kits are marketed for testing chlorine,
bromine, or iodine residuals.

It is necessary only to take a small sample of pool water, add a
measured amount of the color-reacting chemical supplied with the kit,
and compare the water sample's resultant color with a set of "standard
colors" in the kit. The kit's standard colors tell you the amount of
residual in your pool.

BALANCING THE WATER'S pH

The ideal pH level for pool water is between 7.2 and 7.6. Water that
is neutral—that is, neither alkaline nor acidic—has a pH value of 7.0.
This is midpoint on the 0 to 14 pH scale. Above 7.0 pH, pool water is
alkaline. The higher up the pH scale pool water tests, the more alkaline it
is. Below 7.0 pH, pool water is acidic. The lower down the pH scale pool
water tests, the more acidic it is. Maintaining your pool water very
slightly on the alkaline side (note that the recommended 7.2 to 7.6 pH
level is above the neutral point, thus slightly alkaline) is important for a
number of reasons.

When pool water is too alkaline (above 8.0 pH) disinfecting chemicals work more slowly. They may not do their proper killing job even
though tests of the water may indicate a proper "residual." Also, scale
may form on/in pool equipment and piping.

On the other hand, if pool water becomes acidic, it irritates the
eyes, corrodes equipment and piping, and causes pool interior surface
stains.

If your tests indicate that pool water has too low a pH, you use a
chemical that neutralizes the acidity and raises the pH (see below).

Common Chemicals That Raise and Lower pH: There are a number
of water-balancing chemicals. Some chemicals (highly alkaline) raise
the pH level of pool water. Others—acid chemicals—lower the pH.

Soda Ash is one common chemical that raises pH. This cousin of
common baking soda is among the least expensive and easiest to use of
acid-neutralizing pool chemicals. Soda ash can be "sowed" by scattering it as you walk around the pool—as if it were grass seed. It is also
available in block form for immersion in water.

Muriatic acid and sodium bisulfate are common chemicals that
lower pH. Commercial-strength muriatic acid (available at most pool
suppliers) is about 30 per cent hydrochloric acid. No more than one pint
of muriatic acid should be added to every 5,000 gallons of pool water at
one time to reduce alkalinity and to re-establish your pool water's pH
balance.

Algae Control: Algae are small microscopic organisms which

290 * possess an internal green pigment called chlorophyll. This group of organisms are the normal inhabitants of surface waters and are encountered in every water supply that is exposed to sunlight. If ideal conditions for their growth exist in a water supply, it is possible within 24 hours to develop a thriving algal population. Furthermore, if waters contain considerable dissolved minerals and other suspended matter, these serve as nutrients for the growth of algae and other microscopic aquatic life.

The problem of algae control is serious and ever-present in swimming pools. The presence of even small numbers of algae in swimming pools or other water supplies tends to clog filters and impart disagreeable odors and tastes to the water. Furthermore, algae can interfere with the effectiveness of chlorine, iodine, and bromine, the common disinfectants used in swimming pools.

Once algae have developed in a swimming pool, particularly the so-called "wall-clinging" types, even superchlorination of the water cannot destroy the algal mats which often form on the sides and bottoms of the pools.

Algae are not usually harmful to swimmers. But they are objectionable. And they can be a hazard—particularly the slimy sort that make the pool bottom slippery. They also discolor the water or bottom, making it hard to see objects on the bottom. A pool with algae appears unsightly and dirty as well. Because so many strains of algae are immune to disinfectants present in the pool they require special treatment with chemical algicides at all times to control them.

Algicides: Special anti-algae chemicals prevent the development of particularly stubborn pool algae and kill any algae growth already present in the pool. It is necessary to add an algicide to the pool water regularly.

Algicides are chemical compounds or formulations specifically designed to kill existing algae in the pool and to prevent further growth. Algicides are available at most pool dealers.

How To Clean Your Pool

Besides the chemical treatments outlined above, routine pool cleaning includes:

* Skimming the pool's surface manually.
* Brushing down walls and tile.
* Cleaning the skimmer basket and hair & lint strainer.
* Vacuuming the pool bottom.
* Cleaning the filter.
* Hosing down the pool deck.

If the somewhat complex chemical programs are too much for you, get away from it all by hiring commercial pool maintenance services. In most areas there are service companies that perform this work, but it costs, like everything else. So, before you get discouraged, try pool care yourself for a little while. You'll find that it's not as complicated as it sounds at first, although it can be a little tedious.

Do-It-Yourself Pool Construction

As mentioned earlier, concrete and fiberglass pool construction is strictly for the professional, but it is not impossible for an average handyman to put up his own metal or wood pool with a vinyl liner. If it's above ground, the job is that much easier. Things get a little more complicated below ground, but are still not too difficult. The hardest part is the excavation, and no matter how energetic you are, this is definitely a job for the professional with a big shovel (or "back-hoe," to be exact).

Assuming you have the excavation done, the hardest job is to get the diving hopper right. You can eliminate it, of course, but then you're eliminating half the fun. Most vinyl-liner pools come with do-it-yourself directions. Unfortunately, they often seem a bit confusing, but they are still the best guide to each particular pool. Try to follow the manufacturer's directions if and when you buy your own, but read the general instructions below. They are meant to give you an overall preview of installation techniques.

GENERAL LAYOUT DIRECTIONS

Lay out the area for excavation by placing stakes on the ground. Then run cord between them. Remember, the outer dimensions for the excavation must be two feet greater on each side than the actual size of the pool. Determine the level of the top surface of the pool and mark this point on the stake at the highest ground level. Then, as a guide for the excavator, outline the digging area on the ground with powdered lime or flour.

An experienced and skillful backhoe operator will disturb the least possible amount of earth while digging the hole to size. When he is finished, lay out the exact pool size and outline its dimensions on the floor of the hole. Outline the hopper dimensions as well, if your pool is to have one. Be sure to allow an 8″ safety ledge around the hopper. The excavation for the hopper should be made about two to three inches deeper than its actual finished depth.

Next, install (or have installed) the wall panels and bearing plates on a level foundation of undisturbed earth. As soon as the final hand trimming of the excavation is done, lower the panels onto the foundation and lean them against the walls of the excavation. Place a corner section

Figure 11-13: A good backhoe operator should be able to excavate an area pretty close to final pool dimensions. Be sure you have everything measured and ready for him.

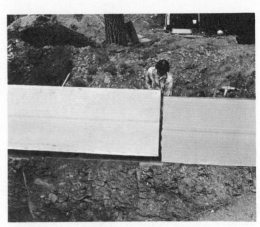

Figure 11-14: Next, each wall panel for the pool is set into place and carefully aligned so that fit is assured.

Figure 11-15: Starting with the corner panels, the pieces are all securely fastened once they are exactly in position.

Figure 11-16: The Buster Crabbe pool system uses specially-treated wood panels with heavy-gage metal corners and braces.

in position and start bolting the panels together—working alternately in either direction. This way, the bolted panels will be self-supporting as work progresses around the pool.

Use a sighting level, carpenter's level or transit to make sure that level is maintained as each panel is placed. Check to be sure each joint is true to the first corner section. After all panels are in place and staked to the ground, you can usually align the top edges of the wall panels by raising or lowering the plates. Fill any voids under the wall sections with concrete and allow to set. Then backfill with moist earth to a 6″ depth and tamp lightly.

Figure 11-17: After all panels are in place, fine worked sand is dumped inside the pool walls and spread over the bottom in a two- to three-inch layer.

Figure 11-18: The sand must be drenched and then tamped to make the pool bottom as level and smooth as possible.

Next, wet and tamp solid all the loose earth in the pool bottom. Then dump in thoroughly washed, fine sand—enough to make a two- to three-inch layer on the bottom. After you spread it, drench it. Then tamp and compact this sand with a lawn roller. Take particular care with this operation, for the smoothness and evenness of the sand will determine the appearance of the pool bottom when the vinyl liner is placed in position.

At the hopper end of the pool, position the jig corner-guide boards or templates to the configuration appropriate to that particular style of pool. Dump sand into the hopper and work it smooth on bottom and sides. After you tamp the walls, remove any guide boards and fill those recesses with sand.

Figure 11-19: While some workers are tamping and leveling the sand, others can start installing the skimmer, the piping, and the rest.

Figure 11-20: The simple hopper area shown here can be smoothed with a hand float or trowel.

Figure 11-21: More elaborate pool hoppers like this one usually require a template.

Next, fasten to the wall corner pieces of the plastic extrusion into which the liner fits. Then fasten the straight lengths, butting them tightly together.

Then enlist friends and neighbors to install the liner. At least four helpers are usually needed. Starting from the corners (with one volunteer in each corner), insert the bead at the top edge of the liner into its mating extrusion. Pull the liner gently into position so that the bottom fits exactly into the excavation. When the liner is in position, remove some of the bead from the extrusion in one corner of the deep end and insert a vacuum cleaner hose. (If you have it, use a heavy duty, industrial vacuum cleaner; otherwise, a household vacuum with filter bag removed may be used.) Make sure there is no air leakage and start the vacuum. In about 15 or 20 minutes the air behind the liner will be exhausted and the liner will be drawn tight against the pool walls. You can make any necessary adjustments in liner alignment and smooth out wrinkles with a pool brush while the vacuum is running.

Now start filling the pool with water, brushing out any wrinkles that appear in the liner. It is desirable, but not absolutely necessary, that you backfill around the walls during the pool-filling operation. Finally, install the accessories, connect the filter, and attach the coping at the edge of the pool. Then fill to the waterline and enjoy.

Figure 11-22: Four men are usually required to install the liner properly—the fourth man, out of camera range, is holding the other end of the pole from which the liner is being unwound.

Figure 11-23: A vacuum cleaner is used to draw out the air behind the liner and ensure a tight fit against the panels.

Figure 11-24: Backfilling is done while the pool fills up in order to equalize pressure on both sides of the panels.

Figure 11-25: Final steps in building the pool include installation of accessories and connection of the filter (*courtesy Buster Crabbe Pools*).

296 * *Pool-Tending Rules For Fun & Safety*

These rules below are intended to help you understand what is meant by a well-tended swimming pool. You can keep "in the swim" and "in the fun" by observing these simple rules suggested by the National Swimming Pool Institute:

* **Read directions.** Complete maintenance instructions are provided by the manufacturer of your particular pool. Review the pool manual carefully and study the directions for all the chemicals you intend to add.
* **Don't overdose.** Measure exact amounts. Pool chemicals—like medicine—should be used only in specified amounts. Too much can cause irritating side effects.
* **Don't guess.** Take time to learn to use a test kit. Be sure to replace reagents (test fluids) each season to assure accuracy.
* **Establish a routine for testing and treatment.** A few minutes everyday—or every other day—can make the job easy and assure a pool in tip-top shape.
* **Don't work too hard.** Last but not least; check yourself. If you find that taking care of your pool is too much work, you are doing something wrong.

Potpourri—or Miscellaneous Projects

The word *potpourri* is French and is pronounced "poe-pou-ree," accent on last syllable. It means, literally, "rotted in the pot" (as for dried herbs), but over the years it has taken on the additional meaning of either a miscellany or a medley or a mixture. That's what this last section is all about. These are miscellaneous good ideas that we've run across, and projects that were put together on someone's whim without plans or materials lists. Included are various smaller items, such as birdhouses, that don't quite fit in any of the previous chapters.

Rather than relegate all this to the "incomplete" file, we're giving you what we have. You can take it from there. A sharp lumber dealer should be able to figure out what you need from either the photos or the plans. Some of these items, such as patio covers, are the type that must be adapted by each builder to suit his own uses, so there's no point in giving details anyway.

Thumb through these pages and get some ideas of what others have done to create their own outdoor projects. You may just be inspired to work out what you need and want. If you find nothing here or in the previous chapters that's close to what you have in mind, look at page 314 which has a list of companies that sell plans on an individual basis. Most of them will be more than happy to send a catalog.

Birdhouses

It is easy to make a birdhouse. Just a few scraps of wood, an old chalk box, a gourd—almost anything can become a suitable artificial nest for birds. You should, however, keep in mind that certain sizes and styles of shelters attract certain birds. If you're looking for purple martins, for example, you'll need a whole miniature "apartment" building made just a certain way. An open-sided home is more comfortable for robins and phoebes. Unfortunately, the less desirable birds, such as bluejays and starlings, seem content with any kind of home.

The crucial dimension in many cases is the size of the opening. The chicadee likes a 1⅛" diameter—exactly—while the flicker prefers a 2½" opening. (See Table 11-1 for all dimensions.)

Birdhouse #1 was made from two discs of wood and two pieces of asphalt shingle. Number 3 is a gourd with a hole drilled in it. Numbers 5 and 8 are open-sided homes for robins and phoebes, while #6 has a round wooden floor with asphalt shingle sides and top.

Birdhouses can get pretty messy inside, so many people prefer one that can be cleaned, like models #10, 9, and 10. The first two have hinged members, while #10 has a removable top. All are easy to build.

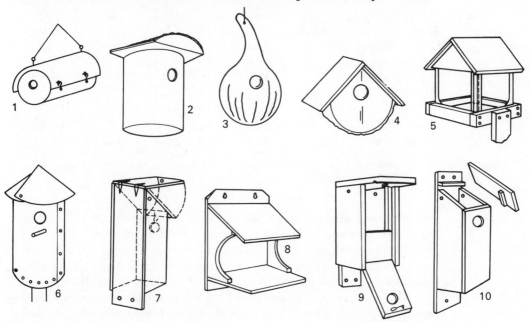

Figure 11-26: Some easy-to-make birdhouses. See text for descriptions.

298 * **Table 11-1:** Recommended Dimensions for Various Birdhouses

Species of Bird	Floor of Cavity	Depth of Cavity	Entrance above Floor	Diameter of Entrance	Height above Ground*
	Inches	Inches	Inches	Inches	Feet
Bluebird	5×5	8	6	1½	5–10
Robin	6×8	8	†	†	6–15
Chickadee	4×4	8–10	6–8	1⅛	6–15
Titmouse	4×4	8–10	6–8	1¼	6–15
Nuthatch	4×4	8–10	6–8	1¼	12–20
House wren	4×4	6–8	1–6	1–1¼	6–10
Bewick's wren	4×4	6–8	1–6	1–1¼	6–10
Carolina wren	4×4	6–8	1–6	1½	6–10
Violet-green swallow	5×5	6	1–5	1½	10–15
Tree swallow	5×5	6	1–5	1½	10–15
Barn swallow	6×6	6	†	†	8–12
Purple martin	6×6	6	1	2½	15–20
Prothonotary warbler	6×6	6	4	1½	2–4
Starling	6×6	16–18	14–16	2	10–25
Phoebe	6×6	6	†	†	8–12
Crested flycatcher	6×6	8–10	6–8	2	8–20
Flicker	7×7	16–18	14–16	2½	6–20
Golden-fronted woodpecker	6×6	12–15	9–12	2	12–20
Red-headed woodpecker	6×6	12–15	9–12	2	12–20
Downy woodpecker	4×4	9–12	6–8	1¼	6–20
Hairy woodpecker	6×6	12–15	9–12	1½	12–20
Screech owl	8×8	12–15	9–12	3	10–30
Saw-whet owl	6×6	10–12	8–10	2½	12–20
Barn owl	10×18	15–18	4	6	12–18
Sparrow hawk	8×8	12–15	9–12	3	10–30
Wood duck	10×18	10–24	12–16	4	10–20

*Many experiments show that boxes at moderate heights (within reach of a man on the ground) are readily accepted by many birds. †One or more sides open.

Plywood Birdhouse for Small Birds: The step-by-step drawings show how to make a birdhouse from scraps of ⅜" exterior plywood. First lay out and cut the pieces, then drill an entry hole for the size bird you'd like to attract (see Table 11-1). This type of house is particularly well suited to wrens, chickadees, nuthatches, bluebirds, or swallows.

The parts are nailed and glued together as shown, using nominal one-inch square lumber and 6d nails. Fronts and backs (F and F-1 on key) are attached with 1" long flathead screws before the top two pieces (T and T-1) are nail-glued. Drill small holes for ventilation and wire hanger. Paint or stain like any other outdoor project.

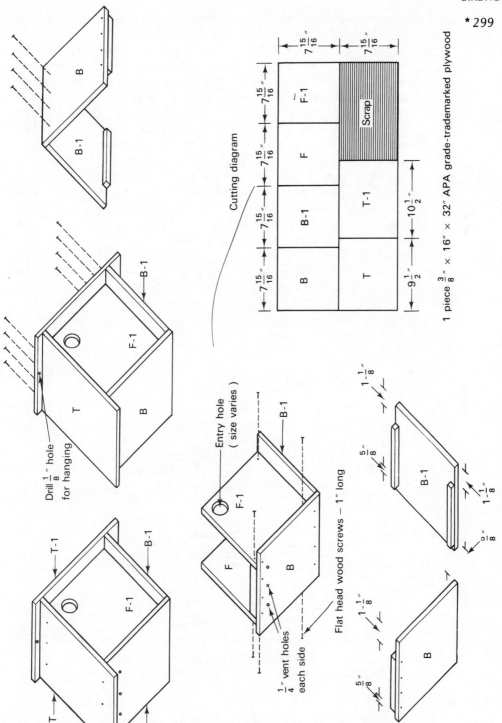

Figure 11-27: Construction details and cutting layout for a birdhouse suitable for small birds.

Purple Martin House: The multiple-dwelling structures that house purple martins are always attractive and interesting—when they contain purple martins. Unfortunately, starlings and house sparrows are also gregarious like the martin and have been known to take over these houses. To prevent that, either take the house down when martins are not nesting, or block up the holes during the off season.

The diagrams here show a martin house and how it is made (see the facing page). This particular model can be built from one to three stories high, and the stories can be added to or dismantled by means of hook-and-eye attachments and a ring molding that prevents lateral movement.

Summer heat is kept down by means of simple air circulation systems. Two holes are drilled in the removable roof and covered with mesh or screening, and a one-inch slot is left under the eaves. The central "apartments" in each story are left open so that the 6″ hole in the roof allows circulation down through the center.

Place the martin house high on a pole which is hinged for lowering to the ground. If you don't wish an arrangement quite so elaborate, make sure that your house is at a height that can be reached by ladder for cleaning and removal. If at all possible, situate the martin house near a pond, stream, or lake in order to provide the best living conditions for your new guests.

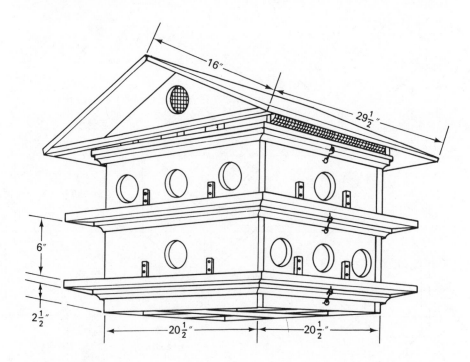

Figure 11-28: Sketch showing finish details and dimensions for a purple martin birdhouse.

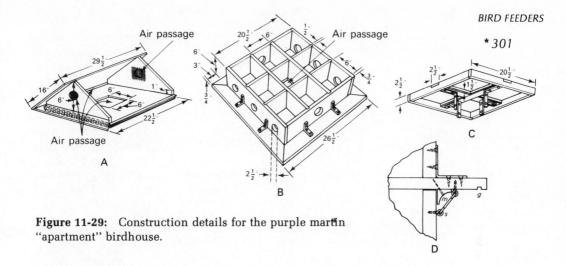

Figure 11-29: Construction details for the purple martin "apartment" birdhouse.

Bird Feeders

Many well-meaning people spread bird food on the ground in the winter. Very little will get to the birds, however, since squirrels and other animals usually get to the food first. To supply bird food to the birds and to keep the birds themselves from becoming food for the neighborhood cats, a bird feeder mounted or hung up and away from other animals is the best idea. Two such feeders are illustrated here, one made from exterior hardboard such as Masonite Weatherall, and the other from several pieces of lumber and glass sides.

Three other feeders are fairly easy to make. The revolving feeder has dual weather vanes that keep the open side of the feeder away from the prevailing winds while the trolley feeder can be rolled back and forth to a window. The box feeder is simply a box attached below a window sill but away from marauding cats.

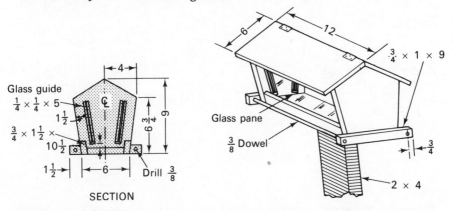

Figure 11-30: Section view and overall dimensions of a wooden and glass bird feeder.

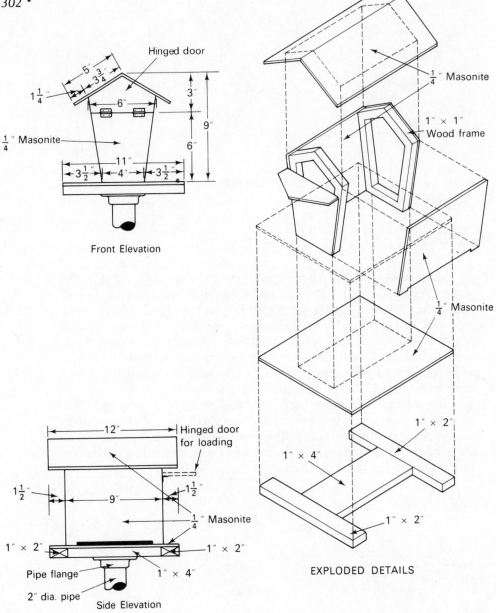

Hinged door

$1\frac{1}{4}$"

$\frac{1}{4}$" Masonite

Front Elevation

12"

Hinged door for loading

$1\frac{1}{2}$"

$1\frac{1}{2}$"

9"

$\frac{1}{4}$" Masonite

1" × 2"

1" × 2"

Pipe flange

1" × 4"

2" dia. pipe

Side Elevation

$\frac{1}{4}$" Masonite

1" × 1" Wood frame

$\frac{1}{4}$" Masonite

1" × 2"

1" × 4"

1" × 2"

EXPLODED DETAILS

Figure 11-31: Elevation plans and and construction details for a bird feeder with a hinged door for easy loading. Materials are lumber, masonite, and a pipe for mounting.

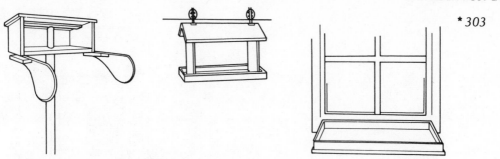

Figure 11-32: Other bird feeders (*left to* right): one whose weather vanes keep the open side turned away from the wind; another that rolls back and forth on a trolley; and a simple box attached to a window sill.

A Garden-Post Lamp

Your lovely garden will look even more lovely after dark if it is softly lighted. If you enjoy the beauty of intricate shapes along with the beauty of plantings, you can create your own wood sculpture—perhaps like this lamp mounted on a post. All you need are some odds and ends of wood, a few hand tools, and a touch of free expression. The plan shown here need serve only as an inspiration for your own design, or you can make a faithful copy according to directions and the accompanying drawings.

To solidly anchor your post lamp, use an auger or post-hole digger to excavate at least 30 inches deep and, for the post illustrated here, approximately eight inches in diameter. Fill the bottom with two to three inches of gravel for good drainage. And thoroughly soak the end of the post that will be below ground in creosote or other preservative. You may either position the post in concrete or simply set it in the hole with the earth tamped firmly about it. In either case, leave the top four inches of the excavation unfilled until the post is wired.

To do that, lead the electrical wiring through a waterproof conduit from the house to the post, burying the conduit at least four inches below grade. Make the connections to the conduit that has been built into the post, then finish filling the excavation to slightly above grade with earth, tamped solid and sloped slightly away from the post for drainage.

The "lamp shade" that crowns your post may be built separately and placed upon the planted post, or the entire unit may be assembled before the post is set in place. Usually this depends on the height of the post and the size of its crown. The louvered design shown here is placed on the planted post and screwed into 1×3 shims. This allows easy removal for replacement of bulbs when necessary. The light, diffused by the louvers, will fall in soft rays and illuminate the garden or garden path, prolonging your visual enjoyment of your backyard labors.

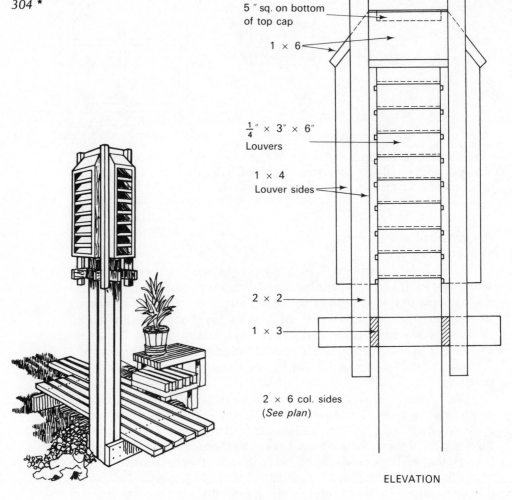

5 ″ sq. on bottom
of top cap

1 × 6

$\frac{1}{4}$″ × 3″ × 6″
Louvers

1 × 4
Louver sides

2 × 2

1 × 3

2 × 6 col. sides
(*See plan*)

ELEVATION

1″ elect. conduit

5 $\frac{1}{2}$″

2 × 6 sides

Plan of post

Figure 11-33: View showing typical siting of garden post lamp. The elevation shows how the louvers are arranged (*courtesy of Western Wood Products Association*).

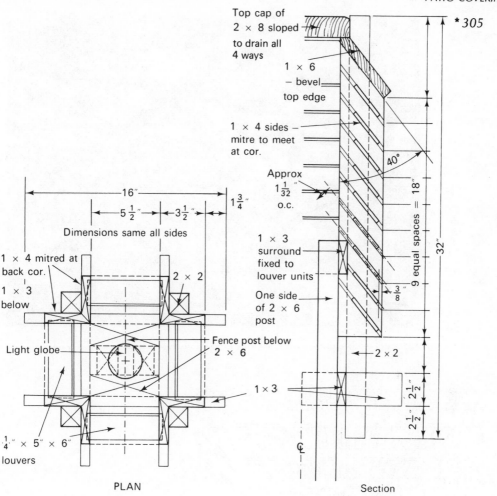

Top cap of
2 × 8 sloped
to drain all
4 ways

1 × 6
– bevel
top edge

1 × 4 sides –
mitre to meet
at cor.

Approx
1 1/32″
o.c.

1 × 3
surround
fixed to
louver units

One side
of 2 × 6
post

Fence post below
2 × 6

1 × 3

40°

18″ = 9 equal spaces

32″

3/8″

2 1/2″

2 1/2″

2 × 2

16″

5 1/2″   3 1/2″

1 3/4″

Dimensions same all sides

1 × 4 mitred at
back cor.

2 × 2

1 × 3
below

Light globe

1/4″ × 5″ × 6″
louvers

PLAN

Section

Figure 11-34: Construction details for the garden lamp.

Patio Coverings

Covering a patio may seem like wearing a raincoat in the shower, but patio covers are useful for keeping out the worst of the sun and the rain without interfering too much with normal breezes. Obviously, this could be a tall order, and some patio covers work better than others. It all depends on what you want to do. Where the sun is blistering hot and your patio is unprotected by trees or any other natural shade, it makes sense to provide cover during the hottest part of the day. A tinted fiberglass or other plastic cover will keep out strong sun and rain and yet

Figure 11-35: Photo shows patio cover made of Filon fiberglass panels.

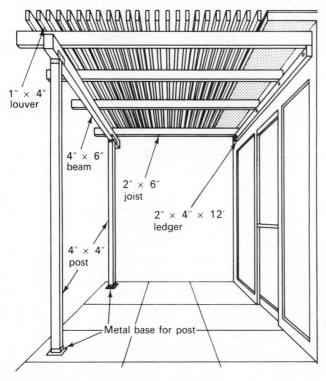

1″ × 4″
louver

4″ × 6″
beam

2″ × 6″
joist

2″ × 4″ × 12′
ledger

4″ × 4″
post

Metal base for post

Figure 11-36: Diagram for a simple, flat wood patio screen with metal posts (*courtesy of California Redwood Association*).

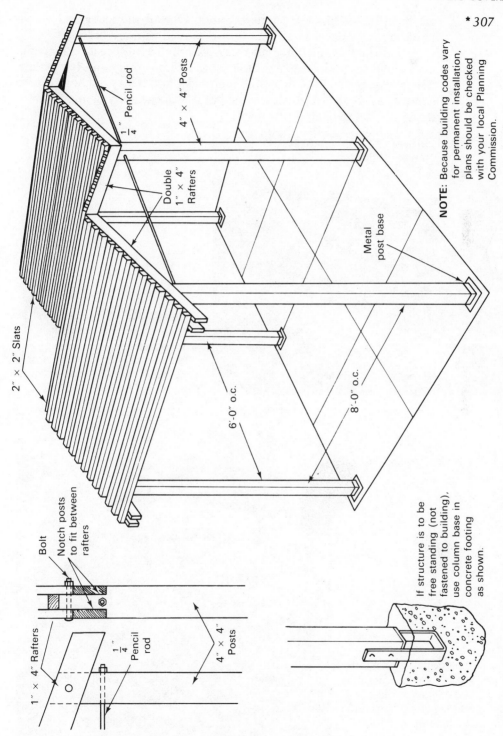

NOTE: Because building codes vary for permanent installation, plans should be checked with your local Planning Commission.

Figure 11-37: Construction details for wooden-louvered patio roof with double pitch (courtesy of *Georgia Pacific*).

308 *   allow sufficient light to come through. One of the staggered wood-louver types will let in still more sun as well as more breeze.

If mosquitos and other bugs are a big problem in your area, consider a screened-in outdoor space. Or if winter comes early and leaves late, you may be better off with a semi-enclosed affair. It may not be as nice in summer as some of the other sorts, but it will certainly be more usable than one that is completely open.

Figure 11-38: If you want fresh air but no pests, enclose your patio with screening like this prefabricated room. This kit can be used with most existing patio covers (*courtesy of Sears Roebuck*).

Figure 11-39: For those who prefer outdoor living away from the house, a portable screen house is bug-free and convenient. This is the Casita model (*courtesy of General Aluminum*).

Greenhouses

Actually, you *can* build an economical greenhouse with wood and sheet plastic, but better-looking, more permanent structures are available in kit form from several manufacturers. A few typical kit-built greenhouses are illustrated here.

Two of the firms that manufacture such prefabricated greenhouses are Lord & Burnham, Division of Burnham Corporation, Irvington, N.Y. 10533, and Baco Greenhouses, 19 E. 47th St., New York, N.Y. 10017.

For true indoor-outdoor living and good space for the cultivation of tender, beautiful plants you can also remove a back wall from your house and incorporate a larger greenhouse, of course.

Figure 11-40: A large, permanent greenhouse like this can be purchased as a pre-fab and butted to an existing structure.

Figure 11-41: A small "window" pre-fab can also be installed at a window with the right exposure.

Figure 11-42: Here a modest but efficient "walk-in" greenhouse can be installed so as to open off doors and windows of a house. As for the larger pre-fab on the previous page, this structure requires a concrete foundation.

Garages, Horse Barns, & Storage Units

Although most new homes are built with carports or attached garages, a free-standing garage is often a better bet for the do-it-yourselfer because he doesn't have to worry about spoiling the lines of the house.

Figure 11-43: Complete building plans are available for structures such as this.

Local building supply dealers may have garage kits on hand, or they may be able to steer you to somebody in your area who makes prefabricated garages. At least one company has complete building plans for garages, horse barns, storage units, etc., that you can put up from scratch. Write National Plan Service, 1700 W. Hubbard St., Chicago, Ill. 60622 for complete information.

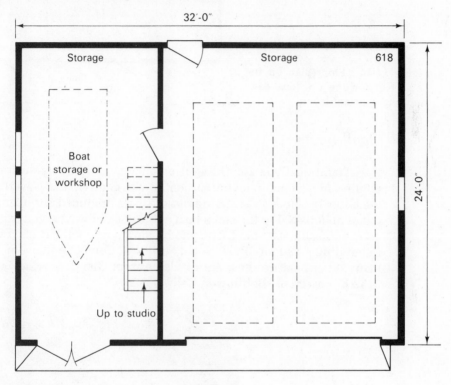

Figure 11-44: Floor plan and layout of the structure on the facing page (*National Plan Service*).

Figure 11-45: Complete construction plans for this horse barn are also available from the National Plan Service.

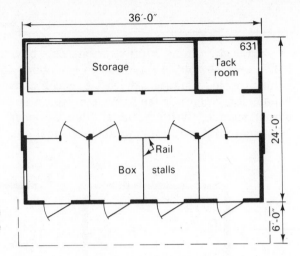

Figure 11-46: Floor plan for the horse barn on the previous page shows its efficient layout.

Small Boats

Traditionally boatbuilding is an ancient and honorable craft that requires much tender, loving carpentry with good woods. Nevertheless, the majority of today's seafaring rigs are mass produced unromantically out of fiberglass. For the small boat enthusiast, however, you can't beat good old-fashioned wood. The photos show some of the steps involved in building a 12-foot "Buck Board" sailboat. Complete plans for it and many other boat designs, are available from Glen-L Marine Designs, 9152 E. Rosecrans, Bellflower, Calif. 90706.

Figure 11-47: Here a satisfied do-it-yourselfer sails his new "Buck Board."

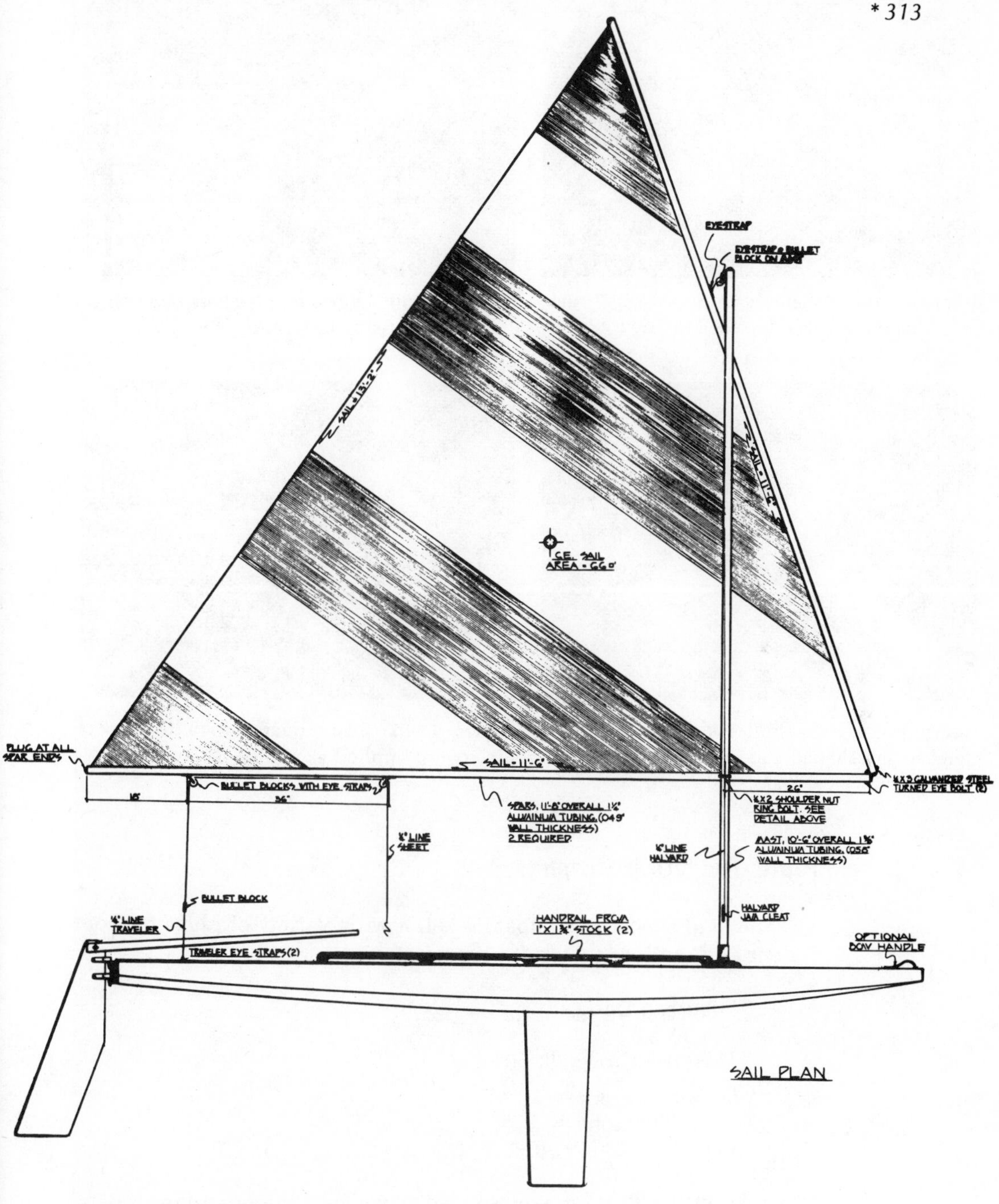

Figure 11-48: Sail plan for the "Buck Board" on the facing page (courtesy of Glen-L Marine Designs).

Figure 11-49: Assembly of one of the "Buck Board" components cut from specified woods.

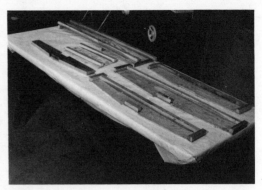

Figure 11-50: Various members assembled and laid out ready to form the hull.

Figure 11-51: The hull takes shape as the members are shaped and fastened.

Figure 11-52: Then quarter-inch top grade plywood is applied as planking and decking.

Plans for Other Projects

Several specialty companies sell a wide variety of plans for both indoor and outdoor you-build-it projects:

* **Suburban Design**
  Box 651
  Downers Grove, Ill. 60515

* **U-Bild Enterprises**
  Steve Ellingson
  Van Nuys, Cal. 91409

Write directly to the companies listed above for catalogs and price lists; and look over our illustrations of their building projects too. You may either find one exactly right or worth adapting to your own taste and requirements. Even if neither is the case, study the photographs anyhow:

they may inspire you to make something even more attractive for your   *★ 315*
own backyard. Some manufacturers' associations also have outdoor
building plans. They are available for a minimal cost.

* **California Redwood Association**
  617 Montgomery Street
  San Francisco, Cal. 94111

* **Western Wood Products Association**
  700 Yeon Building
  Portland, Ore. 97204

Figure 11-53: This redwood gazebo makes a handsome pool-side shelter.

Figure 11-54: This gazebo is adapted from an Oriental design and is made entirely from California redwood.

Figure 11-55: An excellent way to put little-used space to work is to partly enclose a breezeway and make it into a private outdoor lounge (*courtesy of Masonite Corporation*).

Figure 11-56: Here Douglas fir was used to build a lovely shelter in a quiet wooded area of the garden.

Figure 11-57: Redwood monkey bars here furnish many happy play hours for the children whose do-it-yourself parents invested in their construction.

Figure 11-58: This tree house promises great play time for children and a satisfying conclusion for a dedicated do-it-yourselfer.

INDEX